# DANCE WITH CHANCE

# ABOUT THE AUTHORS

**Spyros Makridakis** is Distinguished Research Professor at INSEAD, Abu Dhabi Centre and a former Greek Olympian.

**Robin M. Hogarth** is ICREA Research Professor at Universitat Pompeu Fabra, Spain. He was formerly a professor at the University of Chicago's Booth School of Business.

**Anil Gaba** is the ORPAR Chaired Professor of Risk Management and Academic Director of the Centre for Decision Making and Risk Analysis at INSEAD, France and Singapore, the world's second largest business school.

# DANCE WITH CHANCE

## Making luck work for you

SPYROS MAKRIDAKIS,
ROBIN HOGARTH, ANIL GABA

ONEWORLD
OXFORD

A Oneworld Book

First published by Oneworld Publications 2009
Reprinted 2009
This revised paperback edition published by Oneworld Publications 2010

UK: ISBN 978–1–85168–775–6
US: ISBN 978–1–85168–720–6

Typeset by Jayvee, Trivandrum, India
Cover design by Keenan Design
Printed and bound by CPI Cox & Wyman, Reading, RG1 8EX

Oneworld Publications
UK: 185 Banbury Road, Oxford, OX2 7AR, England
US: 38 Greene Street, 4th Floor, New York, NY10013, USA

Learn more about Oneworld. Join our mailing list to
find out about our latest titles and special offers at:

www.oneworld-publications.com

# CONTENTS

# CONTENTS

# ACKNOWLEDGMENTS

Since starting to work on this book, we have been the grateful recipients of different forms of help from many individuals and organizations. First, many colleagues and friends read various drafts of the book, challenged us to clarify our thinking, examples, and exposition, and further provided many constructive suggestions. These included Fred Collopy, Gerd Gigerenzer, Reid Hastie, Bob Herbold, Tassos Karagiannis, Manfred Kets de Vries, Tomás Lejarraga, and Emre Soyer, as well as Grace Hung, Chris Lobello, and other readers at CLSA. In addition, the text reflects comments made by Irina Cojuharenco, Spyros Efstathopoulos, Natalia Karelaia, Gueorgui Kolev, George Koumbas, Litsa Panagiotopoulou, Carmen Pi-Sunyer, and Eric Thomson. However, our greatest debt goes to Elin Williams who not only vastly improved our attempts to write but also corrected our way of dealing with many issues – and always with good humor.

This book was written in four different places: Athens, Barcelona, Fontainebleau, and Singapore. In particular, we spent three intensive weeks together engaged in the project at INSEAD in Singapore and thank that institution for its support, especially the Centre for Decision Making and Risk Analysis (CDMRA) which also provided financial resources throughout the project. Robin Hogarth thanks the Spanish Ministerio de Ciencia e Innovación for its financial aid.

Finally, we thank Mike Harpley and the team at Oneworld for committing itself so wholeheartedly to our project.

# PREFACE

## Before we begin . . .

*ance with Chance* was created from a meeting of minds. The minds belong to three professors with a shared interest in the human need to predict and influence the future.

It all began way back in the 1970s, when one of the professors, a statistician by training, had an unpleasant surprise. He'd noticed that business people were failing to use the latest statistical techniques in their forecasting and so embarked on some research to persuade them to become more mathematically sophisticated. But – to the professor's intellectual horror (not to mention a little shame) – the research showed that the practitioners' simple methods were better at predicting than his own clever ones.[1] He reluctantly began to wonder whether people should put more faith in human intuition than mathematics when predicting the future.

The statistician happened to mention this dilemma to one of his colleagues, a cognitive psychologist. "Sorry," said the second professor, "empirical findings in my field show that human judgment is even less accurate at making predictions than statistical models."[2] And for a long time, they both carried on thinking about this, which is what professors do best. Years later, the two men returned to the famous business school where they'd first met and got talking to a third professor. He turned out to be a decision scientist, whose research was all about reconciling theory with practice, the irrational with the rational, statistical models with gut feeling.

And so *Dance with Chance* was ignited by this intellectual spark, with the goal of helping people make better decisions in situations where accurate forecasting is just not possible. The key insight, it turns out, is to accept uncertainty and recognize exactly what can and cannot be predicted – the limits to predictability. Only then can we realistically manage the uncertainty we confront in our daily lives and avoid falling victim to the vagaries of chance.

But why, it's only natural to ask, don't people already understand the implications of these limits? The reason is that, for much of our lives, we don't need to. For example, although there are uncertainties involved in everyday activities such as eating, going to the cinema, reading, or even walking down a street, we can deal with each of these as they arise. They require neither accurate forecasts nor much advance planning. At the same time, there are many events that we *can* predict accurately – consider the times of high and low tides, sunrise and sunset, or our favorite TV shows. Regularity and predictability rule much of our daily lives.

Yet, we also have to make many important decisions under quite different conditions – where we have only limited ability to predict and lack control over outcomes. Who knows, for example, what tomorrow's or next year's stock prices will be? When will a subprime crisis develop and cost financial firms, supposedly experts in handling risk, several trillion dollars in losses? Where and when will the next major earthquake or terrorist attack occur? Will your new boss like the way you work – and will she promote you? Then there's that new product you're launching after two years of intensive preparation. Will it be successful or will it flop?

The two kinds of situations are quite different. And yet, people still tend to treat the uncertainties of the second as though they were like those of the first – that is, predictable. Doing so may be psychologically comforting but it is actually illusory. In short, we suffer from an "illusion of control" that fools us into thinking the future is more predictable and less uncertain than it really is. Or worse, we believe we can influence chance events through our own actions.[3]

It's tempting to believe that these kinds of misconceptions no longer exist. After all, rational thinking is supposed to drive today's educated and technologically advanced societies. But superstition is still strangely prevalent. As recently as 2004, the National Science Foundation in the US reported that 28% of Americans believe in astrology, that 15% read their horoscopes every day or "quite often," and that 70% of students claim good luck charms help them perform better academically. On the other side of the planet, millions of Chinese people think that the color red will bring happiness, wealth, fame, and good luck. The Chinese also believe that the number 8 is super lucky. Indeed, one person paid 2.33 million Yuan, or $280,000 (at the time), to get the super lucky 8888–8888 telephone number consisting of eight 8s.[4] Recall too that the 2008 Olympics started in Beijing at 8 pm in the eighth month (August) of the year 2008 thereby further demonstrating the Chinese preference for the number 8. And beliefs like these are everywhere.[5] Italians omit the number 13 from their national lottery, more than 80% of high-rises in many parts of the world lack a thirteenth floor, airports often skip the thirteenth gate, airplanes have no thirteenth aisle, and hospitals and hotels regularly have no room number 13. These are superstitions that have no place in the twenty-first century, yet they're still to be found all over the world influencing the way billions of people behave.

Are we crazy? Absolutely not. We have an innate desire to control our environments and, in order to do so, we need to predict the future. This has helped us evolve as a species over the centuries. But it can also lead us astray. Above all it prevents us from recognizing the substantial and irreducible role of chance in our lives and leads us into making irrational decisions, often based on superstitious beliefs. This is true in practically all important aspects of our lives and work. Even if you *think* you are immune to all superstition, even if you *think* you are an expert in your field, even if you *think* you never behave irrationally, you can't help being human. You're born with an instinct to deny chance its rightful place – and your emotions only make this instinct stronger.

The advantage of superstition is that it comforts us into believing there are things we can do to control the uncontrollable. This is important because failure to feel in control of our lives is psychologically disturbing; it leads to both anxiety and stress. It's no wonder people succumb to the "illusion of control," which assumes predictability, ignores uncertainty, and minimizes the role of luck. Why be realistic and worry when it's much easier to believe that our own ability and actions can overcome the effects of chance?

In this book we show that being realistic and giving up the illusion of control actually increases the *genuine* control we have over our lives. We call this the "paradox of control." To dance with chance is to accept the role and importance of chance and to take advantage of the opportunities it creates while avoiding its negative consequences. Although psychologically discomforting, we will show you that this is actually beneficial and increases your control over your destiny. It lets you harness the role of luck to improve your personal well-being or – as we call it – your "personal Fortune."

Consider, for instance, the following questions:

- Why do banks use simple computer programs to assess the creditworthiness of potential customers rather than trusting the judgments of their managers?
- Why do the investment portfolios created by blindfolded monkeys throwing darts at stock listings often outperform

those chosen by professional money managers earning six-figure salaries?

- Why did a study in a major metropolitan hospital show that more accurate decisions would have been made in admitting patients to the cardiac unit if, instead of trusting physicians' judgments, decisions had been made using a simple statistical rule?
- Why are the richest Americans (as identified by *Forbes* magazine's list of billionaires) no happier than the Inuit people who live in the polar cold of northern Greenland?
- Why do countries that control their economies through central planning fare worse than those that don't?

As we will discuss in this book, the answers to all of these questions illustrate how giving up illusory control actually increases control and results in substantial benefits.

The illusion of control pervades almost all aspects of our lives and can have serious negative implications for our well-being. Ideally, we would like to have covered all the important issues affecting our lives in this book. But this is impossible. So, heeding our own advice, we ceded control to our potential readers by conducting a survey to find out what was most important to them. This revealed four critical areas that we'll cover extensively in this book. We then asked our respondents to estimate how much of what happens to them in these areas is due to their own abilities or actions as opposed to chance. Their answers revealed strong illusions of control and translate into the sad fact that our friends, families, students, and colleagues stand to suffer many unnecessary disappointments. Our goal, then, is to help them – and, of course you – overcome the illusion of control. Once you accept the inherent limits to predictability, we will show you how the paradox of control actually allows you to gain more control.

In short, this book was conceived to help you avoid costly mistakes and to exploit the role of luck in the most important aspects of your life. You should not be afraid to "dance with chance." Instead, you should seek both beauty and opportunity in randomness and take some life-enhancing steps of your own.

Spyros Makridakis
Robin Hogarth
Anil Gaba

# ILLUSTRATIONS

# One

# THREE WISHES FROM A GENIE

*Those who have knowledge don't predict.*
*Those who predict don't have knowledge.*

Lao Tzu, *Ancient Chinese Philosopher*

The tragic events of 9/11 are embedded in humanity's collective consciousness. The authorities have adjusted the official death toll of 2,974 a few times, but it remains close to the original estimates that we all listened to with horror on that September day. This much is well known. All *too* well known.

Statisticians, however, think the real death toll is much, much higher. The official count ignores the thousands of people who, influenced by 9/11, literally gambled with their lives. Perhaps, unwittingly, you too were one of the gamblers: one of the lucky ones, that is. Let's explain . . .

## THE ILLUSION OF CONTROL

After September 11, 2001, many people feared further terrorist attacks and chose to travel by car instead of flying. To put it simply, the number of airline passengers in the fourth quarter of 2001 fell by 18%, by comparison with the last three months of the year 2000. In other words, influenced by 9/11, close to one in five travelers decided not to fly. Let's look at some other numbers now: in 2001, there were 483 deaths among commercial airline passengers in the USA, about half of them on 9/11. Interestingly, in 2002 there wasn't a single one. And in 2003 and 2004 there were only nineteen and eleven fatalities respectively. This means that during these three years, a total of thirty airline passengers in America were killed in accidents. In the same period, however, 128,525 people died in US car accidents. Moreover, it has been estimated that – in the year following 9/11 – some 1,600 deaths could have been avoided if people had not driven but instead carried on taking the plane as usual.[1]

Why did so many people take their car instead of the plane after 9/11? The simple explanation is that, behind the wheel of your own automobile, it's natural to feel in control. Try telling drivers that they have no influence over the skills of other road users, the weather, the condition of the road, mechanical problems, or any other common causes of accidents – and they will agree. But they still *feel* in control of their destiny when they drive. They can't help it. Put them on a plane, and they think their life is in the hands of the airline pilot or, worse, a bunch of terrorists.

Psychologists call this the "illusion of control." It makes sense from an evolutionary point of view. The desire to stamp our authority on our environment explains much of our progress as a species – from the beginnings of agriculture to missions to Mars and beyond. The problem is that we don't know when to stop. For instance, experiments show that people think they're more likely to win the lottery if they pick their own numbers. They also think they'll do better in a game of chance if they throw the dice themselves. The truth is that they can make no difference whatsoever. These are games of pure luck.

In the case of the post-9/11 drivers, most of the deaths were caused by *bad* luck. But those who chose their cars over the plane can't be blamed entirely for their folly, as our inbuilt illusion of control is often magnified by media coverage. Plane crashes are turned into video images of twisted wreckage and dead bodies, then beamed into every home on television screens. It's no wonder so many of us dread flying – and did so even before 9/11. Meanwhile, the thousands of airplanes which arrive safely at their destination every day hold no media interest. This isn't news. So even the most logical of us are led to believe that the chance of a passenger dying in an airplane accident is much, much higher than it really is.[2]

Car crashes, on the other hand, rarely make the headlines, unless they're multiple pile-ups with mass fatalities (which are also statistical exceptions). Meanwhile, smaller-scale road accidents occur in large numbers with horrifying regularity, killing hundreds of thousands of people each year worldwide and seriously injuring many more. We just don't hear about them. Again, this lack of awareness prevents our logic from over-riding our instincts.

As the months and years that followed 9/11 show, the illusion of control – magnified by media sensationalism – can occasionally be fatal. The rest of the time, it can be dangerous to our health, wealth, success, and happiness in varying degrees. After all, for every death in a car accident, there are about nine serious injuries. That's partly why we've written this book – to show that we can't predict most of what happens to us, let alone control it. But there are things we can do to minimize the negative consequences of our inability to predict. Most of all, it's essential to understand the relative roles played by chance and our own actions in shaping our lives.

## FROM ILLUSION TO PARADOX

We believe that one of the biggest challenges facing us both individually and collectively is to accept the full extent of uncertainty that surrounds our decision making without being paralyzed by hesitation.[3] Being hit by a car while crossing a road, being struck by a coconut while on vacation in a tropical paradise, or getting incurable cancer is something that can happen to anyone. Yet the illusion of control makes us believe that such events only happen to others, never to us.

In this book we go beyond simply dispelling the illusion of control. Our message is both more subtle and more compelling. As human beings, we can never shake off our basic desire to eliminate uncertainty. But ironically, it's by realizing and accepting that we *don't* have control that we actually gain *more* control over what happens to us. This can make a big difference in the way we face the future and the decisions we take. Sometimes, we might avoid bad surprises by shaking off our illusion of control (say, by continuing to fly rather than driving). In other cases, we might be able to take out appropriate insurance to cover the risks we've identified (say, by taking out life insurance to protect our family in the event of tragedy, or simply wearing a seat-belt every time we travel by car).

However, the post-9/11 road fatalities suggest that relinquishing control can be even more powerful. If governments had diverted just a little of the colossal spending on increased airport security into raising awareness about the comparative risks of flying versus driving, they might have saved thousands of lives and even more serious injuries. The traveling public doesn't necessarily need a detailed understanding of probability theory or banks of statistics. Sometimes simple facts can be sufficient. Just knowing that in 2002 not a single airline passenger died as a result of a commercial airline crash in the USA, while car accidents killed 43,005 people (and seriously injured many more), can change behavior. The beauty is that, by giving up their perceived control and placing their well-being in the hands of an airline (over which they have no control whatsoever) travelers reduce their chances of having an accident. Paradoxically, by accepting that their previous sense of control was largely illusory, they gain greater control. This "paradox of control" is at the heart of this book.

## YOUR WISH IS YOUR OWN COMMAND. OR IS IT?

Imagine briefly that something very strange has just happened. Instead of revealing these very words and sentences, the act of opening this book has released a friendly genie who promises to satisfy any three wishes you desire. What will your wishes be? But wait . . . don't answer yet. Like all the best genies, this one has a few reasonable rules to follow, not to mention a little sound advice.

First, let's be both sensible and selfish. Your wishes should cover the long term in order to provide the most benefits for you – and you alone. Second, let's be realistic about what we're imagining here. Your wish can't exceed existing physiological limits. So, no, you can't live to the age of 500 or become twenty years younger. Third, let's think it through and not make the same kind of mistake as Midas, the mythical king who asked for everything he touched to turn into gold. It did – including his food, drink . . . and daughter. Fourth, bear in mind that you're not the only person to have access to a genie. (There's an imaginary one free in every copy of this book, after all.) So, by all means go ahead and ask to become the richest person in the world. Just don't expect to stay the richest for long, as someone else is bound to make the same request. Finally, no cheating. Your wish shouldn't contain double demands. To be rich *and* famous counts as two wishes, not one. And rest assured that the age-old trick of wishing for more wishes won't work either.

So take some time to reflect and write down your wishes below.

1. _____

2. _____

3. _____

Before we reveal how your wishes compare to those of others, here's another question: just how much control do you have over achieving your three wishes through your *own* actions? This time we ask you to indicate the degree of control you think you have by assigning a number between 0 and 100 to each of your three wishes, where 0 indicates no control at all (or total dependence on luck) and 100 indicates that fulfilling your wish depends entirely on your actions (and not at all on luck).

1. The control I have over achieving my first wish is (please enter a number between 0 and 100): _____
2. The control I have over achieving my second wish is (please enter a number between 0 and 100): _____
3. The control I have over achieving my third wish is (please enter a number between 0 and 100): _____

Now, you may have entered some pretty strange or unusual wishes. How do these compare with the responses of others? We've conducted several genie surveys – involving close to 1000 people, mainly business executives and MBA students, but also academics. Most of their answers turn out to be variations on the following four themes.

1. I wish to be happy.
2. I wish to live a long life – or at least a healthy one.
3. I wish to be wealthy.
4. I wish to be successful – for example, an entrepreneur who gets rich, an artist who becomes famous, an author who is published, a sportsperson who wins medals . . . you get the picture.

Of course, there are many requests for love too, but as this is notoriously difficult to measure, let's steer clear of it for now.

As for the degree of control people think they have over making their wishes come true, the answer depends greatly on the wish concerned. On average, our respondents score their control over happiness at about 63%, health and longevity at around 52%, for wealth it is 55%, and for success 61%. But are these answers realistic?[*]

The answer is a resounding "no." It turns out that we have almost no control over how long we live or how healthy we are. Certainly, we can make some valid generalizations about the types of people who last longest. Thin, active women who don't smoke tend to outlive obese, male couch potatoes who get through two packets of cigarettes a day. But at an individual level, doctors confess that their predictions are hit or miss. What's more, health is as dependent on chance as longevity is. Of course, people who die young or become seriously sick never believe it will happen to them. But somehow luck just isn't on their side.

Surely, though, we must have a lot more control over our happiness, personal wealth, or professional success? Hard work, determination, education, and experience should count for a great deal. But, again the evidence available suggests that luck is almost entirely responsible for *which* hardworking, determined, educated, and experienced people make it in life.

## BEING PREPARED

One reason why people fail to understand just how little influence they have over their own success is the media (yes, them again). We hear a lot about people who are successful, but very little about those who fail to realize their dreams. The press makes sure that we're all familiar with the achievements of Sir Richard Branson, Warren Buffett, Bill Gates, Tiger Woods, or Nicole Kidman. While we're dimly conscious that these people are exceptional, we rarely hear about the entrepreneurs, sportspeople, or actors who fail – or the sheer scale on which they do so. For example, did you know that in the USA there were more than 55,000 bankrupt firms and over 1.4 million bankrupt individuals in 2009? And the great majority of those involved believed it would never happen to them. In fact, nearly all aspiring entrepreneurs are convinced they will make it in a big way.

A second source of confusion is that we know from everyday experience that many physical phenomena are perfectly predictable. If we release our hold on a ball, it will fall to the ground. The sun will also go down this evening and come up tomorrow morning. And high tide always occurs exactly when it's supposed to. So, our reasoning goes, if we can predict these phenomena with such a high degree of precision, why can't we do the same for our own lives? Unfortunately, however, we have to realize that many events in the physical world are totally impossible to forecast reliably: things like earthquakes, tsunamis, hurricanes, and floods. When the tsunami hit South-East Asia in December 2004, killing over a quarter of a million people, the villain was not terrorists but Mother Nature herself. Yet the thousands of tourists who booked their holidays for this time could not have imagined that they were buying tickets to their own deaths.

When it comes to socio-economic phenomena, our ability to make accurate predictions drops to near zero. Who could have predicted the bankruptcy of Lehman Brothers, Enron or WorldCom, the stock-market crash of Black Monday in 1987 when stocks lost more than 22% of their values in a single day, the subprime crisis that led the world's economies into a serious recession resulting in many trillions in stock market losses and, according to the International Labor Organization, a reduction of 20 million jobs worldwide?

Now, let's be very clear. We're not advocating that you should give up aspiring to success in your chosen field – any more than you should give up listening to the weather forecast or taking exotic holidays. What we are saying is that everyone should make better efforts to *understand* and *estimate* their chances of success or failure in all that they do. Such insights would reduce bad surprises and disappointments, as well as help prepare for all-too-common failure. An unsuccessful business venture, for instance, can bring invaluable experience, or might be an excellent introduction to a new career and a network of people for the future. But without a few contingency plans, these opportunities may well evaporate by the time the liquidators knock on the door.

In other words, the first step is to *accept* our lack of control over our environment. Although tsunamis, earthquakes, and hurricanes do not occur often, they can hit us unexpectedly and with force. The second step is to *assess* our chances of success or failure in a realistic way – without the influence of the illusion of control or wishful thinking. Only then can we take the third – and crucial – step of *augmenting* our assessment of future uncertainty to allow for the possible occurrence of events that we can't currently imagine. (Remember, the enormity of 9/11 was unthinkable before it actually happened.) In this methodical way, we can handle risk with pragmatism and clear thinking. And that's what this book is all about. If you need a little further convincing, ponder the implications of the following story.

## CHECKS IN THE CITY

Hugo is a thirty-two-year-old trader who works for a well-known investment bank in the heart of London's financial district, the "City." He has been working there for seven years now, the last five as a futures trader. It's one of those work-hard jobs with play-hard pay. The exact amount is largely dependent on performance, and last year Hugo earned a little over £400,000 ($660,000 at the time) including bonuses – satisfyingly more than any of his old friends from Cambridge.

Today, there's an amusing diversion on the trading floor (which is something of a rarity). Some researchers from a business school want to see Hugo for a *very* short while (there's money waiting to be made, after all). They start by asking him a few biographical questions, and then ask him to participate in what looks like a rather old-fashioned video game. It involves an index that moves up and down across time – resembling some of the market data he monitors every day. The index starts at zero and increases or decreases every half second for fifty seconds in total. Hugo is told that the object of the game is to win points and that his score will be equal to the value of the index at the end of the fifty seconds. He is further told that the changes in the index across time are partly due to chance but that using three keys on the keyboard may have some effect on the final outcome. If he wants, he can use the keys.

Hugo plays the game four times, as requested, experimenting with the keys. He gets quite a good result on the first two attempts, a negative score on the third, and more or less finishes where he started the last time. After each round, the researchers ask him to rate, on a scale of 1 to 100, how successful he's been at using the keys to increase the index.

Hugo knew that the researchers had asked several of his colleagues to play the game too. That's what motivated him to try rather harder than he admits in their favorite wine bar that evening. What those sneaky researchers didn't tell him, however, was that using the keys had no effect whatsoever. They'd cunningly only said that the keys "may" affect the outcome. In fact, the index moved up and down totally at chance.

This story is based on a real-life study involving a total of 107 traders from four investment banks in 2003.[5] From our point of view, there are two particularly interesting results. First, the game was a method of scoring each trader's susceptibility to the illusion of control. The higher the traders rated the use of the keys, the greater the illusion about their own degree of control. Second, the researchers were able to relate these individual illusion-scores with characteristics of the traders, most significantly their performance-related pay. What they found was that, in general, the more the traders earned, the less they tended to succumb to the illusion of control! Averaging the salaries of the five with the highest illusion-of-control scores and the five with the lowest, they found a difference of roughly £230,000 ($380,000 at the time).

When Hugo read the draft that the business school sent to the bank a few months later, he was disappointed to see that his illusion-score (which he'd taken care to jot down in case of future opportunities for one-upmanship) was exactly half-way between the highest and the lowest – just like his salary. Of course, that's not what he said in the wine bar that evening. But, competitive soul that he was, he did learn from the experience. He adjusted his attitude to risk and tried to moderate his innate overconfidence. It worked. In the next four years he made four million in bonuses. Using his old expertise and his new realism to invest it, Hugo was able to double his money and change his lifestyle radically. When his old friends from Cambridge (who by now really are quite envious) ask, he fully admits he got lucky. The ex-trader now lives in a chateau in the south of France and runs a successful vineyard. He is also taking piano lessons.

## AND NOW, WHAT'S NEXT?

One way of thinking about the issues in this book is that each and every one of us is managing a personal "Fortune," representing the accumulated inflows of good and bad outcomes across our lives. Note that by "Fortune," a concept we'll return to many times in this book, we don't mean just "wealth" (or the magazine of the same title), but instead the many and various factors that affect the quality of our lives, such as friendships, recognition, happiness, fun, health, success, and, yes, wealth itself.

This book is a guide for managing your own personal Fortune. We'll focus on three broad areas: medicine, investments, and business. These areas not only provide good examples of the kind of reasoning we advocate; they also correspond, together with happiness, to the most requested wishes submitted to imaginary genies (based on our own surveys). So it's reasonable to assume that they're of interest to you.

Here are examples of some of the questions we'll be asking. Why do mammography screening programs have so little impact on breast cancer death rates? Why were so many investors delighted with annual returns of 7% at a time when the stock market had been growing at an average rate of 13% a year for some decades? Why do superstar companies suddenly fail? All three questions concern our inability to accept when it's impossible to make predictions. Often our quest for certainty leads us to believe that experts – such as doctors, fund managers, and CEOs – are able to see into the future when we cannot. This is just another example of the illusion of control. Even the best of experts aren't equipped with infallible crystal balls. No one can predict the future accurately – except perhaps in a few situations ruled by hard science or, otherwise, by sheer luck. No one can reduce the future uncertainty in your life. To believe otherwise is to fall prey to the illusion of control with all the negative consequences we've talked about.

The next six chapters give detailed answers to questions like those above. We'll provide empirical evidence that reveals our inability to predict the future accurately, some strategies for coping with the resulting uncertainty – and leave you to make the right decisions (after all, no one else can do it for you). Our recurring theme is that the best way of increasing your control, and improving your personal Fortune, is by accepting your *lack* of control. As you'll see, again and again, it is very costly to assume you have control over events, when, in fact, you don't. Equally important is the fact that no expert can help you increase your control over the future.

Be warned, the right decisions may be counter-intuitive. For example, we suggest that you don't take preventive medical tests, so long as you're healthy. We also think you should select your stocks essentially by chance, rather than relying on a fund manager whose seven-figure bonus is paid by customers like you. Success in management is a bit more complicated, if sometimes more common sense. The critical issue here is how to determine the best advice and come up with the best decision for your particular situation. This is certainly not by following the advice of gurus who write books with simplistic recipes for success. To make good business decisions in the face of mounting uncertainty and increasingly global competition requires novel thinking and innovative approaches. Sadly, we can't claim to help you find them (we'd be no better than the gurus if we said we could); though we do hope to persuade you how vital it is to think in this way.

There's not a great deal we can do directly about other aspects of your Fortune. The empirical evidence about happiness is much more slippery than in medicine, investments, and business. But (unromantic as this suggestion might be), if you take care of your health, wealth, and career success, happiness and perhaps love might take care of themselves? We'll touch on this in the last chapter of our book. Before we get there, however, we provide chapters on the theories and practice behind the issues we discuss.

In a nutshell, pragmatism in life depends on knowing what you can and cannot control. We clearly control our decisions. We can decide whether to invest our savings in the stock market, to accept a job, or to take our umbrella with us. However, we have no control over whether the stock market will go up or down, whether our new boss will be paranoid, or whether it will rain. Interestingly, the implications of our decisions are quite different in each of these cases.

Carrying an unused umbrella is no big deal, while taking the wrong job can have serious consequences for our career Fortune and sometimes even for our wealth, health, longevity, and happiness. In the case of the stock market, if we invest all of our money and our shares go down in price, it's a disaster. But if they go up, we increase our monetary Fortune. And if we invest only a little money, it's not so important what happens in the markets. In the end our success or failure is a combination of our own actions (investing in the market and choosing our stocks) and the effect of the environment (the market going up or down). And so it is with most decisions in life.

But in this book we don't just tell you about problems. We also suggest methods that can help you assess the uncertainties you face. This is often the hardest part of the process, as it's when our decisions tend to get engulfed by emotional forces. In particular, greed, fear, and hope can act as a Bermuda-style triangle that makes the best of rational intentions disappear without trace. Thanks to our suggestions, we believe you can steer clear of the dangers you face by accepting uncertainty with realistic hope and balancing greed with fear.

The book is organized as follows. We first examine empirical evidence about the limits of predictability in three domains: medicine, investments, and business (chapters 2, 4, and 6). The main goal of these chapters is to document what is truly known and thus arrive at the limits of predictability. For most people, the limits are closer than they imagine. So we also draw important conclusions about how to reap some benefits from uncertainty (chapters 3, 5, and 7). In particular, we show how failure to exploit chance can leave us much worse off than we need to be. Indeed, for financial investments, our losses can be quantified quite precisely.

In chapters 8, 9, and 10 we elaborate on the approach to managing uncertainty that we introduce in the earlier chapters and provide a general framework. Chapters 11 and 12 extend this framework by examining the apparent contradictions in our mental capacities and the pros and cons of different ways of making decisions. Chapter 13 discusses what is known about happiness while emphasizing our inability to predict it. Finally, in concluding we emphasize the limits of predictive ability.

And the genie? Well, we won't see much more of him. He's banished along with the wishful thinking that he and his sort encourage. For the rest of this book and – we hope – for the rest of your long, healthy, successful, and happy life, you're going to tackle real-life risk and uncertainty in a rational, practical, and effective way. Together let's hope that we dispel your own particular illusions of control once and for all.

# Two

# THE ILLS OF PILLS

*Anyone can get old. All you have to do is live long enough.*

Groucho Marx, *comedian*

A s we saw in chapter 1 – and as any good genie will tell you – most human beings wish to live a long, healthy life. Regardless of doctors, some people believe that it all depends on your parents. But it's not as simple as that. Whereas our parents' height explains some 80 to 90% of how tall we are, their longevity only accounts for 3% of how long we live. Even identical twins die, on average, some ten years apart.[1] In the next two chapters, we'll look at what determines health and longevity. In particular, we'll emphasize the uncertainty in medical knowledge and how to deal with it. To get us started, here are three stories about the medical profession.

## JUST WHAT THE DOCTOR ORDERED

Let's go back in time to 1685, when the British king Charles II was treated by fourteen of the best physicians available. He had uremia, a clinical syndrome caused by kidney dysfunction. The medical historian H.W. Haggard gives a vivid description of events.

> The King was bled ... to the extent of a pint from his right arm. Next [the physician] drew eight ounces of blood from his left shoulder ... gave an emetic to make the King vomit, two physics, and an enema containing antimony, rock salt, marsh-mallow leaves, violets, beet root, camomile flowers, fennel seed, linseed, cardamom seed, cinnamon, saffron, cochineal, and aloes. The King's head was then shaved and a blister raised on his scalp. A sneezing powder of hellebore root was given to purge his brain, and a powder of cowslip administered to strengthen it, for it was the belief in those days that nasal secretion came from the brain. The emetics were continued at frequent intervals and meanwhile a soothing drink given, composed of barley water, licorice, and sweet almonds, light wine, oil of wormwood, anise, thistle leaves, mint, rose, and angelica. A plaster of pitch and pigeon dung was put on the King's feet. Next there was more bleeding followed by the administration of melon seeds, manna, slippery elm, black cherry water, extract of lily of the valley, peony, lavender, pearls dissolved in vinegar, gentian root, nutmeg, and cloves. To this mixture were added forty drops of the extract of human skull. Finally, in desperation a bezoar stone was tried. The King died.[2]

It's hard not to believe that Charles II would have lived longer without the treatment of the celebrated physicians.

Back in the modern world and across the Atlantic, our second story is even more tragic. Ben Kolb was seven years old when he arrived at the Martin Memorial Hospital in Florida for a routine ear operation in December 1995. Doctors administered a general anesthetic that started to take effect – as planned – within about twenty minutes. The next step was to give an injection of lidocaine, a local anesthetic that reduces bleeding. It was shortly afterwards that things started to go wrong. First, Ben's heart rate and blood pressure increased to alarming levels. The emergency anesthesiologist was summoned and managed to stabilize his condition briefly. However, nine minutes later, his heart rate and blood pressure plunged dramatically, his lungs filled with fluid, and he went into cardiac arrest. For nearly two hours, doctors and nurses fought to get his heart working again, but their efforts were futile. Ben remained in a coma for nearly twenty-four hours, until his parents gave permission for the life-support machine to be switched off.

The post-mortem showed that Ben had died from human error. The syringe that was supposed to contain lidocaine in fact contained a massive dose of concentrated adrenaline. If only the mistake hadn't been made, we would probably never have heard of Ben Kolb, who would now be old enough to attend college with a great life ahead of him.

Now, fast forward six years or so for our third story. A federal district court in Wyoming rules that GlaxoSmithKline should pay $6.4 million in compensation to surviving family members of Donald Shell. On February 13, 1998, Shell, while on the antidepressant Paxil (also known as Seroxat), went on a killing spree in Gillette, Wyoming, shooting dead his wife, daughter, and nine-month-old grand-daughter with his .22-calibre pistol, before turning the gun on himself. On June 2, 2004, New York Attorney General Eliot Spitzer sued GlaxoSmithKline for consumer fraud, charging the company with concealing negative information about the popular antidepressant – which had huge annual revenues.

Although the company conducted three trials on Paxil, it published the results of only the one favorable trial. Worse, despite marketing the drug as suitable for adolescents, the company had no significant evidence from any of the three trials that Paxil was effective for depression in children. Finally, as the court heard, while the published study showed that the only adverse side-effect was headaches, the complete data set revealed that 6.5% of patients treated showed "emotional liability," including suicidal thoughts, compared with only 1.4% of those on a placebo. Actual suicide rates in the two unpublished studies were also higher for those on Paxil than for those not taking the drug.[3]

These stories illustrate three important points. First, the beliefs of even the most distinguished practitioners are often proven wrong at a later date. Medicine is not an exact science. Second, mistakes happen. Despite good intentions, human error prevails. Third, not all intentions are good. As in other fields, some blunders are caused by vested interests.

If this sounds a bit negative, don't be put off. We – like you and your doctor – have your well-being at heart. It's just that, if we're all going to manage the "health" dimension of your personal Fortune effectively, we need to be aware of the limitations of medical science and, as in other aspects of life, the significant role of luck.

We stress throughout this chapter that medicine is an inexact, evolving science. Thus, the fact that a well-meaning physician provides advice based on the best available knowledge of the day does not mean that he or she necessarily has the right answer (remember Charles II). Typically, patients do not perceive the uncertainty inherent in medical practice. But it's still there and to assume otherwise is to fall victim – once again – to the illusion of control. Doctors cannot eliminate uncertainty and, indeed, their advice tends to change (perhaps with very good reason) over the years or vary from one country to another. And quite apart from this inconsistency over time and place, scientists and physicians are human. They make mistakes for good (and sometimes bad) reasons. Some studies have even concluded that medical error is the third biggest cause of death in the USA, behind cancer and heart disease, killing more than 225,000 people every year.[4] The UK and Canada report similar results.

But there's another – more serious – problem with medicine. And this one is not entirely the medical profession's fault. Let's illustrate it by way of a couple of stories again.[5] Again, they're both true, but we won't name any names this time.

## SCREEN SAVERS?

Over a two-year period in the 1990s, one doctor convinced ninety women with positive test results from mammography screening to have radical surgery. It was the only sure way, or so he claimed, to save their lives and protect their loved ones from grief. What he didn't know (or worse, didn't explain) is that 93% of those who test positive with this kind of screening don't develop breast cancer.[6] That means approximately eighty-four of his patients had painful, expensive, intrusive surgery that, on the best possible reading of this story, brought them absolutely no benefits.

Around the same time a single mother was diagnosed HIV-positive after a screening program. At that point AIDS wasn't properly understood and none of today's powerful drugs had been developed. The woman lost her friends and her job, as everyone was scared to touch her. She too was afraid to cuddle her son or prepare his food. Then, nine months later, she caught bronchitis. She thought it was the beginning of the end, but her doctor recommended another AIDS test. "What's the point?" she thought, but – believing that doctors' advice should always be followed – she didn't argue. The test was negative. It turned out that her original results had been mixed up with someone else's. Although great news, it didn't erase the psychological scars suffered by both the woman and her affection-starved son. Meanwhile, the other person involved in the mix-up was about to get some very bad news – and too late to prevent possibly infecting other people with the HIV virus.

The point of both stories is that test results are not 100% reliable. And yet, both doctors and patients tend to treat them as such. The German psychologist Gerd Gigerenzer refers to this as the "illusion of certainty," a close relative of the "illusion of control" that we've already met. The lesson here for the patient? Simple: if you have an unexpected test result, take the test again. It's unlikely to be wrong twice in a row. *if done @ separate Labs*

Another lesson is for doctors and those who train them. To make a sweeping generalization, they need a better understanding of the uncertainties involved in their profession and more training in statistics. Unfortunately, we their patients don't help. We tend to have strongly deferential attitudes toward medical practitioners. We also have mistaken beliefs that physicians are all-knowing and that tests are infallible. We let doctors absorb our uncertainties. As we shall see throughout this book, by trusting experts, we create our own illusions of control. Perhaps we simply get the expert advice we deserve?

## HAPPILY EVER AFTER?

Now let's turn our attention to life expectancy. We are, of course, grateful to the medical profession for the amazing gains in life expectancy made over the last two centuries. However, that doesn't mean to say that today's doctors are all-knowing. When it comes to advice about how to live longer, it turns out that many modern assumptions are based on dodgy data or ropey reasoning. Unfortunately, this can lead to some pretty depressing conclusions. But bear with us at least until the next chapter, where we will return to a more upbeat position.

In the meantime, let's go back twelve to fourteen millennia. In those far-from-good old days, life expectancy was little more than twenty years. Then human beings started to domesticate animals, which provided a more reliable supply of food than hunting. A few thousand years later, people began to cultivate the land, a further innovation in the survival stakes. Life expectancy began to rise steadily and has been climbing ever since. By about 2,000 years ago it had reached twenty-five (a huge 25% increase). Another 1,000 years later, and in England at least, it had risen to thirty (another 20% increase). By 1750, when Britain started harnessing the benefits of the industrial revolution and growing economically faster than any other country, life expectancy increased by another five years to about thirty-five. After that, it grew exponentially, doubling to seventy in only two centuries. So, already, we can see the effects of luck on longevity: how long you live depends on when you are born.

It also depends *where* you are born and live. Today, if you rank countries by life expectancy estimates for those born in 2007, the top fourteen nations come out at over eighty years, while the next sixteen are above seventy-nine. At the other end of the scale, there are ten countries where life expectancy is between forty and forty-five and a further five where babies born in 2007 will be lucky to make it to forty. The difference – from Andorra at 83.5 years to Swaziland at 32.2 – is dramatic.

Even within developed countries, on the basis of life expectancy alone, you are lucky if you're born female. Japanese men, for example, can live on average to 74.2 years of age, while their sisters have a life expectancy of eighty-five (the highest national figure for women in the world). Similarly, there are big differences within countries and ethnic groups. In the USA, women of Asian origin living in Bergen County, New Jersey, have a life expectancy of ninety-one years, while male Native Americans from South Dakota average only fifty-eight.[7]

Whether we call it luck or fate, none of us have any control over our ethnicity, nationality, gender, and date of birth. So, apart from moving to Andorra, what can we do to improve our life expectancy and health? Unfortunately, not a lot. Beyond the obvious advice to avoid excesses – of tobacco, alcohol, drugs, food, and even exercise – there are few straightforward steps to longer, healthier living.

## THE RISKY BUSINESS OF LIFE

Scientists nonetheless have a way of analyzing the possible negative effects of certain activities on life expectancy. Based on observation, they've identified a number of so-called "risk factors" – an obvious example being smoking. They then ask, for instance, how life expectancy varies between people who smoke and those who don't. If it turns out that non-smokers live about one year longer on average than smokers then the scientists conclude that smoking reduces life expectancy by that amount.

One problem is that this is all they can hope to conclude. Some smokers – and even some scientists – interpret this (wrongly) as: "Quit smoking and you can expect to live one year longer." But to reach such conclusions, you have to look at the various studies which have compared groups of people who started and stopped smoking at different ages. Another problem is that people sometimes have complicated combinations of risk factors. Many smokers also drink alcohol to excess and fail to exercise. How do scientists and statisticians unravel the combined effects of different life choices?

In one major study, published in the prestigious international medical journal, *The Lancet*,[8] researchers set out to identify gains in life expectancy across twenty selected risk factors and many countries. They concluded that these twenty factors accounted on average for 16.1 years in sub-Saharan Africa and 4.4 years in the developed world. Many of the risk factors in the developing world – infant malnutrition, unsafe water, inadequate hygiene – are beyond the control of individuals, so we'll look only at the subset of eight risk factors relevant to developed countries.

We'll also compare the results of the *Lancet* research with those of another study from the Harvard School of Public Health.[9] The latter used the statistical technique of "meta-analysis" to estimate differences in life expectancy due to various risk factors. This involves

Table 1  Major risk factors: Contributions and life expectancy gains

| | | Years of life expectancy gained | |
|---|---|---|---|
| Major risk factor | Contribution | (*Lancet* study) | (Harvard study) |
| 1. High blood pressure | 4.4% | 0.90 | 0.75 |
| 2. Tobacco | 4.1% | 0.84 | 0.75 |
| 3. Alcohol | 4.0% | 0.81 | 0.81* |
| 4. High cholesterol | 2.8% | 0.57 | 0.75 |
| 5. High BMI (Body Mass Index) | 2.3% | 0.47 | 0.60 |
| 6. Low fruit/vegetable intake | 1.8% | 0.37 | 0.37* |
| 7. Physical inactivity | 1.3% | 0.26 | 0.62 |
| 8. Occupational risk factors | 0.9% | 0.18 | 0.18* |
| Total | 21.6% | 4.40 years | 4.83 years |

* Numbers from the *Lancet* study since there was no data for these risk factors in the Harvard study

aggregating all the available information from all previously published research. The figures in the last column of table 1 show the results of both studies (cheating a little, as the Harvard study didn't include alcohol, fruit and vegetable consumption, or occupational risk).

Table 1 shows us two ways of looking at the effects of risk factors. The first – labeled "contribution" – captures the percentage of variability in total life expectancy associated with each factor in the *Lancet* study. The big surprise here is that the sum of all eight "major" factors accounts for only 21.6% of the total. In other words, almost 80% remains unexplained and therefore beyond our control. The second and third columns of results (numbers) show the estimated years of life expectancy saved by eliminating each factor – and offer a similar surprise: the maximum expected improvement in life expectancy is only 4.4 or 4.8 years, with high blood pressure, tobacco, and alcohol having the greatest negative effects. The implication is that, in developed countries, all of which have eliminated the biggest risk factors such as malnutrition and poor sanitation, we're left with little room for improvement!

The conclusions vary slightly, but broadly the studies agree that these eight risk factors – all of which involve some degree of human control – account for around four to five years of extra life expectancy. This might be lower than we'd hoped. But not many people are going to argue about having an additional four or five happy, healthy years.

## GETTING ANOTHER OPINION

Hang on a minute, though. If we accept findings like these uncritically, aren't we falling into the same trap as those people who didn't dare question their unexpected test results? And shouldn't we also investigate the quality of medical data available? It's time to follow our own advice and get some second or third opinions.

In fact, if we look at the other available research, we find that the data on risk factors varies enormously. Let's start with the effects of cholesterol reduction on life expectancy. A study published in *The Journal of the American Medical Association* in 2000 underlines the differences in opinion between different researchers.

> An assessment of all the cholesterol-lowering dietary trials published in 1987 showed an aggregate 6% more deaths in those who adopted a cholesterol-lowering diet over those on a free diet. A similar review of drug trials showed an aggregate of over 13% more deaths in those taking cholesterol-lowering drugs. At the other extreme, a study analyzing data from 81,488 men between the ages of 18 and 39 years demonstrated a continuous graded association between elevated serum cholesterol and risk of coronary heart disease, cardiovascular disease, and all-cause mortality. Individuals with baseline cholesterol levels of less than 200 mg/dL had a greater life expectancy of 3.8 to 8.7 years.[10]

The relation between levels of cholesterol, the taking of cholesterol-reducing drugs, and mortality rates is clearly quite confusing. It's no wonder there's talk of a "cholesterol myth."[11] In addition, some stud-ies have shown that some cholesterol-lowering drugs are not only ineffective but may even increase the risk of heart attacks while also producing serious, negative side effects.[12] There are also concerns about conflicts of interest as drug companies may not be releasing negative evidence about the value of their drugs.[13]

Surely, though, there's less controversy about smoking, which has long been accepted as a killer? Research published recently in the *British Medical Journal* gives non-smokers as much as ten years longer than smokers. That's nine years more than the *Lancet's* estimate.

> The excess mortality associated with smoking chiefly involved vas-cular, neoplastic, and respiratory diseases that can be caused by smoking. Men born in 1900–1930 who smoked only cigarettes and continued smoking died on average about ten years younger than lifelong non-smokers.[14]

Similarly, those who never exercise would be advised not to read the 2005 back-catalogue of the *Archives of Internal Medicine*.

> Moderate and high physical activity levels led to 1.3 and 3.7 years more in total life expectancy and 1.1 and 3.2 more years lived with-out cardiovascular disease, respectively, for men aged fifty years or older compared with those who maintained a low physical activity level. For women the differences were 1.5 and 3.5 years in total life expectancy and 1.3 and 3.3 more years lived free of cardiovascular disease, respectively.[15]

As for the overweight, the *Annals of Internal Medicine* painted a bleak picture in 2003.

> Large decreases in life expectancy were associated with overweight and obesity. Forty-year-old female nonsmokers lost 3.3 years and forty-year-old male nonsmokers lost 3.1 years of life expectancy

because of overweight. Forty-year-old female nonsmokers lost 7.1 years and forty-year-old male nonsmokers lost 5.8 years because of obesity.[16]

Finally, the cheerily titled journal *Hypertension* had bad news in 2005 for those with high blood pressure.

> Irrespective of sex, fifty-year-old hypertensives compared with normotensives had a shorter life expectancy, a shorter life expectancy free of cardiovascular disease, myocardial infarction, and stroke, and a longer life expectancy lived with these diseases. Normotensive men (22% of men) survived 7.2 years (95% confidence interval, 5.6 to 9.0) longer without cardiovascular disease compared with hypertensives and spent 2.1 (0.9 to 3.4) fewer years of life with cardiovascular disease. Similar differences were observed in women.[17]

Now let's put the results of these separate studies together in our own table (table 2).

On these five risk factors alone, we get a total potential gain in life expectancy of over thirty-two years! How can this be? Was there something wrong with the way the studies were conducted? Or is there a flaw in the statistical reasoning? Which, if any, studies can we

**Table 2** Major risk factors: Summary of years of life expectancy saved

| Major risk factor | Years of life expectancy saved |
|---|---|
| 1. Smoking | 10.0 |
| 2. High blood pressure | 7.2 |
| 3. Obesity (average of men/women) | 6.45 |
| 4. High cholesterol (average) | 6.25 |
| 5. Physical activity (average of men/women) | 2.5 |
| Total | 32.4 years |

trust? We'll return to these questions later. For now, let's look at a few other well-known life-expectancy brain-teasers.

## SOME NATIONAL PUZZLES

Medical researchers and statisticians have always had problems explaining the data for certain countries. Take Japan, for instance. The Japanese per capita consumption of cigarettes is among the highest in the world, yet Japanese life expectancy is also the highest (at least for larger countries). If the British results, which – if you remember – give non-smokers a ten-year edge over smokers, were applicable, Japanese women, 41% of whom smoke, could expect to live an extra four years on average. That would take them up to an incredible eighty-nine-year life expectancy. Overall life expectancy in Japan would exceed eighty-six, if both men and women didn't smoke. And if we could rule out all the other risk factors, Japanese life expectancy would rise to well over 100 on the basis of table 2.

In the international smoking league tables, the first place goes to Greece, while Norway has the smallest per capita cigarette consumption in the developed world. Yet life expectancy in Norway is only three and a half months longer than in Greece, a country where physical exercise is famously unpopular and where hospital access is patchy – many islands don't have hospitals at all.

What about high-fat diets and cholesterol intake? France is perhaps the most well-known paradox in this respect. Life expectancy in Metropolitan France is more than eighty years – the tenth highest in the international rankings – although the French diet is notoriously rich in fat. If we go into further detail, we find that deaths from cardiovascular disease are lower than in other nations (39.8 per 100,000 as opposed to 196.5 per 100,000 in the USA). In particular, Périgord, the region in south-west France famous for producing the high-cholesterol delicacy *foie gras*, has a particularly fatty diet, with plenty of butter, and duck and goose products. Yet life expectancy is higher than in the rest of France and cardiovascular death rates even lower. Back on the national scale, if we compare France to Norway, we find that per capita cigarette consumption is 2.8 times higher in the former, and fat intake significantly lower in the latter. But – you guessed it – the French live on average about a year longer than Norwegians. The only possible conclusion is that there must be factors other than smoking and cholesterol to explain the difference in life expectancy between France (and in particular Périgord) and the USA, Norway, or many other developed nations, where public health campaigns against these two "vices" have had more effect.

By focusing entirely on the negative aspects of the risk factors – and the worst-case scenarios at that – these public health campaigns tend to raise falsely positive expectations about how we individuals can improve our chances of living longer. The message may be that "doctor knows best." But the deeper we dig into the evidence, the most charitable interpretation is the "doctor is telling us to be on the safe side." And, strangely, there's been comparatively little medical research about why the Japanese, Greeks, and French live longer than medical research suggests they ought to. If we're going to make reasoned choices about how to live our lives, we need more objective and accurate cost-benefit analyses of the many different activities that influence longevity.

## TIME WILL TELL?

The plot thickens yet further, when we begin to look at changes in medical advice over time. Nor do we have to go back to 1685 and the eccentric treatment of Charles II (where we started this chapter), to find doctors changing their minds. If we look at just a few examples from living memory, we see radical and inexplicable shifts in the positions taken by the medical profession.

Take coffee, for instance. Is it good or bad for you? Since the 1950s, coffee has been linked with heart disease and cancer. But the most recent studies – and the resulting hundreds of newspaper articles across the world – suggest that drinking coffee can prolong life, reducing the risk of conditions as diverse as heart problems, type-two diabetes, Parkinson's disease, cirrhosis of the liver, asthma, and even ovarian cancer.[18] Coffee is no longer a guilty pleasure, but a beneficial dietary supplement . . . at least until next year.

So how about salt? The website of the American Food and Drug Administration (FDA), part of the US Department of Health and Human Services, documents the controversial history of medical advice on salt intake and its harmful effects, notably high blood pressure. As early as 1998, a meta-analysis published by the *Journal of the American Medical Association* suggested that "restricting dietary sodium intake" has only a minimal effect on blood pressure.[19] However, the study was immediately attacked as having methodological flaws. The debate rages on right up to the present day. Indeed, the FDA is currently not making any recommendations on how high or low Americans' daily intake of salt should be. They talk instead about moderation and point out that eating *less* salt is clearly not harmful for the healthy, normal adult. Whether this advice is evading the issue or a tacit admission of the lack of evidence, it at least has the merit of being honest.[20]

And so to surgical procedures. Tonsillectomy was a very common practice up until the 1980s. Millions of people (mostly children) had their tonsils whipped out if they regularly became infected and swollen. Back in the 1920s some general practitioners even treated it as a preventive measure, performing tonsillectomy on toddlers in the same way that we vaccinate today. Nowadays, however, the surgical removal of tonsils is rare and only recommended for those with severe throat problems or sleep apnea (a disorder that involves lapses in breathing during sleep). The reason for the decline is that researchers noticed the health of children in geographical areas where the operation was common was no better than in those regions where it was rarely performed.[21] Not that this has stopped the debate. Much of the literature for throat specialists is for removing tonsils, while pediatricians are generally against. If this conflict comes as a surprise, remember what we said earlier about vested interests.

At least vitamins are still good for you. Or are they? There's certainly a huge international industry devoted to dietary supplements – and people say the market is usually right (even if the medical profession sometimes gets it wrong). However, a new meta-analysis of forty-seven research projects, involving 180,938 people who were randomly assigned real vitamins in varying doses or dummy pills, questions prevailing belief. It concludes that the three antioxidant supplements, vitamin A, vitamin E, and beta-carotene, can't be recommended and that taking them may even increase mortality rates![22]

Another more recent study of nearly 300,000 men showed that taking multivitamins more than seven times a week increased the risk of advanced and fatal prostate cancer. The study concluded that heavy multivitamin users were almost twice as likely to get fatal prostate cancer as men who never took the pills.[23]

## BUT WHY?

In order to figure out whom to trust in these shifting sands of advice, we should probably ask *why* the medical profession changes its mind so often. Let's try to find the answer by looking at one particularly extreme example. In 2004, *USA Today* typified the press coverage of a major study about obesity in America with a story entitled "Obesity on Track as No.1 Killer". The tabloid cited a study from the *Journal of the American Medical Association* stating that poor diet and physical inactivity had accounted for 400,000 deaths in 2000 compared with 435,000 deaths from tobacco.[24]

However, just one year later, a study by different researchers also appeared in the *Journal of the American Medical Association*. This study estimated that the effect of obesity was only 26,000 more deaths per year – one-fifteenth of the original estimate.[25] Although publicity raged on using the old numbers, a spokesperson for the Centers for Disease Control and Prevention (whose researchers were involved in both studies) told *The New York Times* that the agency wouldn't take an official position on the new paper, because "We're too early in the science."[26] One reason for the difference between the two studies was that the second also took into consideration the lower mortality risk rate of people who are overweight (but not obese) compared to those who are normal/thin. In other words, there are advantages to not being thin. As stated in an editorial in *The New York Times*, "excess pounds may have prevented some 86,000 deaths annually. That estimate has exploded like a bombshell amid the health officials struggling to control the undeniable upsurge of obesity here and abroad. It leaves the CDC, in particular, with a lot of explaining to do . . . The whole notion of what constitutes normal weight and overweight may have to be rethought."[27]

Another recent study on the topic, published in the *American Journal of Public Health* found:

> The mortality risk among 'normal' weight men (i.e., those in the BMI 'Body Mass Index is used to define normal, overweight and obese people' range of 20 to 25 kg/m$^2$) was as high as that among men in the mild obesity category (BMIs of 30–35 kg/m$^2$), with a minimum risk observed at a BMI of approximately 26 kg/m$^2$. Among women, the mortality risk was smallest at approximately 23 to 24 kg/m$^2$, with the risk increasing steadily with BMIs above 27 kg/m$^2$. In each specification, the slope of the line was small and volatile through the

BMI range of 20 to 35 kg/m², suggesting negligible risk differences with minor differences in weight for much of the population.[28]

In other words, this study found negligible differences in life expectancy between people considered to be of normal weight and those overweight, or even in the mild obesity category. The study also found that even fully obese people could expect to live longer than previous research had indicated. The conclusions are startling and have far-reaching consequences, since overweight and mild obesity are all associated with high cholesterol, high blood pressure, and inactivity:

> The present results highlight previous findings indicating that mild obesity and overweight are not strongly related to mortality. In addition, one cannot assume that a risk measured for a person with a BMI of 35 (a person with a BMI of 35 is considered to be in the mild obese category) should concern a person with a BMI of 30, especially when the personal and economic costs of weight loss are high. It would be more reasonable to focus on the smaller group of people in the severely obese category (BMIs of 40 and over; 3.3% of adults in 2002), which has a clearer relationship to mortality; however, some of this association, too, might be contaminated by omitted variables.

The author of the study also refers to previous findings, going back to 1996, indicating that the relation between mild obesity and mortality is not strong. It's puzzling that we hear so little about this side of the story amidst all the doom and gloom from the media and policy makers.

There is a final twist in the overweight/life expectancy saga. In November 2007, a new article was published in the *Journal of the American Medical Association* entitled "Cause-specific excess deaths associated with underweight, overweight, and obesity."[29] One of the conclusions of this article is the following:

Overweight was associated with significantly decreased mortality from noncancer, non-CVD causes (-69 299 excess deaths; 95% Confidence Intervals, -100 702 to -37 897) but not associated with cancer or CVD mortality.

Finally, another recent study conducted on older adults concluded the following:

We observed that fit individuals who were obese had a lower risk of all-cause mortality than did unfit, normal weight, or lean, individuals.[30]

In other words, while in 2003 overweight was considered to decrease life expectancy by more than three years and have little or no influence on life expectancy in 2006, the new studies now suggest that it is now associated with increased life expectancy. These types of contradictory claims over time seem to be unnervingly prevalent in medicine.[31]

In defense of the scientists, we have to conclude that they're working in an imperfect world. They're under pressure to publish their work and publicize their findings. And the chances of doing so are much higher if they can come up with some surprises or dramas. A 400,000 annual death rate, making obesity the number two or three killer in the USA (and on its way to becoming number one in a few years), is much more newsworthy than 26,000 (about the same as chronic liver disease). At the same time, the 26,000 figure is counter to the interests of all those who are advising on the merits of diets and the dangers of high cholesterol. It's also bad news for the companies which market drugs for weight loss, cholesterol reduction, and heart disease. And if this is happening for obesity and overweight, it's probably true in many other areas of healthcare.

We're not here to support the conspiracy theorists. We simply wish to inform reasonable people like you who want to improve your health, live longer and spend less money on doctors and medicines. All we're saying is that pressures from doctors, the media, the pharmaceutical industry, and society in general are sufficient to explain why the apparent certainty of medical science is just another illusion. Skepticism is not simply justified. It's advisable.

And that's before we take errors in scientific and statistical reasoning into account. Back in the 1960s, US scientists carried out the first large-scale study of mammography, involving 62,000 women.[32] One half received mammography and physical breast examination by a doctor, while the others weren't even aware that they were part of the research. During ten years of follow-up, the death rate from breast cancer was 23% lower in the screened women than in the control group. That sounds pretty conclusive! It was certainly enough to inspire an official recommendation of mammography tests for *all* women.

Yet, when we look at the numbers, doubts begin to creep in. In the tested group there were 147 breast cancer deaths. In the control group there were 192 – that's 45 extra deaths (and 45 is 23.4% of 192, hence the figure of 23%). Or stated in other terms, the reduction in deaths from breast cancer was about 7 in every 10,000 women. Put it this way and the numbers start to look smaller – and less statistically important. Of course, if you're an individual woman who believes her life was saved by screening, it's definitely going to seem worth it. But from a public policy viewpoint, advice recommending mammography tests for all women starts to look questionable, even if we disregard the costs and discomfort of testing.

But the story doesn't end here. The results of two subsequent studies in Canada, involving 90,000 women, showed that routine mammography testing had no effect on breast cancer mortality, even for the highest-risk age group of fifty to fifty-nine years of age.[33] Finally, the Cochrane Collaboration, a respected, international, not-for-profit organization dedicated to providing independent information about healthcare, audited the original 1960s study. It found two major flaws in the research. The corrected results provided no evidence <u>at all that mammography</u> screening reduces <u>breast-cancer-related deaths</u>.[34] Yet many doctors still recommend mammography!

Now consider the results of a study published in the prestigious *New England Journal of Medicine* in March 2009 that investigated the efficacy of screening for prostate cancer.[35] It compared 76,693 men split into two groups. Men in the first group were screened regularly; those in the second group were not. After ten years of follow-up, the researchers calculated the numbers of prostate cancer deaths in the two groups. Surprisingly there were slightly more deaths among those in the first group. Regular screening for prostate cancers did not seem to be useful in this large scale study.

At the same time, there was another, even bigger study involving 162,387 men conducted in several European countries.[36] There were 214 men who died from prostate cancer among those in the screened group versus 326 in the second, control group. Since there were 112 (326–214) less deaths among those screened, the relative reduction in deaths was 20.7% (112/540 = 20.7%, where 540 = 326 + 214). This 20.7% seems a huge reduction but this percentage, as with the reduction in breast cancers, is misleading. In absolute terms, the reduction in death rates is tiny as there were 162,387 men in the study and only 112 less deaths between the men in the two groups. In other words, for every 1,000 men there were about 0.7 less cancer related deaths,[37] or alternatively 1 death less for each 1,429 screened for prostate cancer. Worse still, it is impossible to know in advance which of the 1,429 is the lucky one.

According to the authors of the study this 0.7 decrease per 1,000 was achieved at a high cost as "1,410 men would need to be screened and 48 additional cases of prostate cancer would need to be treated to prevent one death from prostate cancer". There is a big cost, therefore, when screening for prostate cancer even if 0.7 lives per 1,000 are saved in doing so. Regrettably, however, as with breast cancer, physicians rarely explain the tiny improvement due to screening and the possible negative consequences involved.

## FALLING IN LUCK AGAIN

Vested interest and human error aren't the only grounds for doubt in the field of medicine. Sometimes it's just impossible to unravel the tangle of different factors at work. Nowhere is this truer than in healthcare research. If we look back to the research on high blood pressure published in *Hypertension* in 2005 (see above), we find that the authors are honest about the limitations of their data. On the one hand, they say, "Our findings underline the tremendous importance of preventing high blood pressure and its consequences in the population." On the other hand, they admit the following:

> Most of the data used in our analyses were collected at least 3 decades ago. The historic character of the Framingham studies limits the extrapolation of the findings obtained through analyses of the Framingham studies to today's populations. Great advances in health promotion and in the diagnosis, prevention, and treatment of CVD [Cardiovascular Disease] have occurred since the Framingham studies started.[38]

Framingham is a town in Massachusetts, where three generations of the population have so far participated in research into cardiovascular disease. It's a wonderful scientific project that is still underway. Nonetheless, the figures used in the study we've quoted date back to the 1970s and simply aren't representative of the population in general today. Page 283 of the lengthy paper lists the characteristics of the sample. The subjects are divided into three groups: one with normal blood pressure, the second high-to-normal, and the third high. The average height in each group (172 or 173 cm for men and 159 or 160 cm for women) is fairly representative of the current US population. But their weights vary considerably. Less than half of the men with normal blood pressure are overweight, while three-quarters of those in the high-blood-pressure group are overweight. There are similar differences between the groups of women. Even if the authors were able to "adjust" for weight, as they claim, the groups would still fail to be representative.

There's also something strange about the respective sizes of the three groups. Only 22% of the men and 26% of the women surveyed had normal levels of blood pressure. Is this possible? But the major problem with the data is the number of smokers. Across the sample, smoking rates are more than twice as high as they are in the USA currently. In particular, 81% of the men and 53% of the women in the groups with normal blood pressure were smokers. Even in Greece we don't find figures that high today! And when we look at the high-blood-pressure group, we find the proportion of current smokers is lower (74% for men and 38% for women). Should we conclude that smoking reduces high blood pressure and can be recommended? Of course not. But you really have to wonder about the relevance of the data.

Now maybe this well-respected study is perfectly good as a self-contained piece of research. What we're questioning is its suitability as the basis for recommendations made to the general public today. The data are not only thirty years old but highly unrepresentative of the current US population, let alone that of Greece or Périgord. After all, as we've seen, even its authors warn against extrapolating from their results. Yet doctors do, terrifying people that their high blood pressure will lead to an early death – a stressful situation which probably makes their blood pressure even higher!


## A SPOONFUL OF SUGAR AND A PINCH OF SALT

Shifting opinions, human weakness, and statistical minefields all seem to point in the direction of pessimism. It's starting to look bleak for those who want to take positive action to improve their health. But there's no need to become fatalistic. Our message is not that there's *nothing* you can do – just that received medical wisdom is downright uncertain. So, in the next chapter, we make some positive recommendations – about adopting a more scientific outlook, analyzing what medical tests really mean, gathering different opinions, and incorporating the inherent uncertainty of medicine into your outlook. In other words, we offer a spoonful of sugar to help the medicine go down. At the same time, we insist that you take medical science with the proverbial pinch of salt. After all, who's to say that a pinch of salt is bad for you?

# Three

# GETTING THE RIGHT MEDICINE

*My doctor gave me six months to live. But when I couldn't pay the bill, he gave me six months more.*

Walter Matthau, comedian

t's not all bad news. Despite the preceding chapter and its gloomy picture of medical science, there is a silver lining. As many doctors are ready to admit, medicine is an uncertain science. By accepting and understanding these uncertainties and the illusion of control that surrounds them, you can make better decisions about your health. Here, then, is the positive side of the story.

## MIND OVER MEDICINE

During the Second World War, Dr Henry Beecher, an American doctor operating in Anzio, Italy, ran out of morphine. He started injecting his patients — some of whom had terrible injuries — with a harmless saline solution. To his surprise, there was little difference in the results. The soldiers thought they'd received morphine, and the

salted water, acting as a placebo, seemed capable of suppressing quite
excruciating pain even among those recovering from amputations.
But of course, it wasn't really the saline solution doing this. It was the
human mind.

Stories of the incredible power of the mind to cure the body are
not simply found in the literature of pain-killing and drugs. In the late
1990s, for instance, a Swedish hospital operated on eighty-one people
who had a condition in which the heart muscles thicken abnormally.
Typically, some sufferers experience only mild effects, while others
become seriously ill and die. A common cure is to insert a pacemaker,
which is exactly what happened to the eighty-one patients. The twist
was that for half of them, the pacemakers weren't turned on! And yet
they all experienced the same kind of improvements (though to a
slightly lesser extent in the case of those whose pacemakers were
switched off): less chest pain, dizziness, shortness of breath, and heart
palpitation.[1]

Readers of the previous chapter may be suspicious of the
small sample size in this example. So here's another case from the
placebo literature. In a large group of men, aged thirty to sixty-four,
who had suffered a heart attack during the previous three months,
1,103 were given a potent drug (clofibrate) and 2,789 a placebo. The
researchers followed their progress for at least five years and found
almost no difference in mortality rates between the two groups: 20%
of those on the real drug and 20.9% of those taking the placebo died.
The scientists also noticed that those who took their pills regularly
had better survival rates. Of patients on the active drug who took
more than 80% of the prescribed dose only 15.7% had died five years
later (compared to 22.5% of those who took less than 80%).
However, the same thing happened in the placebo group. Of
those who took more than 80% of the fake medicine, only 16.4%
had died five years later (compared to 25.8% of those who took less
than 80%).[2]

The conclusion is that placebos can work almost as well as real medicine. A.K. Shapiro, one of the most noted authorities in this field, summarizes the situation as follows.

> Placebos can be more powerful than, and reverse the action of potent, active drugs. The incidence of placebo reactions approaches 100% in some studies. Placebos can have profound effects on organic illness, including incurable malignancies. Placebos can often mimic the effects of active drugs.[3]

For those of us in search of positive messages, the lesson here is that the human mind can produce effects as strong as the most powerful drugs. Despite over fifty years of research, science is yet to explain fully the self-healing or pain-suppressing power of the placebo, but the implications for our health and longevity are significant. How much more can the mind and body achieve together?

Perhaps some of the answers to the placebo mystery will be uncovered by the more recent medical interest in "self-rated health." The rise of the internet has brought with it all kinds of life-expectancy calculators and do-it-yourself health-assessment tools. It's not yet clear how accurate these are, but several studies have compared the ability of doctors to assess our health and life-expectancy with our own ability to do the same. In such research, doctors typically read the medical history, see the results of tests, and carry out a detailed examination for each person concerned. Independently of the doctor's prediction, the person is then asked to answer a simple, multiple-choice question such as the following:

In general, would you say your health is:
(a) Excellent (b) Very good (c) Good (d) Fair (e) Poor?
(please circle the right answer)

Surprise, surprise . . . self-rated health scores provide more accurate indications of how much longer people will live than the doctors' predictions – at least according to the research in this area.[4] Those rating their health as "excellent" – especially the women – were between two and ten times as likely to be alive six to ten years later than people who rated their health as poor. Even current age and smoking, the two best objective indicators, were less reliable predictors of longevity than the simple multiple-choice question. People, it turns out, and particularly older ones, are the best judges of how long they will live, based on a simple assessment of how they feel right now.

So that's our positive lesson number one. If you feel good, you're probably doing something right. Unless you're a hopeless hypochondriac, you should probably trust the signals your own body is giving you – and the power of your own mind to influence your body. We're not saying that your body and mind, working together, guarantee the certainty that medical science lacks, but that they provide a fairly reliable indicator of whether to consult a doctor.

## THE VALUE OF SCREENING

Ah, but . . . what if your body and mind are plotting to hide something from you? Shouldn't you have an annual check-up or regular tests for killer diseases? As we mentioned in the introductory chapter, this sounds like common sense, but empirical evidence reveals no difference in life expectancy between those who undergo annual check-ups and those who don't. And there sure is plenty of empirical evidence. Doctors have been recommending yearly health checks since 1920, but recent studies reveal that millions of annual check-ups over the years have neither improved patients' health nor prolonged their lives.[5]

Of course, screening programs vary across countries, cultures, and time. Attitudes to preventive testing often depend on how healthcare is funded. The vested interests of private healthcare providers and insurance companies in the US, for instance, are very different from the cost-saving instincts of the state-run National Health Service in the UK. It's important to understand not only the economic context but also the evidence for the test in question. To explain what we mean, let's take two examples: one for the benefit of younger women, the other especially for older men.

The first example is highlighted by a change in the American College of Obstetricians and Gynecologists' recommendations to pregnant women, proclaimed at the beginning of 2007. Previously, the advised form of screening for Down's syndrome was a blood test. The more expensive amniocentesis test, which takes a sample of the fluid in the womb, had been recommended only for women over thirty-five, who are at greater risk, or those for whom the blood test had indicated abnormalities. The new advice was that all pregnant women, regardless of age or blood-test results, should have the more expensive test.[6]

Now, doctors rarely mention this, but *all* tests are subject to two types of errors. In this case, one possible – but very rare – error is that the test fails to detect a baby with Down's syndrome. This is called a false negative. The other possible – and much more common – mistake is that the test indicates Down's syndrome for a completely normal fetus (often leading to an unnecessary termination). This is called a false positive. A third problem, specific to amniocentesis, is that it occasionally causes a miscarriage. All three problems can lead to a great deal of heartache in their different ways.

Putting heartache aside, let's look dispassionately at the statistical evidence. Figure 1 indicates the various outcomes for a theoretical population of 2,500 pregnant twenty-five-year-old women. Given that the rate of Down's syndrome is about 1 in 1,250, two of the women will have fetuses with the abnormality, whereas 2,498 won't – that's the second level down. The third level gives the outcome of

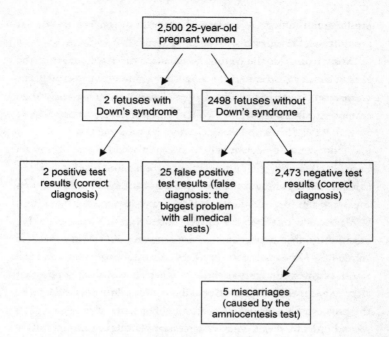

**Figure 1** Are tests for Down's syndrome justified?

amniocentesis for the two groups of women. As the chances of a false negative are very small, we'll imagine that both the Down's syndrome babies are identified. The chances of a false positive are also small: about 1% in fact. But the numbers of women carrying normal fetuses are much higher (2,498), so that in our imaginary sample, twenty-five women with normal babies will test positive, while the remaining 2,473 will get the correct result. This makes the chance of a woman carrying a Down's syndrome baby if she tests positive only about 7% (two out of the total twenty-seven who received positive test results). In addition, there is a two in one thousand chance of amniocentesis inducing a miscarriage, so four to five of the women across the two groups will lose their babies. Again, given the tiny numbers in the first group, let's assume these are all in the largest group (the 2,473 women with negative results).

What exactly do these numbers mean in practice? Looking on the bright side, as we promised, if you're a twenty-five-year-old pregnant woman who tests positive for Down's syndrome on the basis of an amniocentesis test alone, then your chances of having a normal baby are still 93%! Makes you wonder why you took the test in the first place, doesn't it (especially when you add the small risk of miscarriage into the mix)? And if this is the reasoning for an individual, the case for making amniocentesis-for-all a public health policy is even smaller. If the cost of each test is $100, we've just spent a theoretical $250,000 on a test that led to five miscarriages (with the further expenditure that entails) and twenty-seven repetitions of the test at another $2,700, plus the not insignificant emotional stress until the results of the second test are known. That's assuming of course that all twenty-seven women who tested positive follow our advice from the previous chapter, which seems highly pertinent here, and get a second opinion. If not, some unnecessary – and even more costly – terminations may take place. Meanwhile, one or both of the two women with the "true positives" may well decide to proceed with the pregnancy anyway – on religious or other grounds. Was it worth it? We let you, the reader, decide.

And that's the whole point. Any patient, undergoing any tests (especially if they're for purely preventive reasons) should have access to the relevant data and reasoning. The doctor should run through diagrams like figure 1, particularly highlighting the issue of false positives – which occur with all medical tests – in order to both inform the patient and avoid unnecessary alarm. The danger comes from blindly following health-policy directives and slipping into the illusion of certainty – or worse, fog of ignorance and fear – that test results all too often induce.

Now for our second example. In his excellent book *Calculated*

*Risks: How to Know when the Numbers Deceive You,* the psychologist Gerd Gigerenzer highlights a second important example: screening for prostate cancer using a prostate-specific antigen (PSA) test.

> people who take PSA tests die equally early and equally often from prostate cancer compared with those who do not. One cannot confuse early detection with mortality reduction. PSA tests can detect cancer, but because there is as yet no effective treatment, it is not proven that early detection increases life expectancy. [. . .] The test produces a substantial number of false positives, and therefore, when there is a suspiciously high PSA level, in most of these cases there is no cancer. That means many men **without** prostate cancer may go through unnecessary anxieties and often painful follow-up exams. Men **with** prostate cancer are more likely to pay more substantial costs. Many of these men undergo surgery or radiation treatment that can result in serious, lifelong harm such as incontinence and impotence. Most prostate cancers are so slow growing that they might never have been noticed except for the screening (out of 154 people with prostate cancer only twenty-four die of the disease). Autopsies of men older than fifty who die of natural causes indicate that about one in three of them has some form of prostate cancer. More men die **with** prostate cancer than **from** prostate cancer.[7]

A recent study, published in the *Journal of the American Medical Association* reaches similar conclusions about the value of screening with CT scans. The researchers tested 3,246 current and former smokers and found nearly three times as many people with lung cancer than would have been predicted. Yet there was no corresponding reduction in advanced lung cancers or even deaths. "Early detection and additional treatment did not save lives, but did subject patients to invasive and possibly unnecessary treatments," said the authors.[8]

It's no wonder that more and more medical experts are advising against cancer screenings altogether. In a recent book, Dr. H. Gilbert Welch, an American physician, claims that screenings tend to miss the fastest-growing, most deadly cancers, while cancer-free patients with abnormal screening results often endure endless, sometimes risky testing that leads to unnecessary treatment and yet further superfluous tests.[9] Some of his colleagues in the profession are going further, questioning surgical procedures in the same way. Dr. Norton M. Hadler is urging the US medical establishment to rethink some of its most basic beliefs about cardiovascular care. In particular, he says that by-pass surgery "should have been relegated to the archives fifteen years ago." The procedure, he continues, "extends life or prevents further heart attacks only in a small percentage of patients — those with severe disease."[10] Another physician, L. David Hillis, supports this conclusion and extends it to angioplasty, in which narrowed blood vessels are expanded and then, typically, propped open with metal tubes. As he points out: "People often believe that having these procedures fixes the problem, as if a plumber came in and fixed the plumbing with a new piece of pipe, but it fundamentally doesn't fix the problem."[11]

It's that illusion of control again. Our desperate, innate desire to eliminate all threatening uncertainty can be the only explanation of why we're repeating the medical mistakes of the past instead of learning from them. As fast as we get rid of old recommendations, such as annual health checks, regular mammography screening and PSA, we seem to be introducing new ones like advising amniocentesis for all pregnant women.

If this sounds a bit negative again, it wasn't meant to. We refer you to our previous positive conclusion to trust your own assessment of how you feel. In most cases, if you feel good, there's no need to take a test to see if you've got an illness. To that we now add another active recommendation: all aspects of your personal healthcare should be guided by sound reasoning based on empirical evidence. Find out the dangers, as well as the benefits, of undergoing testing, a course of drugs, or a medical procedure.[12] This approach, championed by Dr.

David Eddy among others, has become known as "evidence-based medicine."

We'd like to extend our advice to governments as well as individuals. In the same way that government agencies license drugs (for example the Food and Drug Administration in the USA), they should also make up-to-date recommendations about medical procedures. That way, we'd know an independent, official body had looked at the available evidence and reached a bias-free conclusion. Knowing the world of medical research as we now do, we wouldn't necessarily hold them to it for long! But at least our task of actively managing our own health by weighing up the evidence would be simpler.

## TOO POSH TO PUSH?

Getting hold of the evidence isn't always simple, as the classic case of Cesarean section shows. This, as most people know, is a form of childbirth that involves making a surgical incision to deliver one or more babies. The idea behind the procedure is that it's used when a "normal" delivery would lead to dangerous and possibly life-threatening complications for the mother and/or child.

Although most Cesarean sections these days don't require a general anesthetic, it is without doubt a major abdominal operation that shouldn't be taken lightly. The UK National Health Service estimates the mortality risk of a Cesarean section as three times that of a vaginal birth. On the other hand, this isn't a fair comparison, as the women having surgery tend to be the ones at higher risk. And anyway, the mortality rates for both types of birth have dropped steadily, at least in the developed world. As we said, finding and interpreting the evidence isn't always simple.

Nevertheless, Cesarean sections have some distinct disadvantages. From the mother's point of view, the recovery time is much greater than for a "normal" birth. The operation also leaves an unsightly scar and brings an increased risk of infection. From the baby's perspective, the anesthetics and drugs administered to the mother sometimes mean a sluggish start to life, occasionally with breathing problems. And breastfeeding – with all its proven benefits – tends to be more difficult after a Cesarean, partly because the mother's mobility is reduced. From the healthcare provider or insurer's perspective, there's also a major extra cost to perform an operation. In the longer term, a study recently published in the journal *Obstetrics and Gynaecology* found that women who had multiple Cesarean sections were more likely to have problems with later pregnancies.[13] The conclusion was that women who wanted large families should have vaginal deliveries if possible. And this time, the sample of 30,132 Cesarean births seems statistically ample!

So why are Cesarean sections so incredibly popular – and apparently getting more so? Some recent estimates put Cesarean births at over 30% of the total in the USA in 2005 – an increase of 46% since 1996.[14] Why too is there so much variation from one developed country to the next, as table 3 reveals?

Are Italian doctors justified in performing one-third of births by Cesarean section? Or are their Dutch colleagues right – with a rate lower than 13%? Clearly, it's highly unlikely that they're both correct, as the women of these two countries can't have significantly different medical needs. Curiously too, table 3 shows a positive relation between rates of Cesarean births and infant mortality.[16] As we said earlier, this is a tricky issue to unravel, but it's interesting that Sweden, with one of the lowest rates of Cesarean births, has by far the lowest infant mortality rate while that in Italy is one of the highest.

Perhaps some of the answers can be found by looking at the variation in Cesarean rates *within* countries. Hollywood and celebrity parents famously tend to opt for the operation. And in general, the so-called "elective" Cesarean tends to be a privilege of the rich. A recent study of births in three Greek hospitals – two public and one

**Table 3**  Births by Cesarean section (year 2000): various countries[15]

| Rank | Countries | Number of births by Cesarean section per 1,000 live births | Infant mortality per 1,000 live births |
|------|-----------|------------------------------------------------------------|----------------------------------------|
| 1 | Italy | 333 | 5.94 |
| 2 | Australia | 217 | 4.69 |
| 3 | USA | 211 | 6.50 |
| 4 | Germany | 209 | 4.16 |
| 5 | Canada | 205 | 4.75 |
| 6 | Ireland | 204 | 5.39 |
| 7 | New Zealand | 202 | 5.85 |
| 8 | Austria | 172 | 4.66 |
| 9 | France | 171 | 4.26 |
| 10 | UK | 170 | 5.16 |
| 11 | Belgium | 159 | 4.68 |
| 12 | Finland | 157 | 3.57 |
| 13 | Denmark | 145 | 4.56 |
| 14 | Sweden | 144 | 2.77 |
| 15 | Norway | 137 | 3.70 |
| 16 | Netherlands | 129 | 5.04 |

private – concludes: "The CS rate in the public hospitals was 41.6% (52.5% for Greeks and 26% for immigrants), while the CS rate in the private hospital was 53% (65.2% for women with private insurance and 23.9% for women who paid directly)."[17]

There are two possible interpretations. The first – more charitable – explanation is that a Cesarean section is the ultimate "illusion of control". Rather than waiting for nature to take its course, those doctors and parents with the means to do so slot this time-efficient method of giving birth into their busy schedules. Ironically, by seeking certainty, these mothers are often exposing themselves to greater risk – but that's their business (if possibly a little unfair on the baby, who has no say in the matter).

The other interpretation is less generous toward the medical profession. Could it possibly be that doctors' decisions are influenced by the lure of higher revenues and bigger profits?[18] Far be it from us to cast aspersions on their ethics, but there are many from within the medical profession who do so without prompting. Dr. David Walters, head of cardiology at the University of California in San Francisco, claims that conflict of interest is a major issue in his field, where doctors perform about 400,000 by-pass operations and one million angioplasties a year, creating a heart surgery "industry" with an estimated $100 billion annual turnover.[19]

And so we return to our positive assertion that patients deserve a more evidence-based approach to choosing their individual treatment. If each country or grouping of countries could have some kind of independent, not-for-profit "auditor" of the evidence, so much the better. The assumption that each of us has to fight is that extra healthcare, extra medical intervention, and extra testing mean more health and a longer life. On the contrary, perhaps. As Michael Moore, in his acclaimed 2007 documentary *Sicko*, and many other commentators point out, the longer you can stay outside the healthcare system, the longer you avoid its many risks to your health – from human error to deadly, flesh-eating hospital super-bugs.

Mainstream medical care is based on the assumption that what a physician decides is, by definition, correct. Although many decisions are indeed right, there are plenty of others that are highly questionable. So it's important to find a way to reassure patients that they're receiving the best medical care for their own specific cases – and that such care does not reflect inappropriate interests. Once again, we advocate the approach of evidence-based medicine. Moreover, in order to avoid any suspicions of conflict of interest, there should be some independent, non-profit organization, like the US Food and

Drug Administration or the Cochrane Collaboration, to verify or even audit the empirical evidence. Most importantly, patients should be able to get information about the benefits, dangers, and costs of the various forms of medical care available to them and not be "forced" – through fear or ignorance – into specific treatments.

The problem is that higher spending on health does not imply improved medical care, as Dr. Elliott S. Fisher, professor of medicine at Dartmouth Medical School in New Hampshire, found out. He had assumed that people in areas with low health expenditures would have worse health than those in regions where spending was up to twice as high. However, the opposite turned out to be true. His conclusion: "Patients have a substantial increased risk of death if cared for in the high-cost systems."[20] The reason is that additional physician visits and testing often lead to unnecessary procedures and hospitalizations, which carry equally unnecessary risks. This is a classic example of the paradox of control.

## THE GOOD NEWS

It is important at this point to put our concerns about medical practice in perspective. We don't question that the medical profession has had remarkable successes and made incredible progress over the years. Think of all those wonder drugs we read about in the papers. No one can deny that the world is far better off for the discovery of drugs such as aspirin and quinine. In fact, both have been around long enough for us to be absolutely certain that they work (even if excessive claims are sometimes made for the ability of aspirin to prevent heart attacks and various forms of cancer). Then there are antibiotics, which have transformed society by eradicating not only the infection but also the terror of tuberculosis. Today, the innovations continue with the development of synthetic drugs that allow people with, for example, serious thyroid deficiencies to live perfectly normal lives.

Surgical techniques have also made great strides. What neurosurgeons can do today could scarcely be imagined a generation ago. And it's hard to believe that it was only just over forty years ago (in 1967) that Dr. Christiaan Barnard performed the first ever human heart transplant. Key-hole surgery too has transformed many lives – and the careers of professional sportsmen and women who are no longer sidelined for months by certain types of injuries.

At the same time, countless erroneous medical theories have been discredited. It was only two hundred years ago, for instance, that deliberate bleeding was supposed to cure all manner of ills. And nowadays, it's rare for a doctor to make a diagnosis by examining the patient's tongue with great care – common practice just a generation or so ago.

We take no issue with these particular developments. Nor do we contest that general medical knowledge has increased and that diagnosis is far more accurate than ever before. Our arguments are with the way in which medical data are so often interpreted. But most of all, we dispute doctors' and patients' refusal to accept the uncertainty that inevitably remains to this day. As a society, we could make much better use of what we already know – even though this knowledge is often imperfect. Consider, for example, what a difference it would make if people understood the simple fact that medical tests can incur two kinds of errors (the false positives and the false negatives that we described earlier in this chapter), each with extremely serious implications for our well-being.

## TAKING ACTION

Back in 1923, the French writer Jules Romains wrote a comic play about Dr. Knock, who purchases an unprofitable village medical practice in rural France. He then proceeds to diagnose practically everyone in the village with an illness and prescribes a cure for each character at a price proportional to their income.[21] But is this the stuff of provincial comedy – or an ongoing tragedy on an international scale? Nearly a century later, the doctor and commentator H.G. Welch, whose book we referred to above, writes in *The New York Times*, that over-diagnosis is making people ill.

> For most Americans, the biggest health threat is not avian flu, West Nile or mad cow disease. It's our healthcare system. You might think this is because doctors make mistakes (we do make mistakes). But you can't be a victim of medical error if you are not in the system. The larger threat posed by American medicine is that more and more of us are being drawn into the system not because of an epidemic of disease, but because of an epidemic of diagnoses. [. . .] But the real problem with the epidemic of diagnoses is that it leads to an epidemic of treatments. Not all treatments have important benefits, but almost all can have harms. Sometimes the harms are known, but often the harms of new therapies take years to emerge.[22]

Our purpose is not to criticize any one country's doctors or even the medical profession in general. As we've said before, it's thanks to medical science that people now live longer and more healthily than ever before in history. We'd just like to make the point that the time has come for a worldwide change – both on the part of the healthcare industry and its consumers.

In general, for those who feel healthy (and aren't pregnant), our first piece of advice, based on the overwhelming empirical evidence, is to stay away from doctors. Second, when people really have to turn themselves into patients, they should recognize the inherent uncertainty of medical science. This brings us to our third piece of advice, which is to make yourself as informed as possible about any diagnosis, test, or treatment you are going to receive. There's also some parallel advice for the medical profession, which should be to do everything in its power to help its customers make informed decisions. Finally, if possible, get that proverbial second (or even third) opinion. And even then, if it's not an emergency, wait a few weeks before taking action. You can use the extra time to source further information and to achieve a calmer, more rational standpoint.

Today, we have many sources of information at our fingertips. Examples include the Foundation for Informed Medical Decision Making (www.fimdm.org) in the USA, a non-profit organization that helps people get hold of the information they need to make sound decisions about their health, or an agency for healthcare research and quality, supported by the US Department of Health and Human Services (www.ahrq.gov/clinic/uspstfix.htm). In the UK, there is information from NHS Direct (www.nhsdirect.nhs.uk), a multi-channel information source provided by the state. There are also specialized information sources and web tools for making decisions about specific conditions. According to the Foundation for Informed Decision Making, patients who get the full story – as opposed to listening simply to what the doctor tells them – tend to opt for less intervention. Studies carried out by the Foundation and others show that up to 60% of people change their decision once they have all the information available.[23]

Of course, we hasten to add, we're not recommending web-based self-diagnosis – which has become a true plague of modern medicine. That would be a good deal worse than passively accepting a doctor's diagnosis. Instead, show your physician that you're well informed and impress them with some penetrating questions, like the following:

- Can you tell me the benefits and dangers of the treatment you're proposing?
- Are there alternatives? If so, what are the respective pros and cons of each of them?

- What are the conclusions of any empirical research on the treatment or its alternatives?
- Are the side effects of the drugs I will need to take known? And if yes, what are they?
- Has any independent organization like the Cochrane Collaboration audited the research findings?
- What if I do nothing? Will it affect my quality of life or years left to live?
- If I go ahead with the treatment, will I need further therapy in the future?
- Is the cost of the treatment likely to be covered by my private insurance (or national healthcare system)? If not, how much will the total cost be?

You won't simply get answers to help you make an informed decision. You should also gain the respect of your doctor! Ideally, you will reach a position where you're making a decision yourself with the help and support of your doctor – free of all bias and snap judgments. In his book *How Doctors Think*,[24] Dr. J. Groopman advises precisely this course of action. So once again there's a precedent for what we're saying from within the medical profession. In addition, be prepared when you visit your doctor. Follow the advice of Dr. Terrie Wurzbacher[25] and pre-empt any important questions about your health before you're asked. Write down your answers even. Are you taking any medication or supplement, whether off-the-shelf or prescribed? Are you on a diet? How much alcohol do you drink? How much exercise do you get? Are you under stress – or have you endured severe stress in the past? Do you suffer from any allergies? Do you have a history of certain problems in your family? If your doctors have all this information and more at their fingertips, they can concentrate on discussing your current condition and explaining the pros and cons of the various treatments available.

## CONTROL THE PROCESS

It is important to emphasize that neither you nor your doctor can reduce the uncertainties associated with medical conditions, test results, diagnoses, treatments, or prognoses. However, what you – the patient – can achieve is control over the *process* by which the medical decisions that affect you get made. Taking this active role can, we believe, reduce the negative dimensions of hope (that it'll all work out in the end), fear (of pain or death), and greed (for a long and healthy life). By accepting that you can't always control your health through blind faith in science, you'll improve your ability to deal with most medical problems. You could even come face to face with a life-or-death instance of the paradox of control.

Will our advice make you as "healthy, wealthy, and wise" as in the old nursery rhyme? Well, it will certainly make you wiser and ought to make you healthier. As for wealthier, read on into the next two chapters about money and investments.

Four

# THE CHATTER OF MONEY

*It will fluctuate.*

> *John Pierpont ("J.P.") Morgan*
> *(1837–1913), when asked what the*
> *stock market was going to do*

Money talks . . . and talks and talks. So much so that we can't always figure out what it's saying. Dinner party conversations invariably turn to tales of investment riches (or rags), while experts – from financial journalists to fund managers – claim to be able to see patterns in the stock market. The big challenge is how to separate the patterns from the background "noise."

In particular, how are we – the man or woman on the street – supposed to manage our savings in the midst of all this chatter? This is probably one of the most crucial aspects of our personal Fortune – and one of the most difficult to administer. Even if we're not direct dabblers in the stock market, many of the financial products we buy, such as pension funds, come from the financial markets. Whether we like it or not, we are investors.

This chapter is devoted to proving two facts to you, the investor. They're two pretty big facts, so here they are up front. First, no one can predict specific outcomes of the financial markets consistently across time. The consequence is that investors who believe that they or others can predict market outcomes can lose a lot of money. When it comes to finance, illusions of control are very costly. Second, even though, in the short and medium term, there's no way of telling which way the markets will go, in the long run, they do exhibit consistent upward trends.

## BOOM, BUST, AND BOOKS

Back in 1987, when shoulder pads were all the rage, a book entitled *The Great Depression of 1990* came out. The author, Dr. Ravi Batra, wrote:

> I am an economist, trained in scientific analysis, not a sensationalist or a Jeremiah. Yet all the evidence indicates that another great depression is now in the making, and unless we take immediate action the price we will have to pay in the 1990s is catastrophic.[1]

Dr. Batra was lucky. His book sold hundreds of thousands of copies. But the rest of us were even luckier. His prediction was dead wrong. The 1990s saw the second biggest stock market boom in US history. During the decade, the Dow Jones Industrial Average index of leading shares (DJIA) grew from 2,753 to 11,358. In other words, $10,000 invested in January 1990 across all thirty of the companies whose shares are tracked by the index would have grown to $41,257 at the end of 1999. During the same period in the UK, the FTSE 100 stock market index published by the *Financial Times* almost tripled in value, rising from 2,423 to 6,930. Dr. Batra's doomsday never arrived.

So it's no surprise that, come 1999, people were writing very different kinds of books from Dr. Batra. These included: *Dow 36,000:*

*The New Strategy for Profiting from the Current Rise in the Stock Market* by James K. Glassman and Kevin A. Hassett;[2] *Dow 40,000: Strategies for Profiting from the Greatest Bull Market in History* by David Elias;[3] and *Dow 100,000 : Fact of Fiction* by Charles W. Kadlec.[4] Here's a quote from the first of these (also the most modest in its claims).

> A sensible target date for Dow 36,000 is early 2005, but it could be reached much earlier. After that, stocks will continue to rise, but at a slower pace. This means that stocks, right now, are an extraordinary investment. They are just as safe as bonds over long periods of time, and the returns are significantly higher.
>
> (Glassman and Hassett, p.140)

Between 2000 and 2003, the worldwide value of equities declined by $13 trillion (about $2,000 for every person in the world), while the combined value of the New York Stock Exchange and NASDAQ alone fell by $9.3 trillion. The DJIA hit a low of less than 7,300 in October 2002 and, on November 20, 2008, was more than 35% lower than the peak of 11,722 it reached ten years earlier. Worse still, on March 9, 2009 the DJIA hit a low of 6,700, having fallen close to 53% since its high of 14,165 reached on October 9, 2007. So will the DJIA ever reach 36,000 let alone 100,000? Probably yes, given enough time, but (although this sounds dangerously like a prediction on our part) we doubt it will get there any time soon.[5]

Only one year after the various Dow optimists wrote their books, Yale economist Robert Shiller added another tome to the library of forecasting. In *Irrational Exuberance*, he argued that the stock market was greatly overvalued (the DJIA was about 11,000 at the time) and had all the "classic features of a speculative bubble: a situation in which temporarily high prices are sustained largely by investors' enthusiasm rather than by consistent estimation of real value."[6] While he didn't predict an imminent bursting, he concluded that the outlook for the stock market for the next ten or twenty years was "likely to be rather poor – even dangerous."

So if book writers are not good forecasters, what about the IMF and all the other agencies that specialize in forecasting? They have not done any better. The following are a few quotes from the IMF:

- April 2007: Notwithstanding the recent bout of financial volatility, the world economy still looks well set for continued robust growth in 2007 and 2008. While the U.S. economy has slowed more than was expected earlier, spillovers have been limited, growth around the world looks well sustained, and inflation risks have moderated.

- October 2007: The problems in credit markets have been severe, and while the first phase is now over, we are still waiting to see exactly how the consequences will play out. Still, the situation at present is one with threats rather than actual major negative outcomes on macroeconomic aggregates. At this point, we expect global growth to slow in 2008, but remain at a buoyant pace.

- April, 2008: Global growth is projected to slow to 3.7 percent in 2008, ½ percentage point lower than at the time of the January World Economic Outlook Update and 1¼ percentage points lower than the growth recorded in 2007. Moreover, growth is projected to remain broadly unchanged in 2009. The divergence in growth performance between the advanced and emerging economies is expected to continue, with growth in the advanced economies generally expected to fall well below potential. The U.S. economy will tip into a mild recession in 2008 as the result of mutually reinforcing cycles in the housing and financial markets, before starting a modest recovery in 2009 as balance sheet problems in financial institutions are slowly resolved.

- October, 2008: The world economy is entering a major downturn in the face of the most dangerous financial shock in mature financial markets since the 1930s. Global growth is projected to slow substantially in 2008, and a modest recovery would only begin later in 2009. [...] The immediate policy challenge is to stabilize financial conditions, while nursing economies through a period of slow activity and keeping inflation under control.

Business experts did not fair better either. *Business week*, in its annual survey of business forecasters, summarized their predictions as follows:

The economists project, on average, that the economy will grow 2.1% from the fourth quarter of 2007 to the end of 2008, vs. 2.6% in 2007. Only two of the forecasters (34 in total) expect a recession.

(*Business Week*, Dec. 20, 2007)

It does not seem that the seriousness of the financial crisis, or the resulting economic recession, was predicted by the great majority of forecasters. The consequences, so far, have been big surprises, huge losses, many bankruptcies and several trillions of dollars of taxpayers' money being spent in an attempt to fix the problem. The big question is, therefore, what is the value of economic and financial forecasting when it completely missed the most serious financial crisis that hit the world economy and provided no warning of its arrival and seriousness?[7]

So many experts, so many opinions. With hindsight, it's easy to know which of them to believe. As the 2000–2003 correction showed, Shiller's measured pessimism was the most accurate of those we've mentioned. Furthermore, the eminent economist was right again in the 2005 second edition of his book,[8] where he maintained that the stock markets were still overvalued. But don't tell your stockbroker to sell, sell, sell just yet. After all, Glassman, Hassett,

Elias, and Kadlec are all highly regarded stock market experts too. If they turn out to be right in the end, you'll be missing out on a great opportunity.

Perhaps it's wrong to rely on economic and financial forecasters for advice. Let's look instead at some real-world experts, who put their money (or at least other people's money) where their mouths were.

## THE NOT-SO-LONG TERM CAPITAL MANAGEMENT (LTCM) FUND

Back in 1994, when shoulder pads were finally going out of fashion, a former bond trader for Salomon Brothers called John Meriwether started his own firm, the Long Term Capital Management Fund (LTCM). He had everything going for him: a stellar reputation, millions of dollars, and the best connections. Indeed, he assembled an all-star team including two famous economists (Myron Scholes and Robert Merton), a former vice-chairman of the Federal Reserve Board (David Mullins), and a host of highly experienced, greatly respected traders.

The formula for success was simple. The quantitative models of the academics, combined with the know-how of the practitioners, would achieve substantial returns with minimal risk. In no time at all, LTCM had raised $1.25 billion from about eighty investors – who each put in a minimum of $10 million. Many of the investors were themselves "experts": banks, bankers, university endowment funds, and well-known executives.

For a while, the formula seemed to be working. Returns were well above the market average. In 1994, LTCM earned a huge 28% on its investors' capital, rising to 59% in 1995 and 57% in 1996. With earnings like these, the fund was able to borrow vast sums of money to make its own investments and boost profitability yet further. So much for minimal risk. Then, in 1997, Scholes and Merton's mathematical models had a bad year. Returns were about the same as the market average and Meriwether was forced to repay $2.7 billion to investors. But there was no need to panic – at the beginning of 1998, LTCM still had assets exceeding $130 billion, while its portfolio of derivatives was worth close to $1.2 trillion.

Perhaps everything would have been fine, if it hadn't been for a series of events that began in April 1998, including the devaluation of the ruble and the debt moratorium declared by the Russian government. On a single day, August 21, 1998, LTCM lost more than half a billion dollars. Just over a month later, the fund had lost most of its equity and was teetering on the brink of default. Worse than that, having borrowed $1.3 trillion, the firm's imminent demise was a threat to the entire global financial system. On September 28, 1998, a consortium of financial organizations, led by the Federal Reserve Bank of New York, stepped in with a $3.6 billion rescue fund. By the end of 1998, LTCM had ceased to exist.

The point of the story is not so much that the brilliant academics and their array of expert colleagues and customers got their figures wrong. It's more that *nobody* else in the financial community foresaw LTCM's plunge from grace, even just a few months before it happened. And there's a punchline too: in 1997, just as things were beginning to unravel for them, Scholes and Merton were awarded the Nobel Prize for economics – for their work on controlling financial risk.

## A HEDGE TOO FAR

The following description once stood proudly on the website of Amaranth Advisors.

> We are a multi-strategy hedge fund. Amaranth's investment professionals deploy capital in a broad spectrum of alternative investment

and trading strategies in a highly disciplined, risk-controlled manner. Our ability to effectively pursue a variety of investment strategies combined with the depth and strategic integration of our equity, credit and quantitative teams, supported by a world-class infrastructure, are some of the key strengths that distinguish and define Amaranth. [. . .] We are committed to exploring and developing new ideas, moving nimbly and effectively within an ever-changing investment landscape, thereby staying fresh, current – unfading.

Amaranth is a plant with flowers that seem to last forever (the name's origins are in the Greek word "amarantos," which means "unfading" or "indestructible"). But this particular Amaranth faded fast – and suddenly. It collapsed in September 2006 after losing close to $6 billion in a single week. The fund had been betting heavily on natural gas futures. This paid off handsomely in 2005, after Hurricane Katrina had cut production and prices doubled in less than five months. But good weather and high gas stocks in 2006 sent prices plummeting. On September 29, 2006, the founder of Amaranth, Nicholas Maounis, wrote to the fund's investors notifying them of its termination. On October 1, 2006, just as the fashion magazines were announcing the return of shoulder pads, the financial press reported that Amaranth had appointed liquidators to return what they could of the remaining assets to investors. It really was that quick.

The dictionary defines "hedge" as "to enter transactions that will protect against loss through a compensatory price movement." Yet Amaranth did quite the opposite. It seems as if its experts learned nothing from the catastrophic fall of LTCM and the resulting guidelines – which were readily available even to amateurs. These state that no more than one-tenth of a fund's assets should be placed in a single type of speculative investment. Yet Amaranth brazenly placed huge bets on one highly speculative commodity – natural gas.

LTCM and Amaranth are not alone in financial history. In fact there are hundreds of other funds that have ceased operating because they lost so much money. At the beginning of 2007 there were close to 8,500 hedge funds in the USA with assets exceeding $1.3 trillion. There were also 8,100 mutual funds with assets of $10 trillion. If history repeats itself, many of them won't exist in a few years' time, perhaps because of mergers, but most often because they underperform the market.

Here are some of the figures that *aren't* included in the fund managers' slick sales projections. In 2001, there were 1,921 diversified stock funds in the USA. Five years later, 543 of them were gone. Between 1970 and 2006, 223 US equity funds went under, many of them associated with highly reputable financial brands. The S&P/InterCapital Dynamics fund lost 95.7% of its value, while the Steadman Technology & Growth, CitiFunds Emerging Asian Markets Equity, and Morgan Stanley Gold B funds all failed. In addition, many firms have lost vast amounts in various forms of investments and trading. Barings Bank collapsed after one of its traders, Nick Leeson, famously lost nearly a billion dollars in just two months at the beginning of 1995. And in 2008 this feat was surpassed by a new rogue trader, Jérôme Kerviel of Société Générale, who allegedly lost €4.9 billion (equivalent to $7.4 billion at the time) of his employer's money. Allied Irish Bank lost $691 million in unauthorized trades in its Baltimore subsidiary. Sumitomo of Japan lost millions of dollars through speculative trading, as did Metallgesellschaft of Germany, Showa Shell (a subsidiary of the well-known oil company), Kidder Peabody (an investment bank owned by GE) ... the list goes on. And these are just the ones that made it into the newspapers – the tip of a multi-billion-dollar iceberg.

## DARLINGS OF WALL STREET

Where does that leave you the investor? Probably with very cold feet indeed. Perhaps the solution is to hand-pick a few individual stocks. But which ones? Time to consult the experts again. *Fortune* magazine has been hailing one particular company as "America's most innovative" for six consecutive years now. The *McKinsey Quarterly* is also a fan and says it's an example of how innovative companies can surpass their conventional competitors. And there are lots of business-school case studies explaining exactly how this organization became so successful. International management guru Gary Hamel goes so far as to say that the company in question "has institutionalized a capacity for perpetual innovation."[9] What's more, profits were $1 billion last year, while its total stock market value has just reached $186 billion. Oh, and its revenues have surpassed $100 billion last year, making it the seventh biggest company in the Fortune 500.

The catch? We've gone back in time to early 2001 and the company in question is Enron. Buy shares now at $81.39 and in ten months' time, when Enron files for bankruptcy, they'll be worthless. It turns out that the biggest "innovations" of the world's top energy company are in the creative accounting department. Enron is overstating its revenues and profits, while siphoning huge sums of money from its shareholders to some of its top executives and their friends. Like LTCM, Enron is known for its sophisticated risk management techniques. But they won't save it from insolvency – or its executives from prison. The business school boffins' case studies will soon mysteriously disappear from the back catalogues and the journalists will be writing very different stories about Enron.

But in early 2001, *no one* can tell you this. Nor will they predict the fall of WorldCom, which will beat Enron's record for value destruction when it files for bankruptcy only seven months later. The two companies' stories are strangely similar. Enron was formed from the merger of two traditional gas utilities in 1985, while WorldCom started in 1983 as a small company that would benefit from the break-up of AT&T and the liberalization of the US telecoms market. Thanks to acquisitions, it grew to become the second biggest telecoms company in America. Bernie Ebbers, its charismatic and visionary CEO, was the darling of Wall Street. In the middle of 1999, its stock reached a high of over $64 and the company was valued at $180 billion. But when the company finally filed for bankruptcy on July 21, 2002, it had debts exceeding $40 billion.

The reasons for WorldCom's huge losses were multiple. The internet boom of the late 1990s had increased demand for telecoms services and started a race to lay new fiber-optic cables. The dotcom bust exacerbated the resulting overcapacity and prices dropped by a factor of seven or eight in a period of just a few years. WorldCom's earnings and share prices started to plummet. Ebbers and his CFO were powerless to stop the downward spiral . . . until they started cooking the books. When KPMG came in to audit in the spring of 2002, they uncovered a $3.8 billion accounting fraud. It was Enron all over again, only bigger.

Again, it is not just that these were the two biggest bankruptcies in history. It's not that thousands of investors lost billions of dollars and 1,500 creditors went unpaid either. Nor that nearly 100,000 employees lost their jobs, their savings, and their pensions (which had been invested in the companies). What we're saying is that *absolutely nobody* was able to warn these innocent victims of the impending disaster. And the same forecasters failed to spot other dark clouds on the investment horizon. In 2002 there were thousands of other corporate bankruptcies: four major cases (Conseco, Global Crossing, Adelphia, and K-Mart), involving nearly $130 billion in assets; 259 additional public companies; and 37,000 other businesses in the USA alone. And there are similar tales of unforeseen business tragedy from Europe: Parmalat, Marconi, Swissair, Royal Ahold, to name just a few.

## SOME SUCCESS STORIES

Enough doom and gloom. Table 4 shows a short list of some of the most exceptionally successful USA companies at the time of writing, together with the market capitalization of each of them in January 2008 (that is, how much all their shares were valued by the stock market).

The total value of the eight companies at the beginning of 2008, $1.356 trillion, was more than the total GNP of the world's sixty-five poorest countries, which have a population of over a billion people. What's more, most of this wealth accumulated fairly recently, in historical terms at least. If you'd bought $10,000-worth of Wal-Mart shares in January 1977, your investment would have grown to $35 million just thirty years later. Similarly, $10,000 invested in Dell stocks at the beginning of the 1990s would have given you $10 million at the end of the decade. Microsoft shares went up to 600 times their original price in just ten years too.

*[handwritten margin notes: 1000 x, 600 x]*

**Table 4** Market values of eight successful companies (January 2008)

| | Market capitalization: January 2008 (in $ billions) |
|---|---|
| GE | 349 |
| Microsoft | 311 |
| Wal-Mart | 193 |
| Berkshire Hathaway | 196 |
| Google | 190 |
| Dell | 46 |
| eBay | 38 |
| Yahoo | 33 |
| Total | 1,356 |

The uplifting news is that the immense wealth generated by these and other successful companies more than compensates for the value destroyed in the high-profile bankruptcies. The only snag is that the riches are often unforetold too. With hindsight, it's easy to explain success. But when IBM was offered a significant share of Microsoft for only a few hundred thousand dollars, executives turned the offer down.

Of course, there have been some extremely successful investors over the years. The careers of Warren Buffett and George Soros are legendary, even outside financial circles. But do they have the gift of clairvoyance or did they just get lucky many times over? And what of today's stars? Peter Lynch, John Neff, Bill Miller, and Anthony Bolton have brought great wealth to their clients to date. Will they continue to do so? It might seem reasonable to assume that past successes are a good indication of future returns. But that was exactly where Georgios went wrong ...

## ALL THAT GLITTERS

At the end of 1973, Georgios, an extremely successful self-made Greek industrialist asked one of the authors of this book to forecast the price of gold for the next decade, so that he could figure out exactly how much bullion to buy. Georgios had made his fortune in the steel business, which had thrived thanks to the post-war Greek property boom, caused in turn by the country's rapid industrialization. Through his business, Georgios had become aware of the rising prices of metals and other commodities, and he believed that gold prices would increase much more quickly than inflation.

This wasn't such a crazy notion. Inflation in Greece was rampant at the time, interest rates in government-owned banks barely outstripped it, and strict exchange controls prevented Greeks from converting their money into other currencies. However, to protect themselves from soaring prices, Greeks were allowed to buy gold from the central bank. Many of them did just that, particularly as there were no stock markets or other places to invest their hard-earned cash. Georgios was one of the many. He'd bought and sold gold many times in the past – and still owned a fair amount. Georgios also believed that the termination of the Bretton Woods System about a year and a half earlier would liberate trading and lead to substantial price increases.

The Bretton Woods agreement of 1946 had effectively fixed the price of gold at $35 an ounce. It came to an end on August 15, 1971. Up until that date, gold had principally been used as a reserve for governments to issue paper currencies. Nevertheless, in anticipation of free trading, prices began increasing from January 1971 (having been more or less flat since 1800) – as is clear from figure 2.

In March 1974, the author showed figure 2 to Georgios, who was delighted. He also showed him the yearly real gold prices (adjusted for inflation) since 1800. These had been fairly constant for the past

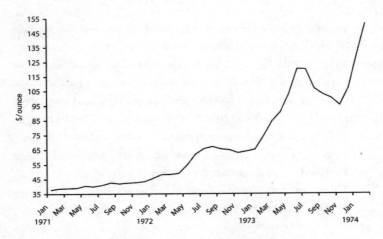

**Figure 2** Monthly gold prices, January 1971 to February 1974

173 years, a fact that Georgios dismissed as irrelevant since the price had been controlled. The author agreed with him, but – as a professional statistician with no training in clairvoyance – felt he'd hit a dead end. There was simply not enough *relevant* data to go on. So, every month, as soon as the latest information on the price of gold became available, he sent a telegram (strange as it may seem, in those days there were neither fax machines nor overnight courier services, let alone e-mail) to Georgios, updating the graph. He also sent him every article that appeared in the trade press or economic journals. Most of them predicted continued price rises. Georgios was convinced that gold would cost over $1,000 an ounce by the end of the decade – and every extra piece of information he received only added to his conviction. He kept on buying bullion even when the price was reaching all-time historical highs. Georgios refused to listen to talk of bubbles that burst. His mantra was: "No one has ever lost money in gold."

But, you guessed it, Georgios *did* lose money in gold. The price peaked at about $675 in September 1980, then started to fall as fast as it had risen.[10] And apart from a small recovery in the late 1980s, it just kept on falling until 1999. Unfortunately for Georgios, gold stored in a bank vault also attracts hefty storage charges. And, unlike many other kinds of investments, lumps of shiny metal sitting underground don't offer annual dividends. He finally bowed to the inevitable and sold up in 2000. His total investment over the years had been $9.1 million. If only he'd sold in 1980, he'd have made more than $18 million. Even if he'd waited until 1982, he'd have come out $6.5 million up. But Georgios didn't. In the end he made a loss of nearly $1 million. Hindsight brings even less consolation. We now know that he sold at exactly the wrong time. Figure 3 shows Georgios's graph, updated to 2007.

As you can see, since 2000 gold prices have been on the up again. Many experts and newsletters are once again making predictions of a

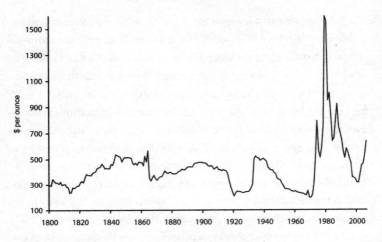

**Figure 3**  Real gold prices (constant 2006 dollars)

new El Dorado. On December 8, 2006, Paul van Eeden of Toronto, one of the foremost authorities on the gold market, announced, "I say with a very high level of confidence that gold prices will go to $1,000 an ounce in the next two to five years." Although Paul van Eeden's forecast turned out to be correct as the price of gold exceeded $1,200 in April 2010, the author for one is sticking to his story: we just don't know – and neither does anyone else.[11]

## THE LONG RUN

If not gold, what *should* Georgios have invested in? Taking a very historical and long-term perspective, the answer is obvious. But before we reveal it, let's get the lie of the investment landscape.

Globally, it's estimated that institutions and individuals hold about $63 trillion in different types of investments. The lion's share of around $60 trillion is invested in equities (also known as stocks and shares) and fixed-income securities (mainly bonds). The remaining $3 trillion or so (about 5% of the total) takes a variety of forms: hedge funds, private equity, real estate, commodities, venture capital, gold . . . even wine and classic cars. The risks and returns of the many different options vary immensely. At one end of the scale, we know that bank certificates of deposit have almost no risk attached. Conversely, the returns are small.

At the other extreme, venture capital gains can be enormous, but so is the risk of losing money (in the USA, for example, venture capital returns were 37% in 1998 and 225% in 1999, the two best years, but -41% in 2001 and -29% in 2002, the two worst). Venture capital and many other unusual investments are not for the average investor, let alone Georgios, as they can destroy wealth in record time. So let's confine our attention for now to equities, fixed-income securities, and gold (we'll return to the others in the next chapter). After all, we have much more historical data for these types of investments and, as we've seen, they represent about 95% of the global total.

Based on the highly respected work by J. J. Siegel, *Stocks for the Long Run*[12] (and updating his figures with some data of our own), let's step into a time taxi and go back to the America of 1802. That nasty business with the British finished about twenty years ago and life is comparatively stable again. While we're waiting for President Thomas Jefferson to buy Louisiana from Napoleon (next year), let's invest $40,000 dollars by putting $10,000 into each of four different types of investments: gold, short-term government bonds, long-term government bonds, and equities. Moreover, we'll spread our investment across the entire market for the bonds and shares. Having instructed our broker to reinvest any dividends each year, we get back into the time taxi and whiz forward to 2006. Adjusting for inflation, we discover that the real values of our four different investments are now as shown in table 5.

The differences are absolutely enormous. And the equities win hands down in the long run. But, as the economist John Maynard Keynes once put it, "In the long run we are all dead." We need to

**Table 5** Growth of $10,000 investment from 1802 to 2006

| | |
|---|---|
| $8,390,179,500 | (yes this is correct, close to $8.4 billion) for the equities |
| $10,888,350 | for the long-term government bonds |
| $3,651,360 | for the short-term government bonds |
| $27,800 | for the gold. |

define some more life-sized long runs. So now let's imagine that the time-taxi driver uses his knowledge of the financial markets to diversify into different kinds of historical investment products. Again based on Siegel's book, these are the annual interest rates that he can offer you for various periods in US history and our four different types of investments (again adjusting for inflation). Table 6 summarizes these findings.

**Table 6** Tardisbank annual interest rates

| | | Different types of investment | | | |
|---|---|---|---|---|---|
| | | Short-term government bond account | Long-term government bond account | Stock market account | Gold account |
| Periods | 1802–2010* | 2.9 | 3.5 | 6.8 | 0.6 |
| | 1871–2010* | 1.9 | 2.7 | 6.6 | 0.4 |
| Major | 1802–1870 | 5.1 | 4.8 | 7.0 | 0.2 |
| sub- | 1871–1925 | 3.2 | 3.7 | 6.6 | −0.8 |
| periods | 1926–1999 | 0.7 | 2.2 | 7.5 | 0.5 |
| | 1926–2010* | 1.0 | 2.1 | 6.6 | 1.6 |
| Post-war | 1946–1999 | 0.6 | 1.5 | 7.7 | −0.3 |
| periods | 1946–1965 | −0.8 | −1.2 | 10.0 | −2.7 |
| | 1966–1981 | −0.2 | −4.2 | −0.4 | 8.8 |
| | 1982–1999 | 2.9 | 8.4 | 13.6 | −4.9 |
| | 1982–2008 | 4.8 | 3.9 | 7.8 | −0.8 |
| | 2000–2010* | 3.2 | 2.1 | −0.1 | 10.2 |

* Updated by the authors, March 2010

Note that, in order to get these annual rates of return, you have to put your money in at the beginning of each period and keep it there until the end of the period, reinvesting all your dividends or interest along the way. That's because – historically – we know that prices of shares, bonds, and gold varied greatly across these periods – and prices may even have fallen steadily for quite some time (something Georgios found to his great cost in the gold market between 1978 and 1999).

The most obvious conclusion is that the time-taxi driver won't get many takers for the bond and gold accounts at any time period. It may also come as a bit of shock that the difference of rates of return across the 1802 to 2010 period between the stock market and long-term government bonds is so small. Of course, 6.8% is better than 3.5% – but it's less than double. Remembering our investment of $10,000, can that really make a difference of over $8 billion in returns? The answer is that, compounded over a very long period of time, it really can make that much difference – a lesson to all would-be investors.

As far as the stock market accounts go, it's clear that there won't be many customers for the 1966–1981 account and plenty for 1982–1999. But it's also striking how consistent the rates of return are for the stock market account across the longer periods of time. In fact, it's not too far from 6.8% (the rate for 1802 to 2010) in all but the shorter post-war investment periods, suggesting that you can probably extrapolate this kind of long-term growth into the future. This is very different from the situation for government bonds, where the lack of consistency suggests that similar long-term predictions aren't possible.

What you can't extrapolate – or even see – from table 6 is the fact that the *variability* of the rates of return from the stock market is also surprisingly consistent across time. In conclusion, short-term investments in the stock exchange are risky, but the longer the term, the better and the less risky the bet.

Back in 1970s Greece, however, Georgios is wearing flares and doesn't have this information. Nor, to be fair, does he have the same range of investment options as his American cousin George, whose lapels are even bigger than Georgios's. But a lot of other countries do have stock markets like the USA. Let's take a look at how they measure up.

## TARDISBANK GOES GLOBAL

The information in table 7 is taken from another highly respected book, *Triumph of the Optimists*, written by three professors at the

**Table 7** Percentage annual returns of stock markets by country (1900–2001)

| Country | Percentage annual return of stock market |
|---|---|
| Australia | 7.4 |
| Sweden | 7.3 |
| South Africa | 6.7 |
| USA | 6.3 |
| Canada | 5.9 |
| UK | 5.2 |
| Netherlands | 5.0 |
| Denmark | 4.6 |
| Ireland | 4.3 |
| Japan | 4.1 |
| Switzerland | 4.1 |
| Spain | 3.2 |
| France | 3.1 |
| Germany | 2.8 |
| Italy | 2.1 |
| Belgium | 1.8 |
| **World*** | **5.4** |

* The world index is composed of the above sixteen countries, with each country weighted by its starting year market capitalization or GDP.

London Business School.[13] The statistical wizardry and dates used are different from Siegel's, so the real average return on the USA stock market is 6.3% this time. But the overall message is the same: in the long term equities produce good returns. Clearly, this is much less true in some countries than others, but the average return for all sixteen countries at 5.4% still represents a nice nest egg if you're prepared to wait 101 years for it to hatch.

In other words, if we were to perform our time-travel trick again and rewind to the year 1900 to invest $10,000 in various countries, we'd have the following amounts by 2001.

- $60,610 in Belgium
- $578,790 in Japan
- $4,784,760 in the USA
- $13,534,190 in Australia
- $2,027,220 if we'd invested the original amount across all sixteen countries.

The difference in returns is immense, when compounded over a century plus one year.


## ONLY IN AMERICA

The generation of wealth is particularly evident if we return to focus on the USA again. This focus will also enable us to be a bit more realistic. Time travel and long periods of investment are good for illustrative purposes, but they're simply not possible. For most investors, after all, the long term is a maximum of two or three decades, not a century or more. And investments are made not in the market averages of all stocks traded, but in much smaller portfolios. So, let's look at the values of the Dow Jones Industrial Average index (which is based on thirty leading companies) since January 1920, as shown in figure 4.

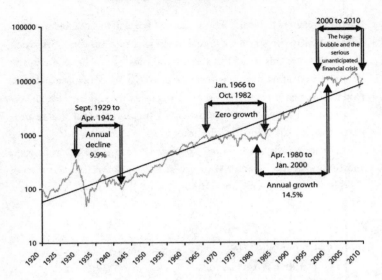

**Figure 4** Actual Dow Jones Industrial Average, January 1920 to January 2010

Figure 4 shows the history of a nation in shorthand. In the long term, it's the story of a vibrant economy and steady growth from 1920 to 2007. But, as well as the broad sweep of history represented by the straight line, we can trace the jagged edges of despair and hope across nearly a century. Note, incidentally, that we have represented the DJIA index on the vertical axis by an exponential scale. This means that the upward trend of the straight line is really increasing at a fast rate.

We've highlighted four particular periods.

The first period shows a huge drop in the value of the thirty companies' shares, then a partial recovery followed by another fall, between September 1929 and April 1942. You can see quite clearly the frenzied selling of shares in the Wall Street Crash, followed by the further decline of the Great Depression. These dark economic times continued through most of the 1930s and things only started to look up again just after the US entered the Second World War at the end of 1941. It took until October 1954 for the DJIA to regain the values of September 1929 – a period of twenty-five years and one month.

The second period runs from January 1966 to October 1982, sixteen years and nine months, during which the value of the DJIA fluctuated and eventually returned to its original value. Economically, this was a highly unusual era of high inflation and zero growth (so-called "stagflation"), low corporate profits, and little productivity growth. Historically, these are also up-and-down years, involving a space race, an oil crisis, and a war in the Far East.

The third period is one of extraordinary growth in DJIA values, starting at the beginning of the 1980s and ending with the bursting of the dotcom bubble at the beginning of 2000, almost two full decades. It's an era of technological explosion and strong economic growth.

Across these four periods it's almost as if someone has plotted a family saga, ripe for a blockbuster novel or TV mini-series. After the first part full of grimy faces and soup kitchens, there's an episode of comfortable middle-class stability, with disturbing yet distant world events played out on a brand-new television set in the corner of the sitting room. Finally, a generation which starts out believing lunch is for wimps comes round to contemplating a distressed future with few opportunities and jobs as the world economy faces its worst recession since the 1930s.

However, regardless of the personal dramas sketched out by the figures, these very different eras weren't selected for their TV potential. They're for investment purposes only and show four periods of decline, zero increase, strong growth, and euphoria as well as distress. Our aim is to demonstrate that the "short term" can last more than two full decades in some cases. For example, investors who bought DJIA equities at the beginning of 1966 would have to wait until the end of 1982 to start to see any gains at all (and that's before inflation is taken into account). Those who bought in September 1929 were even unluckier. During the next twelve years and seven months, they'd be losing money at the rate of 9.9% a year. They'd need to wait over twenty-five years just to get their money back – and by then everyday goods would cost much more, so they'd still be losing out. Conversely, what if you were one of the lucky ones? If you'd bought in April 1980 and sold at the close of the millennium, your investment would have grown at a rate of 14.5% a year. You certainly wouldn't be complaining. But then if you had left your money in the market and sold in March 2009 you would have lost most of your gains.

To cut a long and complicated story short, returns over shorter time spans can be vastly different from the long-term average. Sometimes that means huge losses on the stock market, sometimes huge gains. Quite apart from the periods of decades and centuries that we've just looked at in detail, sometimes there are clusters of months or even days where billions of dollars are lost or gained. For instance, if you'd invested $10,000 in the DJIA in December 1972, you'd have less than $5,900 to show for it twenty-five months later. But if you'd bought in December 1994 and kept your shares for the same period of twenty-five months, you'd be looking at a tidy sum of over $17,600. (Note that these figures aren't strictly comparable with our $10,000-dollar investments earlier in the chapter, as we're not re-investing dividends here. In fact, this would only exacerbate the differences between the gains and losses across these periods.)

"Market timing" is clearly critical to short-term success. However, as we saw at the beginning of this chapter, no one knows what the market will do in the short term. They don't even know when prolonged periods of decline, zero growth, and or strong increase will occur. The uncertainty for investors is huge. And, for certain kinds of stocks, the uncertainty can be even greater . . .

## HIGHER PEAKS AND LOWER VALLEYS

The companies included in the DJIA are thirty of the biggest, most seasoned blue chips, with established competitive advantages and experienced managers. If we see such large variations in the value of the DJIA, what on earth happens to the price of shares in high-tech companies, such as many of those listed on the NASDAQ exchange? Unsurprisingly, the answer is that they vary much more. Figure 5 compares the value of $10,000 dollars-worth of DJIA stocks and the same amount invested in companies listed on the NASDAQ exchange between June 1997 and March 2003.[14] To simplify comparisons, we represent the two indexes by the same scale such that both have a value of 100 at the beginning of the period (June 10, 1997).

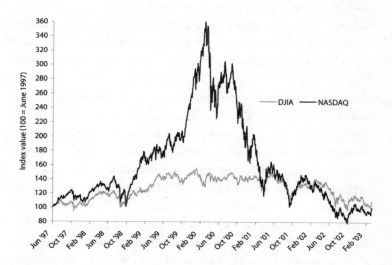

**Figure 5** DJIA and NASDAQ, June 1997 to March 2003

Invest in the NASDAQ on June 10, 1997, sell on March 10, 2000, and you've made a fortune. But invest on March 10, 2000, sell exactly three years later and you're ruined. Meanwhile, the corresponding losses and gains from betting on the DJIA are much smaller. True, the period we chose to illustrate is an extreme case, but it only exaggerates the general rule. And that rule is as follows: the greater fluctuations of the NASDAQ represent greater opportunities, but also greater risks for the investor. Price fluctuations are a double-edged sword.

The NASDAQ "composite" index covers 3,200 individual stocks. Other well-known indexes track the performances of varying numbers of companies. The DJIA is unusual in including just thirty, but – as we mentioned earlier – these are very large, established companies with proven track records. The names – S&P 500, Russell 2000, and the FTSE 100 – speak for themselves. If you invest in a fund that tracks one of these well-known indexes, your money will grow (and shrink) with the index, as reported in the financial pages each day. Similarly, if you pick a number of shares at random from a given index, your investment stands a good chance of reflecting the performance of the index as a whole.

So what happens if you invest in only one company? The answer is simple. Returns are likely to differ significantly from the market average. Figure 6 compares the value of $10,000 invested in the NASDAQ (as before) with the share price for just one NASDAQ company, Amazon, between June 10, 1997 and March 10, 2003 (as before). This time, it's the NASDAQ curve that looks flat, because the values on the vertical axis are much bigger than last time. Of course, we picked Amazon, because it's another extreme example. But it certainly illustrates the potential for volatility in individual stocks compared to the fluctuations of a composite which includes several thousands of stocks.

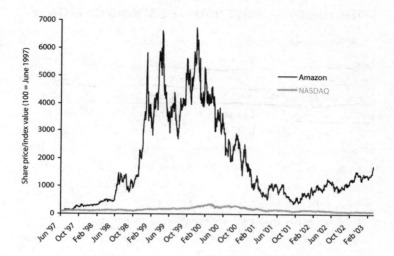

**Figure 6** NASDAQ and Amazon, June 1997 to March 2003

This time round, your $10,000 dollars invested in Amazon on June 10, 1997, will be worth close to $660,500 on April 23, 1999. The value of your investment will drop to a little more than $270,000 by October 9 (a fall of nearly 60% in less than six months). But no need to worry for long. Two weeks before Christmas 1999 it will shoot up to $670,500, higher than ever. Celebrations are premature though. By September 28, 2001, your investment will be back down to less than $30,800 in value. But stay optimistic and keep those shares to the end (March 10, 2003) and they'll be worth over $270,000 again. It's a shame you didn't sell just before the millennium celebrations, of course, but you can take heart from the fact that your return is equivalent to that of putting your money in a savings account with an annual interest rate of 64% for nearly six years! That's got to do your personal Fortune some good, even if it was an emotional and financial roller-coaster along the way.

## THE HILLS ARE ALIVE WITH THE SOUND OF MONEY

The influential Canadian-American economist John Kenneth Galbraith once said: "When it comes to the stock market, there are two kinds of investors. Those who don't know where the market is going and those who don't know that they don't know where the market is going." He was right – at least in the case of those who are out to make a fast buck. There is no evidence at all that anyone can consistently predict turning points and short-term trends. Surprises – both good and bad – occur at a strikingly high rate, as we saw at the beginning of this chapter. On the other hand, it does seem possible to predict long-term trends in the stock market. But when we say "long," we really mean it. It's all too easy to get distracted by the "noise" of an Amazon stock and miss the overall pattern (or lack of it) in the NASDAQ or Dow Jones.

We don't suppose that you're listening to us. Instead, you're probably hearing the background chatter of money. Our experience tells us that one strategy followed by nearly all investors is to continue desperately looking for ways to predict the market. As an intellectual exercise this is laudable. If you're an investor of other people's money it's even understandable. Yet, if your own personal Fortune is at stake, we advise you to be more pragmatic. This, as we show in the next chapter, involves forgoing all illusions of control, not succumbing to greed and adopting realistic investment goals. Filter out the background chatter, and you might just hear the beautiful music made by thousands of investment opportunities. To dance to this music is to accept that you are dancing with chance.

# Five

# WATERING YOUR MONEY PLANT

*I tell people investing should be dull. It shouldn't be exciting. Investing should be more like watching paint dry or watching grass grow. If you want excitement, take $800 and go to Las Vegas.*

Paul Samuelson, Nobel Prize Laureate

This is the chapter where we tell you how to invest your money. We'll look at different kinds of investments, their pros and their cons. We'll also give you some strategies to make your own investment decisions and advice about how to control the emotions that frequently cloud our financial judgment. As you will see, successful investing involves recognizing and avoiding the illusion of control. That is, you need, first, to accept the major lesson of the previous chapter (no one can predict short- or even medium-term financial returns), and second, plot your investment strategy accordingly. But we're getting a bit ahead of our story now. So to get the ball rolling, here's a modern fairy tale.

## ANYTHING BUT THE GOLDEN GOOSE

Once upon a time – well, 1998 to be exact – there was a member of an exiled European royal family, who lived in New York. Although he had never fulfilled his destiny of becoming king, he was very successful and also quite wealthy, having founded a thriving import–export business some thirty years earlier. The king-turned-businessman had also married into a well-known New York family and fathered five beautiful daughters. But there was one tiny, niggling problem. And it was preventing him from living happily ever after.

The problem was that familiar old chestnut of succession planning. The king was fifty-eight and beginning to look forward to retirement. All five of the daughters had joined the family business and were doing well in different departments. But ultimately, a company can have only one leader. In whose hands would the business be safest? He pondered the question for a long time and finally decided to set his daughters a task. He gave each of the five princesses $10,000 and told them to come back in seven years. At that point, the king would appoint as his successor the one who had invested most wisely.

Being thoroughly modern princesses, the five daughters didn't even bother looking for a golden goose. In fact, they'd all attended reputable business schools and knew (unlike Georgios in the previous chapter) that gold wasn't a good investment at all. The king's favorite daughter, Michelle, the one he liked to call "ma belle," put her $10,000 into Venture Capital straight away. Michelle had expensive tastes, a penchant for fast cars, and a knack of finding Mr. Wrong, but not to the same extent as her racier older sister, "Sexy" Sadie, who – at the tender age of twenty-five – already had a string of driving bans and two divorces behind her. Sadie opted for Private Equity without a moment's hesitation.

The youngest princess, the Lovely Rita, was a vivacious graduate of twenty-two. Like her two older sisters, she liked to have fun, but not to unreasonable excess. Her good-looking, football-playing boyfriend wanted to get engaged, but she wasn't sure that she was ready to commit. She considered her pile of crisp dollar bills for a while, then invested it in the stock market.

The two oldest princesses were secretly a disappointment to the king. The first-born, a rather austere-looking woman of twenty-nine was known to the family (rather unaffectionately) as "Long Tall Sally." Ironically, after much deliberation, she invested in short-term government bonds. Her devoted husband, a surprisingly handsome financial adviser, was rumored to be implicated in the decision. Her younger sister by two years was a friendly yet rather non-descript young lady, who was quite frankly a little boring, but got along well with everyone in the family. "Dear Prudence," as they always referred to her, had recently married the handsome financial adviser's brother. She looked at all the investment options, but, truth be known, they rather frightened her, so she put her $10,000 in three-month certificates of deposit at the bank.

At this point, the fairy tale is best continued in numbers, rather than words, as shown in table 8. This details the evolution of each of the five princesses' investments over the seven-year period.

Our tale resumes one morning in January 2006, when the king and princesses assembled in the boardroom. Michelle was looking very smug, yet a little glazed, as she peered out from behind a huge pile of 26,414 dollar bills. She hadn't been the same since a spell in the Betty Ford Clinic around 2002, when the value of her initial $10,000 went down to $5,297. Sadie's smile was as broad as you'd expect for someone sitting on $17,149 dollars, but everyone knew it was the result of tranquilizers – an addiction that dated back to 2000, when she lost 37% of her investment in a single year. Rita looked quietly confident, but seemed to have aged prematurely. She'd moved in with the

Table 8 The princesses' results in figures

| Year | Venture capital (Michelle) Investment ($'s) | Return % | Private equity (Sadie) Investment ($'s) | Return % | Stocks (Rita) Investment ($'s) | Return % | Short-term government bonds (Sally) Investment ($'s) | Return % | 3-month certificates of deposit (Prudence) Investment ($'s) | Return % |
|---|---|---|---|---|---|---|---|---|---|---|
| 1998 | 10,000 | | 10,000 | | 10,000 | | 10,000 | | 10000 | |
| 1999 | 23,509 | 135 | 21,286 | 113 | 16,604 | 66 | 10,610 | 6.1 | 10,546 | 5.5 |
| 2000 | 71,694 | 205 | 13,511 | -37 | 14840 | -11 | 11,101 | 4.6 | 11,039 | 4.7 |
| 2001 | 6,202 | -91 | 9,856 | -27 | 10,630 | -28 | 11,201 | 0.9 | 11,230 | 1.7 |
| 2002 | 5,297 | -15 | 7,891 | -20 | 9,881 | -7 | 11,402 | 1.8 | 11,359 | 1.1 |
| 2003 | 14,300 | 170 | 11,496 | 46 | 11,669 | 18 | 11,652 | 2.2 | 11,536 | 1.6 |
| 2004 | 20,547 | 44 | 12,958 | 13 | 13,290 | 14 | 12,094 | 3.8 | 11,941 | 3.5 |
| 2005 | 26,414 | 29 | 17,149 | 32 | 14,965 | 13 | 12,677 | 4.8 | 12,557 | 5.2 |

football player, but they'd gone through a bad patch after 2000, when Rita had turned to drink in a vain attempt to forget the falling value of her investment. He'd finally left her in 2002, when it sunk just below its original value to $9,881. Now she was dry and had a healthy $14,965, but was no longer "lovely."

Sally and Pru looked happy, but not expectant – despite being heavily pregnant with their third and fourth children respectively. They knew their father would say that their safe investments had barely outpaced inflation, even if they'd never actually lost money in any one year. Secretly, they'd never wanted the responsibility of running the family business anyway.

However, the king, who had followed the progress of all five investments carefully over the previous seven years, was not at all happy with *any* of his daughters. He accused the older pair of lacking ambition and failing to get results. But he was fairly risk averse by nature too. So he was just as cross with the younger trio. Whilst he congratulated them on their final total, he couldn't shake off memories of the bad years. Would they take the same crazy risks with the family business after he was gone? "Worse still, why on earth didn't any of you think of spreading your investments?" he asked in despair. The king let all five princesses keep the money, but brought in a hotshot CEO – a miller's daughter with many years of managerial experience and a strong investment background – to lead the family firm.

The moral? Never put your nest eggs all in one basket. And beware of mixing emotions with investment.

## SPECULATION ISN'T FUTILE

The story is made up of course, but the figures are genuine. Although they only cover seven years, these numbers demonstrate other morals of a slightly more financial nature. First, as we saw in the previous chapter, the difference in returns between selling when prices are at their highest and selling when they're at their lowest for certain kinds of investments can be immense. As the figures show, $5,297 can be transformed by the magic of venture capital into $26,414 in just three years. That really is the stuff of fairy tales.

Second, the fluctuations in the returns each year for venture capital, private equity, and the stock market are also immense. Returns in venture capital went from 205% in 2000 to -91% in 2001. Third and conversely, for other kinds of investment, the variability of returns is low. For short-term government bonds and three-month certificates of deposit, there was little variation between 1998 and 2005. On the one hand, rates of return never slipped into the negative. On the other, they peaked at a disappointing 6.1%. There's no possibility of a fairy-tale ending if you invest in three-month certificates of deposit.

Investors, even professionals, usually associate great variability of returns with risk. We believe they've got the emphasis wrong. The flip side of risk is opportunity. Understanding this is the key to managing the financial elements of your personal Fortune.

## EXPLORING THE ALTERNATIVES

Let's look in a little more detail at the vehicles that provide the greatest opportunities and the most dangerous risks. But remember that these represent only 5% or so of the total sum invested globally, which is why they're often known collectively as "alternative investments."

First, there are the hedge funds we looked at briefly in the previous chapter. They're the fastest growing segment of the alternative investment sector, thanks to the well-publicized success of a few funds. At the end of 2006, total investments in hedge funds had exceeded $1.2 trillion worldwide. However, empirical findings suggest that the average returns of hedge funds are no higher than those of the S&P 500 (Standard & Poor's index of 500 stocks). Investors should also bear in mind that hedge funds aren't regulated, which means that reporting of financial performance is voluntary. A recent article in the *Financial Analysts Journal* found that this leads to biases in how we perceive them.[1] In other words, there are so many funds that fail completely, that much of the available data covers only the industry's survivors thereby exaggerating overall success. The authors warn "Investors in hedge funds take on a substantial risk of selecting a dismally performing fund or, worse, a failing one."

Second, let's consider private equity. Like hedge funds, it's as controversial as it's fashionable. The total amount invested this way was approaching $1 trillion at the end of 2006. Individual investors don't usually have access to the partnerships that are set up to run private equity funds, so they're probably of little real interest to us. But, for the record, *The Journal of Finance* recently reported that average returns are "approximately equal to the S&P 500."[2] The article also notes the huge variation in performance between different funds and the cyclical nature of the industry, but concludes that funds with an established track record of success tend to do best.

Third, real estate remains an old favorite of the amateur investor. Transactions in the worldwide property market reached a record level of $600 billion in 2006. But is this money really safe as houses? According to data from the US Department of Housing and Urban Development, American real estate sale prices increased more than 56% from 1999 to 2004. During the same period, the S&P 500 price index dropped by almost 6%. But over the last sixty-five years, the reverse happened. Property prices increased, but only a quarter as much as those of the S&P 500. And these figures don't take into account the fall in prices associated with the subprime mortgage crisis that started in 2007 and saw huge reductions in the price of real estate that in some areas exceeded 30% in just one year.

Fourth and finally, we come to venture capital, which has been very much in vogue since the late 1990s. In 1999 returns skyrocketed to over 300% for investments in start-ups at an early stage of financing. By 2000, there were 1,600 venture capital firms worldwide with annual investments approaching $120 billion. Pop went the dotcom bubble and returns fell below -40% for several years.[3] Overall, the average return of venture capital investments is the highest of the four alternative investments we've looked at. But it also fluctuates the most. This means the potential for returns well above the average is higher – and so is the risk of huge losses. As we said the flip side of substantial risk is huge opportunity.

## NOT-SO-ALTERNATIVE INVESTMENTS

Where does that leave you, the investor? We've told you that everything between becoming super-rich and losing all your money is possible. But we admit that's not terribly useful. Your task is clearly to find the balance between the levels of return you want and the risks or opportunities that these imply. If you enjoy gambling and aren't relying on your investment to see you through retirement, then venture capital might be a good choice. But if you can't afford to lose the money, you should pick less "alternative" mechanisms.

Bonds traditionally offer a spectrum of adequate to low returns and much smaller risks. Stocks, meanwhile, are in between bonds and the alternative investments we looked at – in terms of risk and therefore return. Both stocks and bonds can be swiftly liquidated if necessary and, crucially, they are sufficiently regulated to protect you against fraud. Most importantly, there is a wide range of choices in both vehicles, allowing you to target different levels of risk and earnings. But the average investor usually relies on experts to do this for them. Here's a normal story of everyday investors, to compensate for our earlier excursion into the land of fairytales. As before, the characters are fictional, but the figures are real.

Norma is a divorced librarian with a grown-up son and daughter. She lives in New York, but doesn't move in glamorous social circles and has never met any exiled kings or princesses. Norma started saving way back in 1980 when she inherited $50,000 from the sale of her deceased father's house. Being sensible, Norma believed in entrusting her money to the experts. After all, she knew little about stocks and investments. But she did know she'd need to supplement her pension after retiring. And now she thinks she has done very well thanks to the mutual fund she invested in. Her investment grew, on average, by 7% a year and, by the time she retired in 2005, it stood at $271,372. Of course, there were some unavoidable costs. When she joined, there was a 4% up-front fee for some funds, then an annual management fee of over 2%. But that's a small price to pay for such expertise.

Or is it? Over the same period the S&P 500 grew by an average of 13% a year. This means that if Norma had invested her $50,000 in a portfolio covering all S&P stocks her money would have grown to $1,061,527. (This figure is reached by calculating the compound interest at 13% on $50,000 over twenty-five years.) Of course, buying stocks this way isn't practical for a small investor, but there are plenty of index funds available that track the S&P 500 as closely as possible. These typically charge an annual fee of 0.5% or less with no up-front charges.

In fact, Norma's younger sister Jean, who is also a university librarian, invested her 1980 inheritance of $50,000 in an index fund – on the advice of a visiting finance professor from Europe. She too retired in 2005, but five years earlier than expected, when her investment hit a value of a little over a million dollars. She liked her job, but who's heard of a millionaire librarian?

Jean hasn't told Norma exactly how much money her investment made in the index fund. She's a little bit embarrassed, to tell the truth, especially when she hears Norma talking about the huge success of her mutual funds. But she does remember the visiting professor from

Europe telling her all about the "illusion of control." In her sister's case, that pesky illusion has a lot to answer for. Not only did it lead Norma to put her faith in an unknown expert with a seven-figure salary and huge bonus, it also made her lie to herself.

## THE POWER OF LUCK

Back in the real world, it's time to look at this question of expertise in more detail. Bill Miller, the manager of the Legg Mason fund, has beaten the S&P 500 for fifteen years in a row – from 1991 to 2006. This is a spectacular achievement that makes him a superstar fund manager and a darling of the popular business press. All credit to him. But would it be possible to achieve this by luck alone? Time for a few very simple calculations.

Let's assume there are 8,192 funds in the USA (actually, that's not far off the truth). Now suppose that the chance of each fund beating the S&P 500 in a given year is exactly 50%, the same as tossing a coin, and that each fund's performance is independent of all the others. This means about 4,096 funds can be expected to beat the S&P 500 in a single year. About 2,048 of these will beat it again for a second year, then 1,024 for three years in a row, 512 for four years in a row and so on, dividing by two each time . . . until you get to one fund that's made it for a whole thirteen years. If Bill Miller is the only "survivor," then his achievement of getting to fifteen years already sounds less impressive.

Now, it's important to remember that one fund out of 8,192 beating the S&P for thirteen years is just an average outcome of our original assumptions and that in reality the actual number can fluctuate above and below the average. Finally, if we look more closely at the record of Bill Miller's fund, we see that in 1994 its returns more or less tied with the S&P 500. So it's perfectly reasonable to claim that he beat the S&P only eleven years in a row, rather than fifteen – a performance well within the limits of pure chance. In fact, his subsequent performance was below the S&P 500 for three years in a row bringing the returns of the fund to those of the early 1990s. Sorry Bill, luck does not favor anyone in the long run.

The same is true for the many other funds that have outperformed the market for several years in a row. Most of them subsequently revert back to an average or even poor performance. At the same time we never hear about the funds that did worse than the average for fifteen consecutive years. Who'd want to advertise results like these?

Professor Burton G. Malkiel of Princeton University, author of the classic book *A Random Walk Down Wall Street*, is one of several observers who claim that beating the market is due to chance, rather than skill. In one study, he compared the results of the top twenty equity mutual funds of the 1970s with their own performance in the 1980s.[4] In the 1970s their average returns exceeded the average of all equity funds by a margin of 10.4% to 19% per year. In the next decade, they slumped into mediocrity. They performed worse than the average fund by 11.1% to 11.7% per year. In a second study, he made the same calculations for the 1980s and 1990s. The star twenty funds of the 1980s, whose collective results had outperformed the average of all equity funds by 14.1% to 18% a year, underperformed the average by a margin of 13.7% to 14.9% over the following ten years.

John C. Bogle, the founder and former chairman of the Vanguard Group and crusader against fund managers, carried out a similar, but shorter-term study over the two periods 1996 to 1999 and 1999 to 2002. First he looked at the top ten out of a total of 851 USA equity funds (those with assets of more than $100 million). They were paragons of success and big bonuses between 1996 and 1999. But in the following three years, the former number one dropped to a position of 841. The best performance of all ten of the formerly outstanding funds was a position of 790, out of a total of 851 funds, between 1999 and 2002. It seems fair to conclude that, as the small

print so often tells us, past success is no guarantee of future performance. What's more, it really does look as if the majority of star fund
managers just got lucky.

Professor Eugene F. Fama of the University of Chicago put it this
way: "I'd compare stock pickers to astrologers, but I don't want to
bad-mouth astrologers."

## THE EXPERT STRIKES BACK

Nevertheless, there are many who defend the skill of the expert
stock-picker. They claim that some fund managers consistently outperform the market for such sustained periods that their results
couldn't possibly be due to chance alone. Their hero is the legendary
Peter Lynch, the former manager of Fidelity's Magellan fund, which
between 1977 and 1990 made an immense 2,703% return, compared
to the 574% of the S&P 500. They also cite the famous Schroders fund
that, since its inception in 1993, has posted a 16.26% annual compound return, versus the 12.30% of the S&P 500. There are several
other relatively successful funds and anecdotal evidence to boot.

Yet there are few academic studies to support this point of view
– at least not wholeheartedly. And you have to dig deep to find any at
all. A recent paper in the *Journal of Finance* claimed that there was
strong evidence for consistent, superior performance for some kinds
of funds but not for others.[5] Another paper, from the Cass Business
School in London, scours the previous research on mutual fund performance in the US and UK over the previous twenty years. It concludes that "only very sophisticated investors should pursue an active
investment strategy of trying to pick winners – and then with much
caution."[6] Instead, most investors are advised to buy into low-cost
index funds that track the market average.

In other words, if there are some stock-picking skills out there,
they're of little practical use to the investor on the street. After fund

and transaction fees have been included, actively managed funds just don't perform consistently better than the market average.

So much for stock picking. What about experts who claim to have perfect timing? Mark Hulbert, whose *Hulbert Financial Digest* has become a highly respected source of investment wisdom, examined the claims of the financial newsletters with established reputations as the "best." In 2003 he created a hypothetical portfolio based on the newsletters' advice. Then he timed his buying and selling over the next twelve months (also hypothetically) according to their hot tips. The result was a loss exceeding 32%. Fortunately, that was hypothetical too. Meanwhile the Wilshire 5000 index, which included all of Hulbert's stocks, increased by 13%.

The academic literature tends to agree with Hulbert's findings. The researchers from the Cass Business School in London who warned against stock picking also conclude: "There is little evidence of successful market timing." In the most comprehensive study of all, researchers at the US National Bureau of Economic Research scrutinized the market-timing recommendations of 237 investment newsletters – a massive 15,000 predictions. They concluded: "There is no evidence that newsletters can time the market. Consistent with mutual (managed) fund studies, 'winners' rarely win again and 'losers' often lose again."[7]

Professor Michael Jensen of Harvard Business School was one of the first researchers to compare the performance of actively managed mutual funds with the market average over the period 1945 to 1964. He concluded:

> The evidence on mutual fund performance indicates not only that these 115 mutual funds were on average not able to predict security prices well enough to outperform a buy-the-market-and-hold policy, but also that there is very little evidence that any individual fund was able to do significantly better than that which we expected from mere random chance. It is also important to note that these

conclusions hold even when we measure the fund returns gross of management expenses (that is assume their bookkeeping, research, and other expenses except brokerage commissions were obtained free).[8]

Nearly forty years later, in the revised 2003 edition of *A Random Walk Down Wall Street*, Burton Malkiel (quoted earlier in this chapter) restated his earlier thesis that a blindfolded chimpanzee throwing darts at the *Wall Street Journal* can select a portfolio as successfully as a roomful of experts! His once controversial theory is of little concern to us. But his empirical findings are powerful. "Through the past thirty years that thesis has held remarkably well," he claims. "More than two-thirds of professional portfolio managers have been outperformed by the unmanaged S&P 500-Stock Index."

The same goes for investing in bonds. Professionally managed bond funds underperform the various indexes by 1% to 1.7%. Given the lower returns of bonds in general, this is equivalent to the 3% underperformance of equity funds. There has been less academic research concerning managed bond funds, but one of the earliest, published in *The Journal of Business* in 1993, concludes, "Overall and for subcategories of bond funds, we find that bond funds underperform relevant indexes post-expenses. Our results are robust across a wide choice of models."[9]

So what about funds that aren't actively managed? These are the so-called "index" funds that aim to track the market average, either by holding all the shares in a given listing (such as the Dow Jones Industrial average) or a representative sample of them. They're how Jean the librarian from the earlier story got so rich. Table 9 shows the result of making an investment of $50,000 in 1980 and not touching it for twenty-five years, just as the two librarians did. It's easiest to think of the average yearly returns as equivalent to putting the money in a savings account with a fixed annual interest rate for a period of twenty-five years.

Table 9 Cumulative returns of $50,000 invested for 25 years (using the historical returns of 1980–2005)

| | Average yearly returns | $50,000 invested for 25 years | Return as percentage of S&P 500 |
|---|---|---|---|
| Market average (S&P 500) | 13.0% | 1,061,527 | 100.0% |
| Index fund (tracking the S&P 500) | 12.8% | 1,015,541 | 95.7% |
| Average mutual fund (deduct 3%) | 10.0% | 541,735 | 51.0% |
| Average investor (deduct another 3%) | 7.0% | 271,372 | 25.6% |
| Survivorship bias* (deduct 0.75%) | 6.25% | 227,611 | 21.4% |

* This is an average estimate of the effect of bankrupt, folding, or merged funds on the average return of the remaining mutual funds

The first expensive lesson learned is that a small percentage difference in annual returns can add up to a gigantic difference when compounded over twenty-five years. But even for a statistician it comes as a bit of a shock. How can the difference between Norma and Jean's investments be quite so big?

The answer is not simply that the experts are less expert than they claim to be. It's that they also expect a handsome payment for their non-expertise! John C. Bogle, whose research we referred to earlier, has been a long-term and vocal critic of the mutual fund industry – from within. One of his major complaints is that the cost to the investor is huge: 2% to 3% of the assets – and that's before you count the entry and exit fees.

Another of his criticisms is that a large proportion of mutual funds fail or are forced to merge with others – over 60% of them in the period from 1970 to 2005! But the returns of these funds aren't included when the average is calculated. So, in addition to the risk of investors losing money, the 10% average annual return is estimated to be 0.5% to 1.0% higher than it should be. The exact figures may be elusive, but one stark fact stands out: the returns for the average investor are a whole lot less then those for the average mutual fund.

## TAKING STOCK

Before making our investment prescriptions, let's look back on the conclusions which underpin them from this and the preceding chapter.

- In the very long term, the average annual return of all stocks and of all bonds is fairly consistent and positive. And it's much higher for stocks than for bonds.
- In the short to medium term, the average annual return of all stocks and of all bonds can fluctuate significantly, with very high unpredictability. This makes profitable forecasting for stocks and bonds in the short to medium term next to impossible. What's more, the medium term can be longer than many people's investing life spans.
- The return on an individual stock fluctuates more than the return on a broad mix of stocks from the same category which in turn fluctuates more than the underlying market index or the average return for all stocks in that market. The same is true for bonds.
- Risk and return are positively, although imperfectly, correlated. For example, return on stocks is much more variable than return on bonds, offering a greater potential downside but also a potentially higher reward. So, there is greater risk associated with stocks but also a higher return. However, this positive correlation

between risk and return is not perfect, in the sense that a riskier asset pays a higher return only on average. Similarly, alternative investments, such as private equity, venture capital, real estate, and hedge funds, are riskier than stocks and thus can provide greater windfalls but can also lead to more extreme losses.

- Experts and sophisticated models don't perform better than the average returns of the markets they operate in. That is, the number of experts or models that outperform the average return in a given market in any given period of time is no higher than you'd expect to occur by sheer luck. Even for the few "superstar" money managers, it's far from proven that they aren't just the lucky ones. Let's put it another way – the returns of actively managed funds tend to do less well than index funds, at least on average.

- Past and future performances of markets, of experts, and of models are unrelated. In other words, chasing past successes for future positive returns doesn't seem to work.

## THE FOUR PILLARS OF INVESTMENT WISDOM

Given all these conclusions what should you do with your money? Well, of course, that depends on why you're investing it and what you want to achieve. All we can do is give you four pillars of investment wisdom to help you decide. These four pillars follow so directly from the conclusions above that we probably don't even need to tell you them, but here goes.

1. **Be average.** Don't try to pick individual stocks or bonds to outperform the market. Invest in as many as possible so that you can match the market average. If you can't buy stocks on your own, invest in a vehicle like an index or exchange-traded fund, which tracks some market average of your choice (e.g., growth stocks, value stocks, emerging markets, BRICs, etc.).

2. **Be patient.** Don't be tempted to sell at the "perfect" time. Chances are you'll lose out. All the evidence suggests that you should adopt a buy-and-hold strategy. The more often you trade, the lower the returns. If nothing else, the transaction costs of trading – commissions to brokers – really dent the returns of heavy traders.

3. **Be risk-aware.** Note that this isn't the same thing as being "risk-averse." For most readers, the stock market average will provide all the risk and opportunity you could ever want, especially if you've got a decade or two on your hands.

4. **Be balanced.** Rebalance your portfolio periodically – at most once a year – to keep your objectives on track. If you've invested in a fund that tracks the market average, then this will happen automatically.

Of course, the third and fourth pillars aren't quite so simple. The key is good asset allocation. In other words, you have to build a portfolio of investments that matches the market averages as closely as possible, while minimizing the risk you're willing to accept. In particular, what mix of stocks and bonds should you pick? For those of us who aren't investing directly, and who prefer to use off-the-shelf products such as pension plans, it's still worth asking these kinds of questions about the composition of the fund you're buying into.

As we saw before, bonds – especially short-term bonds – don't fluctuate anywhere near as wildly as stocks. This means you have the option of selling to cover unexpected needs for cash. Try this with stocks – and you might find yourself having to sell when the price is low. On the other hand and in the longer term, the average returns of bonds are less than half those of stocks and there's little chance of returns above that average. A rule of thumb often used in asset allocation is that the percentage of bonds in your portfolio should be about the same as your age. If this is starting to sound a little ageist, the rationale is that you can afford to wait for high returns when you're young. But when you're older, security will be more important. Of course, whatever your age, you might fancy a bit of a thrill, in which case how about – say – 10 or 15% of your portfolio in something a bit riskier? Around 10% in venture capital could be your little bit of Las Vegas.

Here, then, is a balanced portfolio for Norma the librarian's forty-year-old daughter, Marilyn, who's a bit more switched on than her mother: a total of 60% in stocks and 40% in bonds.

- 15% S&P 500 (fairly safe, large US companies)
- 10% Value Stocks (somewhat speculative)
- 10% Small Stocks (some small companies can become real winners)
- 15% International Large Cap Stocks (in case the US economy goes a bit pear-shaped)
- 10% Emerging Market Stocks (as far as she's willing to go for her 10% thrill)
- 20% short-term bonds (in case of emergencies)
- 20% long-term bonds (for that nice, warm, secure feeling)

Younger investors, such as Marilyn's thirty-year-old brother, may want to reduce his proportion of bonds to 30% and put his 10% in small-company growth stocks. Norma's son-in-law (Marilyn's husband), meanwhile, is a lot more conservative than his wife, even though they're both the same age. He's put 50% in bonds and doesn't have time for any emerging-market nonsense. In other words, your own asset allocation decisions should be based on your particular investment objectives, your investment horizon, the amount of your assets, and your tolerance of risk – tempered by your attitudes to getting higher-than-average returns.

Having done all this, sit back and do no more (apart from the permitted "rebalancing"). If you must insist on following the progress of your investments, adopt what we call a "Ulysses" strategy, in memory of the mythical hero. As his boat approached the island where the beautiful yet dangerous sirens sang their songs of seduction to passing sailors, he commanded that the crew tie him to the mast . . . and fill their own ears with wax. One way of doing this would be to program a computer to handle your investment according to simple rules that you input at the very beginning. But of course, you're not a mythical hero or a dumb computer. You're a human being in a media-rich world. And that puts you at a psychological disadvantage. And so we conclude with a list of dangers to avoid – the songs of the sirens.

## EIGHT SONGS – BUT NOT FOR THE INVESTMENT DANCE

Warren Buffett, who is almost as famous for his witticisms as his investment successes, once said: "The principal enemies of the equity investor are expenses and emotions." We've already seen the cost of the expenses taken by fund managers. Emotions are harder to quantify, but often more dangerous. As in other areas of life, our good intentions can be drowned in the Bermuda triangle of greed, fear, and hope. Moreover, like all effective lures, they take on different forms that are hard to recognize. Here are the main ones.

1. Following the herd. Unfortunately, statistics show that the average investor buys when the market is high. Added to this, Mr. and Ms. Average are often attracted to the more aggressive equities, such as NASDAQ technology stocks, which fluctuate most in value. They panic when their investments drop more than the overall market and sell at just the wrong time. Sometimes this turns into a stampede. Even when it doesn't, the herd is tempted by alternating greed, hope, and fear to trade just too often. Finally, the average and understandable reaction is to chase and buy into the best-performing funds. But, as we've already seen, today's star fund managers are all too often tomorrow's failures.

2. *Not* following the herd. If it's wrong to follow the crowd, it's tempting to adopt what is often called a "contrarian" strategy. This means doing the precisely the opposite of the market. However, given that we can't predict where the market is going anyway, it seems a little rash. And in the long term, the market is at least headed up, which means a true contrarian's investment would be headed down.

3. Believing what you read in the papers. The media are historically implicated in many buying and selling frenzies, from the Wall Street crash to the dotcom boom. The trouble is that journalists are more interested in an interesting story than a boring truth. This leads not only to distortions of reality, but huge gaps in the information that appears in the financial press. In addition, following fluctuations in stocks is like living on a roller-coaster. If you need that thrill, follow the fortunes of a professional sports team. But take our advice: don't read the financial pages – or at least, only very occasionally. You'll be much happier, and probably richer.

4. Unconscious connections. You hear that Amazon is doing well and suddenly you start thinking about other online retailers. Sometimes there's some good logic underpinning this thought process, but you need more specific information before investing in a given company. This kind of thinking is a particular danger for those who persist in picking individual stocks.

5. Short memories. We tend to remember the most recent things that happened to us. It's only natural. If it rained this morning, it's a good idea to carry an umbrella this afternoon. But short-term thinking is bad in a long-term business. At fashionable London dinner parties in 2007, everyone was talking about how their house had tripled in value since they bought it. They'd forgotten the misery of negative equity and repossessed homes in the last UK property crash that occurred less than two decades previously. By 2008, prices had started falling – suddenly bringing back all those bad memories.

**6.** Fear of losses. For some people, losing money is a form of bereavement. In fact, most of us fear the possibility of losing money much more intensely than we imagine the pleasure of gaining it. This emotional asymmetry leads investors awry. They tend to sell "winning" stocks but hang on to "losers" for too long – only selling when the price gets back to what they paid (if it does at all).

**7.** **Wishful thinking.** Again this is the kind of erring that's just human. Any dedicated fan of a hopeless sports team will understand the need for optimism. Ask any Chicago Cubs fan. Also, as the irrepressible English soccer anthem goes, "Thirty years of hurt never stopped me dreaming". True, there are many circumstances where misplaced hope can bring temporary benefit and a sense of security. But, with the magnifying effects of greed, investing isn't one of them. When it comes to investing, realism is always healthy.

**8.** **Imagining patterns.** In particular, seeing causal patterns where there aren't any. Your hopeless football team suddenly wins . . . and the value of Amazon shares goes up. The same thing happens the next week . . . and the next . . . and the next! Could these two phenomena be related? It's difficult to see how. But some people will find illusory correlations everywhere they look – and invest accordingly.

In short, if you want to be like Ulysses and hear the songs of sirens, you really need to be bound firmly to the mast. Most people can't cope with this. But when it comes to investments, it (literally) pays not to listen to alluring distractions, no matter how melodious they might sound.


## AVOID THE ILLUSION OF CONTROL AND WATCH THAT PAINT DRY

We invite you to build your investments on the four pillars, to allocate your assets wisely, and to tune out any mysterious or magical music. For investments, the dance of chance involves accepting the inevitable uncertainty, defining an appropriate policy, and, above all, sticking to it. In fact, investments are a perfect illustration of the paradox of control. By investing in index funds or randomly selecting your portfolio, you give up control over which stocks are picked. But you also make better returns, thereby gaining *more* control over your financial Fortune. This is because your investment behavior acknowledges that neither you nor anyone else can predict the market, at least in the short and medium term. Indeed, the recent subprime crisis and the accompanying credit crunch are perfect examples of our inability to predict even major economic and financial events.

We hasten to add that this won't make you super-rich, but it should ensure that your money plant grows steadily. Who knows? You may even be able to retire early, like the librarian in our story. Don't expect any excitement, though. As our opening quote suggests, if you must gamble, go to Las Vegas. In the meantime, let's see what experts in business can tell us.

# Six

# LESSONS FROM GURUS

*Those that fail to learn from history are doomed to repeat it.*

*Winston Churchill*

*History is bunk.*

*Henry Ford*

I n May 2007 a troubled relationship finally came to an end. The final split came as no surprise to those who had been watching. But just nine years earlier it had seemed a match made in heaven. Everyone had said they were perfect for each other: a distinguished European pedigree linked to a name that stood for the American dream. No one would have predicted nearly a decade of miscommunication, mistrust, and misery – and finally the painful break-up itself. It's another all too true story of misplaced certainty, high emotion, and utter inability to predict.

## BREAKING UP IS EXPENSIVE TO DO

The relationship in question was the now infamous merger between US car giant Chrysler and the prestigious German motor manufacturer Daimler-Benz. The man at its center was Jürgen Erich Schrempp, CEO of Daimler-Benz AG, who had instigated and sealed the deal – to the point that some commentators called it a "take-over." But this was a saga on an epic scale with thousands of characters. Not just executives and workers of both companies, but armies of advisers, consultants, and bankers . . . and finally the private equity firm Cerberus, which eventually "rescued" Chrysler.

It all began in 1998. The price tag of $36 billion for Chrysler seemed a bargain. The merger would enable Daimler-Benz to conquer the US luxury car market, while Chrysler would learn from the Mercedes engineering legend *and* gain a foothold in Europe. After all, if Volkswagen had managed to turn Skoda, infamous for its poor quality, into a respectable car company, the profits to be made from transforming Chrysler were vast. The optimistic assessment was that the market capitalization of the combined company would increase by more than $100 billion after five years, while the absolute worst-case scenario was still over $40 billion.

The stock markets and business press were on the side of the optimists. The day the merger was announced, the Chrysler share price soared by 17.6%, while that of Daimler-Benz went up by 6.4%. Analysts were waxing lyrical about "synergies" and "economies of scale."

The first signs of trouble came barely six months later in May 1999, when the press started seeing signs of culture clash. Then in 2000 Chrysler suffered unexpectedly high losses – with worse projected for 2001. Schrempp fired the American President, James P. Holden, and replaced him with his own protégé from Germany, Dieter Zetsche. The new guy sacked 26,000 employees and replaced further American executives with Germans. Morale dwindled and years of restructuring loomed. By 2006, Chrysler's annual loss was $1.2 billion with an additional restructuring charge of $1 billion.

Meanwhile, things weren't going brilliantly back in Germany. Mercedes was slipping down the industry quality rankings. There was an embarrassing product recall, and losses in the business involving the small Smart cars eventually totaled $3.6 billion.

Schrempp finally stepped down or, more accurately, was forced to do so in 2005, leaving Zetsche in overall charge. Shares rallied at this news, with an 8.7% increase. But the damage was done. In May 2007 Daimler unloaded 80% of its shares on Cerberus, actually *paying* them $650 million for the privilege of taking over an acquisition that had originally cost $36 billion! Worse still, in November 2007 it was announced that as many as 12,100 more employees would lose their jobs in 2008, in addition to the 13,000 redundancies already planned over a period of three years. So much for the deal that had once been hailed as the "merger of the century."

How could so many experts get it so wrong on such a multinational scale? All these famously clever people – top executives and their bankers, paid seven- and eight-figure salaries – made catastrophically bad decisions that tarnished two great brands. Had Schrempp and his team ever heard of uncertainty? Did they know that at best only two out of three mergers achieve their financial objectives? They weren't alone either. Hundreds of journalists, investors, and business school professors, among other experts, had also failed to predict the disastrous turn of events. So how are ordinary mortals supposed to manage in their everyday lives and work?

## BUY THE BOOK

There's certainly no shortage of people who claim they can help. Gurus are everywhere. Whether you're interested in management, alternative therapy, education, marriage, or parenting, there's always someone with a new theory (accompanied by a glossily marketed new book) which promises to solve all your problems. And – like the investors of the previous chapter – as managers, patients, educators, spouses, or parents, you're driven by desire, fear, and hope to listen (or at least buy the book). This makes you a captive audience for those who preach simplistic solutions. But which particular gurus should you believe?

As business school professors, the authors' own experience lies with management gurus – which is why they're discussed at length in this and the next chapter. But the same arguments can be applied in other fields. We also believe that the management gurus are the most influential of all. Many of them work for leading universities, top media companies, or strategy consultants and so command great respect. Even if you're not the kind of person to buy business books or magazines, the latest management theories almost certainly have a profound effect on your life. No longer confined to business, their teachings pervade the entire working world and shape the products and services on which we all depend.

By now, you'll have noticed a pragmatic – if not downright critical – thread to our arguments. Don't expect us to be any different about management theories. But bear with us, and again we promise a positive message in the end. Like everything else in life, business success is greatly influenced by luck, and this is important to remember. To do otherwise is to give in to the illusion of control – the same illusion of control that duped Jürgen Erich Schrempp into believing that nothing could go wrong with his merger of the century.

## THE RISE AND FALL OF REENGINEERING

Let's start with one of the most radical management theories of them all. In 1993, the book *Reengineering the Corporation: A Manifesto for Business Revolution* hit the airport bookstores. Its authors, Michael Hammer and James Champy, claimed that the time had come to throw out all the principles that had guided business over more than two centuries in favor of a new model. "The alternative," they warn on page one, "is for corporate America to close its doors and go out of business" – not exactly a modest statement. The new theory went by the name "reengineering" and the book-jacket blurb staked some pretty ambitious claims for it:

> Reengineering does not seek to make business better through incremental improvements – 10 percent faster here or 20 percent less expensive there. The aim of reengineering is a quantum leap in performance – the 100 percent or even tenfold improvement that can follow from entirely new work processes and structures.[1]

Reengineering went on to be a worldwide hit. A 2005 survey of top management tools from the leading international consultancy, Bain & Company, put reengineering, which was used by 61% of companies questioned, in the top ten.

Yet today, reengineering is practically forgotten. There are no major conferences or popular seminars on the subject. The last book we know was published in 2003 and the business journalists have moved on to newer theories. The once popular www.reengineering.com no longer operates, nor do the niche consultancies that sprang up to spread the word. Reengineering has lost its appeal and become part of management history.

It's not the only business theory to rise and fall in this way either. How many seasoned managers remember Management by Objectives, T-Groups, Theory Z, the Managerial Grid, the Systems Approach, Experience Curves, PIMS, the BCG Growth Matrix, Competitive Strategies, S-Curves, Product Life Cycles, Total Quality Management (TQM), and One-Minute Management? In each case, initial euphoria swiftly gave way to over-familiarity, disappointment, and finally obscurity.

Perhaps each of these theories deserves to be forgotten. But the phenomenon as a whole, with its repeated pattern of growth and decay, should be remembered by any manager seeking a quick fix or miracle cure. In the academic community at least, it's reassuringly possible to discern a few voices who speak out against the gurus. One of these belongs to Professors Eric Abrahamson and Gregory Fairchild from Columbia Business School in New York, who in 1999 penned the following warning.

> Our results suggest that management fashions intended to be both rational and progressive may in fact be irrational and, thus, retrogressive from the point of view of the thousands of organizations and millions of managers and employees who use these fashionable techniques both nationally and globally. Such widespread perpetual change, if it is technically inefficient, has the potential to generate pervasive waste, burnout, and cynicism about the potential for all forms of advancement in management.[2]

Fortunately for the world of business, it doesn't necessarily come to this. Many new theories are just variations on old ones repackaged with fancy names and brightly-covered books. You could argue, for example, that the theory of reengineering began with Henry Ford's production line. But elevate a technical process to a metaphor, add a dose of fear and some marketing know-how, and hey presto, you've got a best-seller on your hands! The downside is felt only by the employees whose jobs were reengineered out of existence, or the investors who ultimately paid the fat consulting fees charged by the reengineering experts.

Today, reengineering has been reincarnated as "business process management" (BPM to its friends). It's better this time around, as the new theory takes the useful idea of "process" and puts it to practical use, while discarding the more faddish and dysfunctional elements. Meanwhile, the term "reengineering" lives on non-metaphorically – and very valuably – in the worlds of manufacturing and software. This happy ending defines the key challenge for managers: how to find and exploit the real benefits in management theories, while avoiding the negative consequences of becoming a management-fashion victim.

## THE PIED PIPERS OF MANAGEMENT

One obvious and common-sense course of action is to identify successful companies and find out what makes them great. That's exactly what Tom Peters and Robert H. Waterman Jr. set out to do in the 1982 book, *In Search of Excellence: Lessons from America's Best-Known Companies*.[3] It was an instant phenomenon and went on to sell multiple millions of copies, thanks to its simple and apparently impeccable logic. The authors singled out thirty-two outstanding US companies and listed eight common factors for managers in other organizations to replicate.

How have the thirty-two exemplary companies fared since then? In the past quarter-century, five ended in bankruptcy or chapter 11 proceedings while six merged or were bought by other firms. This means that more than one in three of the excellent 1982 firms did not exist at the end of 2007. But what about the remaining twenty-one? Well, if we look at their share prices over the last ten years ending on December 31, 2007, we find that twelve did better than the S&P 500 during this period, one did the same (that is, within ±5% of the S&P 500) and eight did worse. Thus, even if we exclude the six firms that merged or were bought, thirteen companies did worse than the S&P 500 and twelve did better – the pattern of pure chance. Finally, only two of the initial thirty-two companies made it into *Fortune* magazine's 2007 survey of the top ten most admired US companies (more about this below). Excellence may well have been found in 1982, but it didn't definitely endure until 2008.

As if to pre-empt this disappointment, in 1994 another book appeared. *Built to Last: Successful Habits of Visionary Companies* was another instant bestseller.[4] Its authors, Jim Collins and Jerry Porras, used a similar methodology, only this time the book was the result of a six-year research project and the goal was to find not simply what made companies successful but also to identify what made them stand the test of time. As it happens, half of *Built to Last*'s eighteen "visionary" companies were also included in *In Search of Excellence*, although the common factors of their success were quite different in the two books.

The eighteen companies of *Built to Last* are all still in business. On the other hand, several have been through bad patches, while Citigroup, Sony, Ford, and Motorola have faced serious financial problems (which resulted in their share prices falling by more than 84% between 1995 and 2009). In terms of stock market returns in the seven years ending on December 31, 2007, nine of the eighteen companies did better than the S&P 500, eight did worse and one did the same (within ±5%). OK, they *have* lasted. But overall their financial performance is average. Was the six years of research really any more effective than randomly selecting eighteen companies that happened to be going through a good patch at the time of writing?

## IN SEARCH OF EXCELLENT THEORIES THAT ARE BUILT TO LAST

At this point, it all seems a bit confusing. Why can't those management gurus get it right? And given their atrocious track record, why do managers keep buying into their latest theories?

The second question probably has a more obvious answer than the first. It goes back to the greed, fear, and hope that we've seen before. It's all too easy to be seduced by a theory that promises effortless success. There are probably further psychological explanations too. Management gurus are usually poor historians while many managers often have big egos. They like to think their situation is unique and that there's nothing to learn from their predecessors' vast bank of experiences and mistakes. Sometimes this attitude pays off. If you're an innovator like Henry Ford, you've earned the right to dismiss history as bunk. But for the rest of us this can lead to grave errors.

Now to the gurus, themselves. To be fair, we're sure they have the best intentions and they don't in any way set out to exploit the psychological weaknesses of managers. But best intentions are no substitute for rigorous methodology. To see exactly what we mean, let's consider how to draw a valid scientific conclusion from a sample of data.

Imagine, by way of example, that you work in the facilities department of a university, which is currently refurbishing its student rooms and buying a new set of beds. You're sent out to estimate the average height of male students, but you're only given the time and funding to measure 50 of the 6,000 men currently enrolled. The obvious reaction is to measure the first fifty you see. But only a couple of students into the process, you notice that everyone waiting in the queue to be measured just got off the coach from the inter-university basketball tournament. And so it dawns on you that you need to find a way of selecting the fifty male students by chance. Only once you've done this – and measured their heights – can you make a scientifically meaningful statement about the average height of the 6,000 students. It's this chance selection that ensures your sample of fifty is likely to be representative of the wider population.

If we apply this thinking to *In Search of Excellence* and *Built to Last*, the once impeccable logic starts to look a bit shaky. The (rather small) samples of thirty-two and eighteen companies respectively were selected anything but randomly. No doubt, the "best practices" the authors identify really are common to all the companies concerned. But how do we know they aren't shared with thousands of average performers, failures, and bankrupt companies? In short, these particular management theorists over-sampled success and under-sampled mediocrity and failure (this over-sampling of successful firms becomes obvious by the fact that six of the top ten US companies identified in Fortune's 1983 survey[5] were included *In Search of Excellence* and five of the top ten in Fortune's 1993 survey were included in *Built to Last*).

Tom Peters, Jim Collins, and their co-authors aren't alone. Most management gurus make the same mistake. It's nonetheless strange to find so many intelligent people falling into such an old trap. Way back in the 1930s, the Austrian-born philosopher of science, Karl Popper[6] leveled exactly the same charge at Sigmund Freud, whose psychoanalytical theories had gained widespread acceptance. Popper pointed out that real scientists start with conjectures, which they then try to refute – as well as seeking evidence to support them. Only by failing to *dis*prove their hypotheses, can they prove they were right all along. (This is why the medical researchers whose work we glimpsed in chapters 2 and 3 always have control groups in their experiments.) Meanwhile, "pseudoscientists," as Popper called them, only look for events that prove their ideas correct. Theories like this are little more than untested assertions. That's not to say that the assertions won't eventually turn out to be right – but we can only reach this conclusion once someone has tested them.

The other problem is the way in which the theorists make inferences from their own sample of successes to the entire population. For instance, imagine that gurus identified an incontestably brilliant management practice among eighteen companies in the US during the 1990s. Will the brilliance of this practice hold true for all other firms in the US? Will it also work in India or China in 2010? Or in the US in 2015? Not necessarily. We all know that many important factors change across time and place, history, and geography. To make this kind of extrapolation is equivalent to assuming that our results for the average height of fifty male students will also apply to the entire male population not only now but also in fifteen years' time.

Clearly, outstanding companies owe their performance to certain factors. And equally clearly, it's of considerable interest to identify and exploit these factors. But it's far-fetched to assume that they'll be unremittingly beneficial in different times, cultures, and environments. Time and again, we've seen extrapolations like this fail in the world of business. Many of the Japanese star companies of the 1980s, which the management gurus once urged us to emulate, themselves faced serious problems less than a decade later. Sony, the Japanese *super* star (one of the visionary companies included in *Built to Last*) stayed successful to the end of the twentieth century, but at the beginning of the twenty-first – after its share price had fallen 84% – the board of directors took the last resort of appointing a foreigner to head a much-needed turnaround. Past success is no guarantee for the future . . . or new markets, or new technologies. This much is an empirical fact. After all, even Wal-Mart, that paragon of all-American retail virtue, withdrew from Germany under a cloud of failure. And what could all those once-rock-solid typewriter companies have done to halt the digital word processor's march of progress?

No company has managed to remain "excellent" or "visionary" for long periods. Instead, the changing business environment requires a model of continuous adaptation – and sometimes revolution – which can't be achieved using recipes from the past. So was Henry Ford right all along? Well, only up to a point. Over-simplistic historical – or geographical – reasoning really is bunk. Perhaps management gurus and their followers spend too much time looking purely at business. With a little more training in the subtleties of historical, geographical, scientific, and statistical methodology, they might design some more robust research projects with the following characteristics:

- **Sampling failure as well as success.** A group of randomly chosen firms, similar to those singled out for their great performances (but different in that they lack the "best practices" identified), would have to perform relatively badly over a long period of time. To be fair, *Built to Last* tries to do this up to a point.

- **Large, representative samples over long periods of time.** The number of firms investigated would need to be large enough – and the time span of the investigation would need to be long enough – to prove that the companies' achievements are due to the specific factors identified, rather than luck.

- **A solid attempt to refute the theory.** In particular, researchers would need to look carefully for firms that exemplified the selected "best practices" identified, but which nonetheless fail.

- **An ongoing reality check.** Researchers would need to verify that the factors for success discovered hold true in new environmental conditions. They'd have to be prepared to refine or abandon their theories accordingly.

Alas, these conditions are almost impossible to respect, but it would be nice to think that management researchers aspire to them. On the other hand, perhaps it's just as well they don't. If someone ever did figure out the exact recipe for business success, everyone else would apply it and all businesses would become disappointingly average!

## THE FUTURE: A HISTORICAL APPROACH

As the two quotes with which we started this chapter suggest, we believe it's important to learn what we can from the past, but without extrapolating wildly into the future. And if we really want to understand what makes companies successful across time, it's a useful exercise to track the performance of companies at different points in their histories. Consistent success might indicate practices that stand the test of time. Inconsistency would suggest the contrary.

We're therefore lucky that, since 1983, *Fortune* magazine has been publishing an annual league table of America's most admired firms. The ranking is based on a survey of managers and analysts (the data are collected and analyzed by the top consulting firm Hay Group). Set criteria are used to give each company scores, which are then aggregated to get the overall result. So how many stars of the 1980s are on *Fortune*'s current list? Very few, it turns out, and in some industries there are none at all. Once great names, such as AT&T, General Motors, Ford, Sears Roebuck, Eastman Kodak, and Xerox, have all suffered serious reversals in their corporate Fortunes over time.

The difference between explaining the past and predicting the future is fundamental. All credit to *Fortune* magazine that they don't make guru-like claims to offer the recipe for future success. Instead, without doing any fancy research, they ask respondents to identify high performance in firms they know a great deal about. And when we measure the subjective criterion of "admiration" against objective factors, such as stock market performance, we find a great deal of correlation. The ten most admired companies in 2005 produced average returns of 23.1% in 2003 to 2004 (compared to the S&P 500 average of 10.88%). Go back a bit further and the story is the same. Between 1999 and 2004, the top ten produced average returns of 6.1%, while the S&P 500 average was a dismal -2.3%.

No clairvoyance here, then. Just good solid knowledge of the past and present. On the other hand, in the *near* future at least, you'd probably expect many of the most admired companies to continue performing well. Even if they don't have the best practices, they've got some momentum from accrued competitive advantages. And indeed, for the 2005 top ten, this was the case. Nine of them also appeared in *Fortune*'s ten most admired companies for 2006 – and even the one that got away, Wal-Mart, only slipped from fourth to twelfth. The same happened in 2007 and 2008. From the top ten of

2006, eight still remained in 2008 (Dell and Microsoft dropped out) and Microsoft was in sixteenth place. *yes, there was never any Ed*

But there was no way of knowing that Dell, the most admired company of 2005 and eighth in 2006, would slide out of the 2007 and 2008 surveys altogether (it's not even in the newly expanded "top twenty"). In 2006 it had serious operational and strategic difficulties. By the middle of the year its share price dropped to under $20 (from over $42 at the end of 2004). As if the customer service problems and the massive notebook battery recall weren't enough, there was also a Federal investigation into its finances and accounting practices. At the time of writing (mid 2008) we have no foresight as to whether Dell will recover or regain the admiration of *Fortune*'s survey respondents. But at the time of reading, you probably have the benefit of some hindsight as to whether the stock market was correct in reducing Dell's value by over 50% in less than two years. Our point is simply that your hindsight and our lack of foresight are very different beasts.

Today, as we write, the participants in *Fortune*'s survey have just discovered Google and its dominance of the internet. It was included for the first time in 2007, as America's eighth most admired company, and it rose to fourth in the 2008 survey. This reminds us of Dell's meteoric rise between 1995 and 2000, when its share price went from less than $1 to over $50. Just remember Google's words on its own search page: "I'm feeling lucky". Are their strategists doing everything right? Or was the company in the right place at the right time? Only time – not gurus – will tell.

## QUALITY, NOT QUANTITY?

Chan Kim and Renée Mauborgne's *Blue Ocean Strategy: How to Create Uncontested Market Space and Make the Competition Irrelevant* provides another prescription for success – "innovative strategies."[7] Although one can raise questions about *Blue Ocean Strategy*, along with other business blockbusters such as *In Search of Excellence* and *Built to Last*, it's also important to recognize that they provide an important service. Namely, they identify a number of "excellent" or "visionary" companies based on valuable accounts of past successful performance that is due to some form of innovative strategy. It would be pointless to argue against this historical logic.

However, even in the case of innovation, we warn against assuming a one-to-one relation between prescriptions based on past success and future triumphs. It's the deterministic relation between the "lessons from" and the "how to" in the subtitles of these books with which we take issue. And that's because it's yet another case of the illusion of control. It's going one step too far to believe that these factors – deployed by different organizations in different times, places, and situations – will lead to outstanding performance again and again, with complete certainty each time.

But there's also an inverse problem. That is, companies often fail to spot the innovations on their own doorsteps. Consider the case of Xerox. In the 1970s it dominated the market in office copying. Cleverly spotting the rise of computers and the possible threat to the entire photocopying industry, Xerox executives set up a research program at their California office in Palo Alto to investigate the future of the "paperless office." The brilliant researchers were highly innovative and essentially created the PC, complete with easy-to-use interfaces, mouse controls, connections between different computers, and even a form of email. Sadly for Xerox, the senior managers on the East Coast lacked the imagination to see what their own West Coast unit had achieved. Fortunately for the rest of the world, someone else – a twenty-something techie from outside the organization – glimpsed the potential of Xerox's innovations. His name was Steve Jobs.

Jobs claims that, if Xerox had realized what they'd created, they'd have dominated the computer industry through to the 1990s. As it turns out, Jobs initially got his own strategy wrong with Apple, which went through some bad times of its own. It's not clear that Xerox would have done any better. What *is* clear, however, is that high levels of creativity and innovation are – by definition – limited to a few talented individuals or companies. If everyone had the talent of Van Gogh, Picasso, or Monet, then the level of creativity would rise to new levels that only a few even more exceptional artists could achieve. The trick for the art investor is to spot today's great painters who will be remembered tomorrow . . . or – if you're a senior manager – to predict which innovative strategies will work in the future, and be lucky enough to be alone in doing so.

Contrary to the image projected by best-selling books, the business environment is extremely complex. It's influenced by many chance events and driven by new technologies that defy prediction. What can the *Encyclopedia Britannica* do to compete with the free internet site Wikipedia? How should IBM and DEC have responded to mass demand for PCs? What could Compaq have done to compete with Dell's new business model of selling directly to the customer, allowing it to offer lower prices for computers of the same or better quality? These were novel challenges with no precedents. Perhaps history can offer inspiration in such circumstances, but it certainly provides no magic keys.

Sometimes, the only hope is to break with the past completely. That's why a change of CEO sometimes works. IBM, once considered the best-run company in the USA, had a narrow escape from bankruptcy during the period from 1991 to 1993 when it lost close to $12 billion. It returned to profitability after hiring an outsider who changed precisely those practices that had led to its former glory. As *Blue Ocean Strategy* documents so well, the problem is that competitors are forever catching up, copying not only successful products but proven practices. "Visionary" companies have to stay on their toes, forever seeking new vision and new innovative strategies.

If there's one lesson from history, it's this: history never repeats itself in exactly the same way. If there is another lesson, it is that successful innovation cannot be predicted.

## DOES SUCCESS HAVE TO BE EPHEMERAL?

Time and time again, we see the outstanding firms of the past become the underachievers of the present. Rubbermaid, for example, was in *Fortune*'s list of America's most admired companies for eleven consecutive years between 1986 and 1996, even making it to number one in 1994 and 1995. That didn't prevent Newell, a lesser-known company that also made plastic household goods, from buying it just a few years later. Similarly, General Motors used to be a paragon of management and market leadership. But by the turn of the twenty-first century, it was flirting with bankruptcy, and then lost its position as the world's biggest car manufacturer to Toyota, which was practically unknown three decades ago.

Now, by our own admission, a few examples from the past don't prove anything (least of all about the future). So let's look in a little more detail at the ebbs and flows of the *Fortune* rankings of America's most admired companies over the period 1983 to 2008. During this time, the magazine's knowledgeable respondents considered more than a thousand companies. Yet, in twenty-six years of compiling top tens, they included a total of only forty-nine organizations. In other words, over 95% of eligible companies never made it into the list. An elite seventeen, however, have been in the top ten more than five times.

## THE MOST ADMIRED OF ALL

As table 10 shows, the most dominant companies of all – over this period – are Johnson and Johnson (J&J), Merck, and Proctor &

**Table 10** *Fortune*'s most admired companies, 1983–2008

| No | Company | First year on the list | Last year on the list | Number of times on the most admired list | Number of years between the first and last year outside the list |
|----|---------|-----------|-----------|---------|---------|
| 1 | Johnson & Johnson | 1983 | 2008 | 15 | 11 |
| 1 | Merck | 1983 | 1999 | 15 | 2 |
| 1 | Procter & Gamble | 1986 | 2008 | 15 | 8 |
| 4 | General Electric | 1983 | 2008 | 14 | 12 |
| 5 | Coca-Cola | 1984 | 1999 | 13 | 3 |
| 5 | Microsoft | 1994 | 2006 | 13 | 0 |
| 5 | Wal-Mart Stores | 1988 | 2005 | 13 | 5 |
| 8 | Berkshire Hathaway | 1997 | 2008 | 12 | 0 |
| 9 | Rubbermaid | 1986 | 1996 | 11 | 0 |
| 10 | 3M | 1985 | 1995 | 10 | 1 |
| 10 | Southwest Airlines | 1998 | 2007 | 10 | 0 |
| 12 | Intel | 1995 | 2002 | 8 | 0 |
| 13 | Boeing | 1984 | 1993 | 7 | 3 |
| 13 | Dell | 1999 | 2006 | 7 | 1 |
| 13 | FedEx | 2002 | 2008 | 7 | 0 |
| 16 | Hewlett-Packard | 1983 | 1998 | 6 | 10 |
| 17 | IBM | 1983 | 2004 | 6 | 16 |

Gamble (P&G). These three giants have appeared in the top ten an impressive fifteen times in the twenty-six years between 1983 and 2008. It is interesting that these three companies were also included in both *Built to Last* and *In Search of Excellence*.

J&J and P&G have remained in the most admired list for several years through to 2008 but not Merck, which was dropped in 1999. Merck's profits have fallen considerably since the late 1990s and, by 2005, its stock price had dropped by 73% (although it then recovered a little). It all began when Merck canceled the launches of several drugs that were supposed to be block-busters. There were also safety scares about certain products already on the market, as well as some patent infringement lawsuits and investigations into the possible withholding of evidence about the efficacy and safety of drugs. As the search for those responsible intensified, management problems became ever more severe. The once revered Merck lost its shine and became just another drugs company. Its rapid decline proves, once again, that past performance is simply not sufficient to predict future success.

Table 10 also shows that five firms in the sweet seventeen (Rubbermaid, Berkshire Hathaway, Southwest Airlines, Intel, and FedEx) are included every single year between their first and last appearances. Others (GE, Wal-Mart, and Coca-Cola) exhibit a similar pattern, but lapse for a few years before reappearing consistently once again. The remaining companies also show a tendency to cluster around consecutive years, although there are a few exceptions. The message seems to be that, once the admiration wanes, it's hard to regain.

Curiously, table 10 shows a distinct shift between the new century and the old. Merck, Coca-Cola, Rubbermaid, and Hewlett-Packard appeared consistently before lapsing in 2000 and failing to return. Conversely, Berkshire Hathaway, Dell, GE, Microsoft, Southwest, Wal-Mart, Johnson & Johnson, and Procter & Gamble all appear for the first time, or reappear after an absence of several years, around 2000. Could it be that the most admired companies at the end of the last century simply made a natural regression toward the average? Perhaps an era of mediocrity has even dawned for the mighty Microsoft. After all, it slipped off the bottom of the list in 2007 after thirteen consecutive years in the top ten. Former McKinsey consultants Richard Foster and Sarah Kaplan[8] have made a special study of once-star companies and suggest that it's rare to sustain stellar performance beyond a decade: "As soon as any company had been praised in the popular management literature as excellent or somehow super-durable, it began to deteriorate." If this is true, then Microsoft is already living on borrowed time.

More than that, is it possible that Microsoft's success was just due to being in the right place at the right time? The right place is the IT business. And the right time was the mid-1990s to mid-2000s – heyday of all things involving computers. Given the march of IT progress, it also makes perfect sense for Dell and Microsoft – leaders in their industry as were Hewlett-Packard and IBM before them – to appear when they did. In the case of Berkshire Hathaway, GE, Southwest, or Wal-Mart it could be a different kind of luck: drifting into one of those blue-ocean innovations or happening on a bunch of talented managers.

Out of curiosity, we compared our table of "the most admired of the most admired" with the names in *Built to Last* and *In Search of Excellence*. Remember that both books involved long, systematic research, whereas the magazine's ranking is based on a survey of experts, whose subjective scores are averaged to get the top ten. Despite these very different methodologies, it turns out that eight companies (3M, Boeing, Hewlett-Packard, IBM, Johnson & Johnson, Merck, Procter & Gamble, and Wal-Mart) are common to all three sources. In addition, the top three (J&J, Merck, and P&G) are included in both books. Is this coincidence or simply due to the over-sampling of success that we warned about earlier?

There is a particularly strong overlap between *Built to Last* and *Fortune's* most admired of all. Nine companies appear in both lists and most of the other *Built to Last* companies have appeared in *Fortune's* top ten at some point. In fact only four of the eighteen firms haven't – and one of those, Sony, which is Japanese, isn't eligible anyway. *In Search of Excellence* has less in common with our *Fortune* list, which you might expect, since it predates the magazine's ranking and the research it draws on goes back even further. Nonetheless, nine companies out of the twenty-three included in *In Search of Excellence* (and that were still in business) also appear in our *Fortune* list.

If anything, the massed ranks of the *Fortune* respondents are rather better than the painstaking researchers at picking companies that last. Only one of their top seventeen, Rubbermaid, has fallen into truly serious difficulties, while – as we saw earlier – three of the eighteen from *Built to Last* and at least eleven of the thirty-two from *In Search of Excellence* are in serious trouble or out of business altogether. One reason for this is probably that the *Fortune* survey isn't hung up on finding a simplistic recipe for success. The respondents use multiple criteria and their own totally subjective hunches to select companies. In 2008, the executives, directors, and securities analysts surveyed used a total of eight categories (quality of management, quality of products and services, innovation, long-term investment value, financial soundness, people management, social responsibility, and use of corporate assets) to rank companies. This means that single issues, such as stock market performance, don't skew the results. For example, Microsoft, Wal-Mart, GE, and Dell have all done worse than the S&P 500 but still managed to retain their admired status. Yahoo and eBay, on the other hand, don't appear in the top ten, despite their superior stock market performance and record for innovation.

The other reason that a popular business magazine seems to get better results than the academic researchers is simply that there are so many more opinions involved. Erroneous assessments cancel each other out. In other words, the averaging process extracts "pattern" from a "noisy" background. Gurus, in contrast, tend to operate alone, in pairs, or very small groups. Their more individualistic predictions – amplified by the need to identify success factors – are then totally exposed to the uncertainties of the future. In chapter 9, we'll return to this problem of separating pattern from noise when we consider the power of averaging. We'll discuss why and when we can rely on the "wisdom of the crowd" to assess uncertain quantities such as sales and reputations. In the meantime, let's just say there's more wisdom than madness in the way *Fortune* canvases the opinion of a large number of independent respondents.

## MEDIOCRITY AND FAILURE

Companies are like living creatures. They come into the world and, once they survive their teething troubles, they mature and eventually cease to exist. Sometimes, if they're not killed off by bankruptcy, they even reproduce through the medium of merger or acquisition. Arie De Geus, a retired Shell executive,[9] has conducted research that shows the life expectancy of new firms in Europe or Japan to be less than thirteen years – down from twenty in the late 1970s and early 1980s. Even if they grow up to be large multinationals they're likely to last only forty to fifty years in total. And Foster and Kaplan estimate that by 2020 the average S&P 500 firm will stay in the index for just ten years – down from sixty-five in the 1920s, when the list first appeared.

There are, as usual, exceptions. Like giant tortoises, there are some companies that have made it to over 150 years of age. But they tend to move like giant tortoises too. All the evidence points to the conclusion that the financial performance of long-lasting firms is below the market average. As Foster and Kaplan say: "the corporate equivalent of the El Dorado, the golden company that continuously performs better than the markets, has never existed. It is a myth."[10] Managing for survival doesn't guarantee strong performance for the entire corporate lifespan – in fact, just the opposite.

The ephemeral nature of success and the natural tendency toward mediocrity and eventual failure is the rule for all systems devised by mankind, whether countries, industries, economic structures, or superpowers. Since the beginning of human history, empires have come, seen, conquered . . . and disintegrated. Persia, Greece, and Rome took it in turn to dominate the ancient world. Since then, there's been a succession of empires, culminating in the presence of a single superpower at the end of the twentieth century. But change is already underway. Many people say that the twenty-first century belongs to China.

Since the industrial revolution, entire economic sectors have risen to preeminence only to lose their appeal as others gained in significance and profits. The canals and railways dominated the eighteenth and nineteenth centuries, finally giving way to oil and steel, followed by car manufacturing in the twentieth century. In the last 100 years, electrical appliances, telecoms, banking, pharmaceuticals, consumer electronics, and financial services have all risen to prominence. Now, at the beginning of the twenty-first century, all of these have been eclipsed by the new stars of the information industry (despite a small blip at the end of the millennium). Right now, search engines and social networking sites are all the rage, but who knows what tomorrow will bring?

## THE END OF THE RAINBOW

Identifying the secrets of successful companies and replicating them elsewhere is the holy grail of management gurus, consultants, and their customers. Or maybe it's more like searching for the pot of gold at the end of the rainbow, though. We can never get there.

That doesn't stop people like Jim Collins repeatedly trying, however. He's one of the authors of *Built to Last*, which was written partly with a view to correcting the methodological problems of *In Search of Excellence*. Yet *Built to Last* was not without a few problems of its own. One of Collins's colleagues at the top management consultancy, McKinsey, allegedly told him, "You know, Jim, we love *Built to Last* around here. You and your co-author did a very fine job on the research and writing. Unfortunately it's useless."

So serial-guru Collins embarked on another mammoth research project. Five years later, in 2001, it came to fruition with his next best seller. *Good to Great: Why Some Companies Make the Leap . . . and Others Don't.*[11] Collins isn't exactly modest in his claims. He says he's identified the "timeless 'physics' of good to great" and can show us "how you take a good organization and turn it into one that produces sustained great results." And you don't even have to be good for it to work. He adds that "almost *any* organization can substantially improve its stature and performance, perhaps even become great, if it conscientiously applies the framework of ideas we've uncovered."

Whatever happened to the eleven companies identified by Collins as having made the leap from good to great? It turns out that none of them has appeared in the *Fortune* top ten of most admired US companies since 2001, when the book came out. One of them, Gillette, no longer exists. It remains a successful brand-name, but the company itself has been bought by Procter & Gamble. Of the remaining ten, the stocks of seven of them performed worse than the S&P 500 during the last five years (ending in December 2007) while that of one did the same (within ±5%). That "physics" is beginning to look less "timeless" already. For all we know, to be fair to Collins, the companies could all have stopped applying his framework. But in their particular case, it may be time for a sequel, *Great to Good*. We hope, for their sakes, that the inevitable follow-up, *Bad to Worse*, doesn't come too soon.

Meanwhile, McKinsey partner Bruce Roberson, in collaboration with two academics, kept pursuing the end of that rainbow. They started the Evergreen Project, a five-year study of more than 200 well-established management practices used by 160 companies over a ten-year period (1986 to 1996). It culminated in 2003 in another book, *What Really Works: The 4+2 Formula for Sustained Business Success*.[12] The book concludes that the companies with the best long-term performance are extremely good in four fundamental practices and very good in two out of a further four practices. Here's the "four" part of the equation – the must-haves:

- Devise and maintain a clearly stated, focused **strategy**
- Develop and maintain flawless operational **execution**
- Develop and maintain a performance-oriented **culture**
- Build and maintain a fast, flexible, flat **structure.**

And here are the four additional options, from which companies should choose two to master.

- Hold on to **talent** and find more talented employees
- Build a **leadership** philosophy of commitment to the business and its people
- Change your industry through **innovation**
- Grow through **mergers and alliances.**

There's not much room for argument with any of this. It sounds like good common sense. But what the authors don't say is *how to* devise and maintain a clearly stated, focused strategy, *how to* develop and maintain flawless operational execution, *how to* develop and maintain a performance-oriented culture, *how to* come up with the innovations that would change your industry, and so on . . . you get the picture. And that's the hard bit.

## ANOTHER YEAR, ANOTHER GURU

Another more recent management book along the same lines of research is Alfred Marcus's *Big Winners and Big Losers: The 4 Secrets of Long-Term Business Success and Failure*, published in 2006.[13] The promised recipe for success is: start from an advantageous industry position ("a sweet spot") and make sure your management is adaptive, disciplined, and focused. Conversely, the recipe for failure is: start from a disadvantageous industry position ("a sour spot") and make sure your management is rigid, inept, and diffused. Again, so far, so indisputable. But *how* do you do all this in your particular situation?

At least the recipe for becoming a business guru is by now quite obvious. Carry out a long study of successful companies (and ideally some failures too). Criticize some previous such studies. Come up with some "secrets" common to all of them. Fill in the gaps by describing the exploits of a bunch of companies that prove your case particularly strongly. Easy, if a little time-consuming.

In both *What Really Works* and *Big Winners and Big Losers*, however, the chosen few companies don't stand the test of time. Campbell Soup is classified as really working by the former, but as a big loser by the latter. Yet there's only three years between their publication dates. What's more, the stock market performances of the supposedly exemplary companies in both books are already falling short of expectations. No matter, next year, there'll probably be another guru with another crop of successful companies, which will – sooner or later – fail.

## LEARNING FROM THE PAST

OK, we've been a little mean to the gurus. There is clearly much food for thought and plenty of inspiration in their accounts of business success or failure. The theorists also provide an important historical record besides identifying the broad issues to which managers should pay attention. But it's equally clear that we can't count on research studies based on detailed dissection of past performance as a guide for the future. To do so is – once again – to fall victim to the illusion of control. Yet, paradoxically, the limited life span of all humanity's structures – from small companies to empires, from management theories to (presumably) the entire capitalist system, is itself a case of history repeating itself on a grander scale. The implications of this duality – that is, what we can and cannot learn from history – are the theme of the next chapter. As both the *Fortune* survey and the histories of the companies identified in the three best selling books prove, there is no such a thing as lasting success. Instead, the excellent, visionary, and good-to-great companies identified by the gurus regress toward mediocrity. This is either a very depressing or a rather comforting thought, depending on which way you look at it.

# Seven

# CREATIVE DESTRUCTION

*The river*
*where you set*
*your foot just now*
*is gone —*
*those waters giving way to this,*
*now this.*

Heraclitus, *Ancient Greek Philosopher*

nough of gurus! Let's look at the bigger picture. In this chapter, we will show that long-term societal and economic history, not unlike living organisms, is a constantly repeating pattern of creation, growth, decline, destruction, and recreation. This cycle of creative destruction plays out endlessly at many levels: from individual companies to whole industries, from single sectors to entire national economies.

Yet we live in the short term. And we do business on even shorter time scales, which – as we saw in the case of the stock market – presents us with a lot of random fluctuations and little or no patterns. Despite what the management gurus try to tell us, history just doesn't repeat itself at the level of individual firms or business units. As the Greek philosopher Heraclitus wisely said, you can't step into the same river twice. Even if the water is the same depth and temperature as before, even if the pattern and the currents look constant, even if no stone on the river bed has moved, the water itself is not the same. It's constantly churning and changing. But the long term is a completely different story with creative destruction driving societal and economic progress. Like the river, it follows the same inexorable course with few changes, at least most of the time.

Far away from ancient Greek wisdom and the vast panorama of history, managing a business in the twenty-first century is – like managing our health or personal finances – fraught with all the uncertainty we've seen in previous chapters. But there are critical differences. Our bodies are highly complex, but our choices in managing them are confined. Running a company offers more options, even more than investing. Investors are usually blessed with the opportunity to withdraw their funds at will if their original decision starts to look bad – a luxury that few executives can afford. No, managers are stuck in the here and now of business and saddled with the consequences of decisions, both good and bad, from the past.

## THE CREATIVE DESTRUCTION OF COPPER

If we raise our sights from the narrow concerns of running a single company to the broader sweep of an entire industry, we do, however, start to learn some lessons from history. Back in 1932, the real price of copper (in constant 2007 dollars) was $1.97. By 1974 it was $7.26 (again in 2007 dollars), an almost four-fold increase. The main reason for this huge increase was the demand from the growing network of copper telephone wires that encircled the globe. But it was also because an industry cartel was controlling the supply.

Economists tell us that high profits are supposed to encourage additional capacity, with new facilities opening to increase production and meet rising demand. The people who run cartels, however, love their rising profits, so why would they reduce them? They work to defy economic principles and to maintain the status quo. That's exactly what the copper cartel did, restricting the number of mines and factories to constrain supply and maximize the profits of the copper companies – pushing the price up even further.

But high profits attracted competition from outside the copper industry. From the 1950s onward, scientists started exploring the possibilities of fiber optics. But the theoretical problems weren't solved until 1970, when three scientists, Robert Maurer, Donald Keck, and Peter Schultz, found a way of using fused silica (a material of extreme purity with a high melting point and low refractive index) to transmit more than 65,000 times more information than copper wires – and with much better transmission quality.

Fiber optics transformed the telecoms industry and heralded the coming of the information age. Since the 1980s many million kilometers of telecommunications lines have been installed worldwide and nearly all of them involved fused silica. Today, technical improvements mean that a single hair's-breadth fiber is enough to carry tens of thousands of phone calls, transmitting more than ten billion digital bits per second. That's equivalent to 20,000 books the size of this one.

Poor old copper. In less than a decade, the vast superiority of fiber optics made copper wire virtually obsolete. Demand for the metal collapsed, most copper companies went bankrupt and employment in the industry fell by 70% in some countries. To save itself from liquidation, Anaconda, once the fourth largest company in the world, was sold to ARCO in 1977. Prices continued to fall, and ARCO ceased all copper-mining activities in 1983. C. Jay Parkinson, the former president of Anaconda, must have regretted what he said in 1968: "This company will still be going strong 100 and even 500 years from now." Not that anyone can blame him. At that time, the copper cartel was controlling the market, and prices – not to mention profits – had been on the rise for over thirty-five years. Parkinson had underestimated the incredible power of the market to drive prices down (more about this soon) and thus wreak revenge on the few companies that previously controlled the market. It's small consolation that plumbers still like to use copper.

The key to understanding this tragic tale of an industry that got its just desserts lies in the fact that Maurer, Keck, and Schultz came from another world entirely. They worked for Corning Glass, a company that had no connections whatsoever with the telecommunications industry, let alone the copper business. It produced ordinary, everyday glass products. In other words, the threat to copper came from outside and, with absolutely no warning, took an entire industry down. Corning Glass didn't care if the copper industry was destroyed. On the contrary: the faster the destruction, the bigger its own revenues and profits.

Parkinson and his peers in the industry should have known it would happen sooner or later. But they only cared for their short-term profits, not to mention their huge salaries and hefty bonuses (usually increasing even faster than their companies' revenues). Any economics undergraduate could have told them that competition to an industry all too often comes from outside. Over-inflated profits are very attractive, and outsiders don't worry about oversupply reducing prices. Nor do they give a damn whether an industry collapses. As it happens, neither should we (though we should retain the nugget of economic wisdom that the story of copper offers). No doubt shareholders and employees suffered, but society as a whole gained immensely. If we'd stuck with copper, there'd be no internet, no e-mail, no free calls from Skype, no Google. One industry collapsed, but others rose phoenix-like in its place, creating new jobs and profits for new shareholders – bringing people together across oceans and time zones at little or no extra cost. Technologically, the world is a better place for the demise of copper wires.

This true story of a metal that lost its luster brings us back to the concept of "creative destruction" that we mentioned earlier. Like most good ideas, there's nothing new about it. The term was coined by the economist Schumpeter in his classic 1942 book, *Capitalism, Socialism and Democracy*. He defined creative destruction as the "process of industrial mutation that incessantly revolutionizes the economic structure from within, incessantly destroying the old one, incessantly creating a new one."[1] Schumpeter believed that entrepreneurs are the people who make things happen in the economy, by transforming innovative ideas into practical opportunities. They introduce new products or services and reduce costs by improving efficiency. In so doing, they overturn old regimes of market leadership and make old products or services obsolete. According to Schumpeter, the opposite of creative destruction is lack of progress and stagnation – not only in the economy but also in society as a whole. The story of copper is a perfect example.

## DEATH, TAXES, AND PREDICTION

As Benjamin Franklin notoriously observed: "In this world nothing is certain but death and taxes." The same is true for companies. As we saw in the previous chapter, they typically don't last long. Even big multinationals rarely make it beyond the age of fifty, so there's little hope for smaller, local firms and even less for start-ups. By all means, executives can opt to manage for long-term survival, but not without adversely affecting financial performance. This is not simply an empirical fact, but a logical necessity: the safer you play, the fewer risks you take . . . and the lower the potential gains. This is precisely what we saw in chapters 4 and 5: higher returns go hand-in-hand with greater investment risk. The same principle holds in the business world.

As the fall of copper illustrates, it's no different on the scale of entire industries and economic sectors. In their day, railways, steel, and motor manufacturing all boomed and then bust, or at least slipped into mediocrity. Since then, the entire sector of manufacturing has declined, while the information and communications technologies are riding high. Did we see these changes coming? Initially, no. Then we got our timing wrong in a frenzy of over-reaction. In the process, we created a bubble that finally burst at the very beginning of this century. Nearly half a decade later, the good times were back for the information business, but unfortunately these times did not last long as a bigger bubble emerged and brought about the largest post-war recession. It's as difficult to predict when an entire economic sector or industry will take off and slow down as it is for individual companies.

These days, everyone loves Google. Internet users, investors, journalists, and business school professors alike, we all revel in its tremendous success – and the benefits this brings us. With Google's market value of more than $220 billion toward the end of 2007, the power of internet search is apparent for all to see. Yet Google historians tell us it wasn't always this way. As late as the end of the 1990s, no one in Silicon Valley was interested in buying the company with its unique search technology. The asking price from its founders was just $1.6 million.

Excite, a one-time competitor of Yahoo, came closest with a bid of $750,000. But Yahoo, the now-defunct Infoseek, and a whole bunch of venture capitalists didn't even bother making an offer. The Valley buzzword of the day was "portal" not "search." Larry Page, one of Google's two founders, recalls: "We probably would have licensed it if someone gave us the money . . . but they were not interested in search." He adds dryly, "They did have horoscopes, though."[2]

But even Page and his partners didn't predict the Google phenomenon (as the attempt to sell proves). No one had the slightest inkling of the vast practical and financial value of its search technology. And it's lucky for the founders that they didn't. If Google had sold for $1.6 million at the end of the 1990s there'd have been no stock market flotation in 2004 and no $220 billion-worth of shares in 2007. Google is no isolated case. One of the best books on the subject of commercial success stories, Nayak and Ketteringham's 1986 bestseller *Break-Throughs*, concludes that, if there's one thing all business breakthroughs have in common – it's the surprise factor.[3] No one foresees their occurrence, let alone their immense commercial consequences. If we can't spot *big* breakthroughs before they happen, what hope is there of predicting smaller business successes?

Apple is another prime example, beloved by the business press. Its innovative products have revolutionized the telecom and music businesses and brought huge gains to its shareholders (its share price went from $3.3 in 1997 to more than $160 twelve years later). Going back in time, without Apple there'd be no Windows and today's creative industries would look very different. Back in 2003, however, the price of an Apple share was only $7 and Apple's CEO, Steve Jobs, is rumored to have given up stock options that only four years later (with the share price up to $93) would have made him $2.6 billion richer.[4] Arguably the most visionary man in business, Jobs couldn't see the future of the infant iPod and its creative-destructive potential.

Apple and Google are still creating and destroying as we write. The fearful have coined the three-letter acronym DBG (Death By Google) to explain the way in which small changes to the search function slightly affect the order in which sites appear on the results pages. This can send the revenues of the companies who own those sites soaring or plummeting, even forcing some into bankruptcy. The power of Google is generated by people like us, the vast number of visitors who use it to search the web daily free of charge. The business model of providing this and other services for no payment is another aspect of creative destruction with far-reaching consequences. It subverts traditional business paradigms and raises a red flag to those whose livelihoods are threatened. Apple has had a similar effect — even on its comrades in the digital music revolution, let alone the old-guard record companies. By the middle of 2007, the iPod had an 82% market share in the US. Now more recent projects, such as iPhone and iTV as well as Google's new mobile phone, are giving sleepless nights to executives in the telecom and TV industries.

Meanwhile, Jobs, Page, and the Apple and Google elite enjoy sweet dreams. Perhaps, however, on some dark and stormy nights the troubling memory of Ken Olsen flits across their collective unconscious. In 1986 he was the founder and chairman of the great Digital Equipment. The cover of *Fortune* magazine hailed him as "America's Most Successful Entrepreneur". And no wonder. At that time, Digital had managed to break IBM's monopoly by introducing smaller, cheaper, and more user-friendly computers. Revenues were growing at close to 40% a year, while profits were growing at more than 20%. But he was a player in a much bigger industry story.

Just over ten years earlier, a small start-up had launched the idea of the "personal" computer. A garage partnership between Steve Wozniak and Steve Jobs (yes, him again) had a small but enthusiastic following for their Apple I and II models. As their sales increased, IBM decided to get a piece of the action and introduced its own product in 1981. By October 1986, when Ken Olsen's face appeared to the world on the cover of *Fortune*, new customers and companies, such as Compaq, were jumping on the personal-computer bandwagon. IBM and Apple Computer had competition. And Digital had a low-cost, easy-to-use product that screamed out competitive advantage.

However, back in 1987, Olsen didn't believe in personal computers. He's credited with the by-now infamous words: "There is no reason for any individual to have a computer in their home." Whether or not he actually made the fateful statement, he expressed it in his subsequent strategy of not entering the PC industry in time.

In the three years leading up to 1995, Digital lost close to $2 billion and only managed to limp on until 1998 by making drastic cuts in cost and head count. Finally, it was obliged to "merge" with (or more accurately "sell itself" to) Compaq.

All this time, the world's addiction to the personal computer was growing stronger and stronger. By April 2002 sales hit the one billion mark. Predictions (for what they're worth) indicated that another billion would be sold by 2008. "America's Most Successful Entrepreneur" had clearly seen the trend toward smaller, cheaper, friendlier computers, but he hadn't taken his insight to the logical conclusion that would – in just a few years – allow us to have powerful computers within our mobile phones. As for the journalists who hailed him as a business super-hero, they soon moved on to new faces. The Swede Percy Barnevik, CEO of ABB, was greeted as the "Jack Welch of Europe." Until 2001, that is, when he became a media villain overnight. Since then, others have come . . . and gone: Lee Iacocca of Chrysler, Bob Nardelli of Home Depot, and, more recently, Carly Fiorina of Hewlett-Packard.

So one day, it will be Google and Apple managers having the nightmares. Their pre-eminence will be creatively destroyed (or at least reduced to mediocrity) by new strategic or technological ideas. A new generation of innovation heroes will appear on the magazine covers. But that's as far as our forecast can go. When and how it will happen remains uncertain. And that's a tough reality to confront – not just for Google and Apple, but for the whole unpredictable world of business. Don't let it get you down, though. The dark clouds of uncertainty don't just cast shadows of danger. They also have silver linings of opportunity. But in order to grasp those opportunities, it's important to understand history and the fact that accepting new possibilities might mean destroying old ones. Copper wires can't coexist with fiber optic cables, as the latter are much more cost-effective and billions of times faster and greatly more cost-effective than the former.

What's around the corner for the company you run or work for? Are you at the total mercy of creative destruction? Or is there something you can do to save the day? As in previous chapters, we're convinced that dispelling the illusion of control can be fundamental. If leaders of the copper industry had abandoned their attempt to control by cartel, paradoxically, they could have shaped their own destiny for a little longer. Instead, their greedily inflated profits offered rich pickings for unexpected competitors.

We're no gurus, however. We realize that there's much, much more to doing business than triumphing over the illusion of control. Managing isn't like investing, where we were able to offer specific advice for general success. Instead, business is characterized by its complexity – which adds further uncertainty to the unpredictability that creative destruction brings. At the same time, feedback comes infrequently and is hard to evaluate. It's difficult (if not impossible) to assess past performance and to attribute outcomes to specific decisions, actions or people. Of course, executives congratulate themselves when things go well and blame bad luck or others when things go badly. They also tend to surround themselves with people who echo these conclusions. That's just human nature. But it only compounds the uncertainty and unreliability of the feedback. Worse still, it blinds them to looming creative destruction. And, as Schumpeter told us many decades ago, creative destruction is one of the few certainties of business. And it's not just inevitable – it's beneficial, for society as a whole, that is!

So, in the rest of this chapter, we advocate two strategies based on accepting the inescapability of creative destruction. The first involves understanding the factors that produce creative destruction, so as not to be finished off by it (or at least to delay it as much as possible). The second is more radical. It consists of harnessing the power of creative destruction, instead of giving in to it. Neither strategy promises certainty or a panacea for all other business problems, of course. But they're both better than the third choice – which is to sit back and wait to be engulfed.

## STRATEGY 1: WHEN HISTORY REPEATS ITSELF

In chapter 5, we dabbled in the stock market and found that the short and medium term were all about flux and unpredictability. However, we also discovered that – in the long run – the only way was up. It turns out that there are similar long-term trends in economics, which have implications for all managers. So, for a second time in this book, we're ready to make some predictions for the long run.

### 1. Prices will go down in real terms

They've been going down since 1800, in fact, when the effects of the industrial revolution started to kick in. And economists are virtually certain that real prices (adjusted to exclude inflation) of nearly all standardized products and services will continue to decrease exponentially in the long run. Of course, it's not quite as simple as that. Two notable exceptions are oil and gold. But even in these exceptional cases, the real price hasn't gone up but remained constant in the long term, at least until now.

In the short term and medium term, however, there are huge fluctuations, which can inflict extensive losses or gains on both producers and consumers. As we saw earlier, the real price of copper quadrupled between 1932 and 1974, fell by 73% between 1974 and 2002 . . . and went back to the 1974 level in 2006. But even in the extreme case of copper, the general trend is consistent, as figure 7 shows.

### 2. Pay will go up in real terms

Again, salaries have been going up exponentially since 1800 (see figure 8), although there are considerable variations in the shorter term. It's the same story as prices but in reverse.

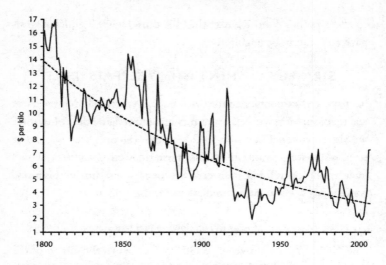

**Figure 7** Real copper prices (constant 2007 dollars)

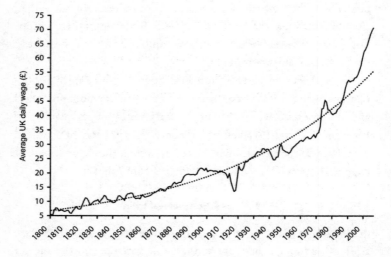

**Figure 8** Real wages/salaries in constant 2006 pounds, UK

### 3. The implications of 1. and 2.

Put them together and these two long-term trends are extremely good news for those of us who earn money and buy stuff with it. Our buying power increases at a double exponential rate as prices decrease and income increases! All those lovely standardized goods and services are ours for the taking. The result is material abundance, at least in economically advanced countries.

On the other hand, when our weekend shopping frenzy is over and we're back at work, it's a different story. Falling prices and rising pay add up to a double whammy for managers. One way or another, their ultimate objective is to increase the profitability of the companies they work for. And the easiest way to do so in the short term is to increase prices, while also decreasing their payroll expenditure. Trouble is, that's the opposite of what's going on in the marketplace, as we just saw. In the long term, the winners are the companies who can capture market share by lowering prices and still attract the best talent by increasing salaries.

Try telling that to a copper industry executive back in the 1960s. He would have laughed in your face. As we said in chapter 6, most business people just don't get history. And you can't blame them really. The board, shareholders, and financial analysts are usually too busy looking at the next quarter's results to care about the past or even the medium-term future. And there's certainly no incentive to pry into the long-term threat posed by some scientists in a glass-manufacturing company.

But how on earth do you go about squeezing prices downwards, while also generating extra cash to hire and retain competent employees – at the same time as keeping your shareholders smiling? The only solution is to increase productivity, usually through automation, organizational improvements, or technological innovation. Think about using a bulldozer to dig the foundations of your house, rather than a spade. Or, to use a more recent innovation, booking flights over the internet, compared to queuing on the high street and generating pointless paperwork. This may not sound very glamorous or clever, like inventing a new search technology, reinventing the MP3 player as an iPhone and iPod, or creating an entirely new material to transmit digital information. But it can be equally effective in the survival stakes. The streamlining strategy can stop competitors from outside your industry from overtaking you and forcing you out of business. Creative destruction it isn't, but it can save you from being creatively destroyed for many profitable years to come.

## DIGRESSION: THE ILLUSION OF SUCCESS

Before we talk about our second, bolder strategy, let's digress pleasantly for a moment into the world of childhood. As a seven-year-old, what did you want to be when you grew up? It's unlikely that "executive" was very high up your list of ambitions. You don't see many kids dressing up in suits and ties to enact boardroom dramas. Instead, these days at least, they're outside playing soccer in David Beckham shirts or indoors perfecting their karaoke. Unlike the children of yesteryear, who wanted to be nurses or train drivers, the youth of today generally aspire to stardom. Europe, Asia – and now the US – is full of little boys who don't simply wear the Beckham shirt, but genuinely believe they will live the Beckham life one day.

So what do we as parents do? Should we encourage our kids to moderate their ambitions from movie star to train driver, nurse, or executive? Should we tell them that, for every Beckham, Ronaldinho, and Zidane, there are several thousand professional soccer players who never make it to the premier league, let alone the national side? Should we point out the daunting mass of competition from all the other kids who are similarly convinced that stardom beckons?

The answer is that we can try, but it probably won't do any good. No parental illusion of control here then, but plenty of a different kind of illusion from the kids: the illusion of success. As we mentioned at the beginning of this book, this is largely caused by the media. Television, newspapers, and glossy magazines rarely tell us about "failed" actors, singers, dancers, and football players, let alone the "average" ones. They're not news – just like the thousands of airplanes that safely reach their destination every day.

The same goes for entrepreneurs who dream of turning their start-ups into Apple or Google. Do they realize that fewer than one in ten new products succeed? Do they know that most of the start-ups that survive achieve only average performance? Have they ever heard a venture capitalist joke about the "living dead," those entrepreneurs who limp on for years by borrowing from family and friends, never paying salaries or turning a profit?

Again, it's tempting to blame the media. The business papers are always writing about Bill Gates and Michael Dell, not Joe Average or David Failure. But it's also our fault. We don't want to read about ordinary entrepreneurs making average profits or the start-ups that finished up. The only failures we show any interest in are the spectacular ones like LTCM, Enron, WorldCom, and Lehman Brothers, which involve the mighty falling. We get the media we deserve. So when we automatically equate "start-up" with success, we ultimately have ourselves to blame. Mediocrity and failure are a bit like the dog that didn't bark – they don't draw any attention to themselves until we, like Sherlock Holmes, are willing to seek beyond the obvious.

The illusion of success, however, isn't all bad. Like the illusion of control it can lead many people to make the wrong decisions, but for a select few it pays off. Take Tiger Woods. His father introduced him to golf at the precocious age of eighteen months and encouraged him to practice intensively throughout his childhood. If Earl Woods had worried about his son's minuscule chances of becoming a champion, golf would be a much duller sport today.

More importantly, the world needs crazy entrepreneurs who believe they're invincible. Without them we'd have no new products or services – no cars, no telephones, no internet. If everyone feared failure, there'd be no such thing as progress. This process is analogous to evolution, where certain mutations form the basis of a new species, while other animals become extinct. Some entrepreneurial innovations prove successful and evolve into engines of progress, while others lead to the dead-end of bankruptcy. It's bad luck for the individuals that fail, but it's highly beneficial to society as a whole. In fact, it's precisely what's needed for creative destruction to take place. It may be unpleasant, but it is the truth: modern society benefits from the failure of the many as much as it thrives on the success of the few.

## STRATEGY 2: DRIVING CREATIVE DESTRUCTION

It should be clear from our digression that the key to harnessing creative destruction – as an individual company or sole entrepreneurial operator – lies in balancing our attitudes to success or failure. It's significant that the most entrepreneurial economies in the world are those – like the USA and unlike much of Europe – where failure is not only tolerated but it is accepted. Those countries that lose their appetite for risk become incapable of innovating and changing the status quo. Successful innovation, therefore, requires a lot of trial and error and, paradoxically, cannot be achieved without failure!

At the same time, as an individual player, it is absolutely critical to understand your chances of failing and the risks involved. People who practice so-called "dangerous" sports set an interesting example. We generally believe that those who scale a cliff face, base-jump from a bridge, or sail solo around the world are seeking the thrill of adventure to the point that they're prepared to risk their lives. By contrast, we see the vast majority, who opt for more conventional sporting hobbies, as playing safe. However, appearances are perhaps deceptive. Many people have accidents playing basketball, American football, soccer, rugby, squash, cycling, and even cheerleading (thanks to the pyramid formation and that irresistible temptation to throw people in the air). The reason is simple. In a dangerous sport, the danger is obvious, so evaluating the risk and taking measures to avoid injury are part of the game. Meanwhile, on the municipal sports ground or on in the school gym, people feel so safe that they fail to take the most basic precautions.

Any individual seeking success should take some inspiration from dangerous sports and realize that much of the pleasure is in the journey rather than the arrival. He or she should confront the possibility of failure and construct a personal safety net. Having a plan B or an exit strategy is crucial. It may not lead to the success originally desired, but could salvage the situation from total disaster. In the case of dangerous sports, total disaster spells death; in business it means financial ruin.

But it's not just about meeting with triumph and disaster and treating those two imposters just the same. In any competitive context – business included – most performances are just average. This is a mathematical certainty. Only a select few can be tennis champions or principal ballerinas. Mid-table mediocrity is in most cases the most likely alternative to success or failure – and a possibility that has to be faced bravely too.

There are also lessons for success-seekers from the world of investment. As we saw in chapters 4 and 5, there are rarely big gains without big risks. The same is true in many other areas of life, including business. Above all, those aiming high should accept and embrace the role of luck in the final outcome – whilst of course doing all they can to improve their chances of success.

The best business-school brains all over the world devote a great deal of time and intellectual energy to the question of entrepreneurship, whether the traditional start-up model or so-called "corporate entrepreneurship" (which tries to foster innovation within the context of a large organization). We firmly believe that they're right to do so – especially if they're as willing to tackle the issue of failure as they are to tell success stories. The entrepreneurs that our society relies on for progress must first be able to see and then judge the risks and opportunities involved in their ventures. Come to that, business schools have a role to play in educating *everyone*, so that society can continue to nurture the desire for success, whilst becoming more accepting of failure.

On the other hand, it should be obvious by now that we don't believe entrepreneurship experts from business schools – or anyone else – can provide simple recipes for success. As we've pointed out before, it would be a logical fallacy to believe in a failsafe method of succeeding in business. As soon as everyone reached average performance, someone would find a way of taking their company to the next level.

## TENSIONS AND TRADE-OFFS

On a brighter note, entrepreneurship experts have developed some guidelines for managers (and governments) who seek to cultivate the right attitudes to success, mediocrity, failure, luck, and skill, in such a way as to generate creative destruction. Rather than giving a set of rules, we prefer to express these guidelines in the form of a series of tensions. There are no easy ways out. It's up to each individual to decide where to place themselves between the opposing forces – knowing that one end of the spectrum represents eventual destruction from someone else's creativity, while the other unacceptably risks everything on driving your own creative destruction.

### Efficiency versus innovation

Everyone knows that companies must be effective and efficient in order to keep costs down and compete with other firms. It's also generally accepted that effectiveness and efficiency are typically achieved by implementing systems of control that minimize wastefulness without deviating from budgets. The problem is that tight operational controls can also stamp out innovation. They place people under constant stress and leave them little or no free time to think creatively. This is another instance of the paradox of control. You gain more options by giving up some control.

Companies like Google, and even more established players like 3M, try to keep the entrepreneurial fires burning by letting employees use, say, ten per cent of their time to pursue projects that interest them. At the same time, they make sure that people use the remaining ninety per cent as efficiently and effectively as possible on core corporate activities. When the internet bubble burst at the beginning of this century, some Silicon Valley firms survived precisely because they had adopted this strategy. Their employees had used their "free" time to develop alternative products and services that worked for the company's benefit.

Even so, this small percentage of slack involves a real extra cost that most conventional big businesses are reluctant to shoulder. Creating an environment for innovation to thrive is – and will continue to be – one of the biggest corporate challenges. At the very least it involves recognizing that creativity is incompatible with tight schedules and that truly creative people can't operate under tight controls. The trick is to find the right balance between efficiency on the one hand and nurturing innovation on the other.

## Survival versus risk

It's only natural that managers don't like risk. They want to keep their jobs and move up the greasy pole. Collectively too, companies tend to be conservative animals that shy away from risk. But it's the same old story as in chapters 4 and 5. It's almost impossible to achieve above-average returns without taking some above-average risks. As we saw earlier, there's strong evidence that simply managing for survival doesn't guarantee strong, long-term performance for shareholders. Far from it. Richard Foster and Sarah Kaplan whose work we referred to in the previous chapter (along with many other experts) have produced research that conclusively proves the need to take a few risks along the way.[5]

Ironically, not taking risks is perhaps the biggest risk any organization can take. Look at the stagnation of the former communist states in the years leading up to the fall of the Berlin Wall. The challenge is to allocate enough resources to experimentation and risk-taking without staking everything on the success of a crazy new idea. Of course, some risks can lead to serious problems, even bankruptcy. But not to take any risk at all guarantees you'll be overwhelmed by the forces of creative destruction.

## Long versus short term

It's an age-old story, we know, but the companies that last are generally prepared to spend generously on R&D, brand-building, and developing their employees – the engines of creative destruction. In short, they see the value in sacrificing immediate profits on the altar of long-term competitive advantage. The contradiction is that the stock market doesn't seem to look beyond the next few quarters' earnings. Yet those companies concerned purely with milking their cash cows inevitably have a short shelf-life that doesn't bode well for shareholders. Again, it's a question of balancing the tensions in a way that works for the company.

## Managing versus motivating people

Once upon a time, companies' competitive advantages depended on their fixed assets: their factories, their machinery, their land. Building a new plant required a major capital outlay, which fortunately also discouraged new competitors to enter the market. This is still true up to a point in certain sectors, but today, there is overcapacity in practically all industries. Competitive advantages come instead from new products and services, clever marketing, and innovative strategies. And these activities all depend on people, not fixed assets. *Seover Farms ??*

Compare and contrast Google and GM. The former had only 16,000 employees (in 2007) and no tangible assets to speak of. The latter had nearly 300,000 employees and acres of factory space. But, surprise, surprise, the stock market, at the end of 2007, considered Google to be eleven times more valuable than GM. Investors aren't fazed by Google's size or lack of property. On the contrary, they consider these advantages that make the company not only nimble but also able to keep its talented workforce happy and creative. You may not be able to touch or feel these assets, but they're the ones that keep Google ahead of its competitors in the world of search engines and information technologies.

But unlike machines and production lines, talented people are notoriously hard to manage. Their demands are high, so not all companies can afford them in the first place, let alone keep them productive as time goes by. Perhaps this is the most difficult of all the challenges we've mentioned.

## THE VENTURE CAPITAL APPROACH

It's illuminating to examine the approach taken by venture capitalists. Contrary to popular belief, venture capitalists don't rely on accurate predictions of the future for their success. Like us, they know that the future's not ours to see. Of course, there's a certain amount they can do to check that a business is well run and founded on solid premises. But they can't tell which brand-new products and services will catch the consumer's imagination, no matter how much research they do. Instead, a good venture capital fund adopts a "que será será" attitude and invests in a number of projects. It's taken for granted that some will fail, but that some of the successful ones will make it big and compensate for any losses. If that sounds implausible, consider how many companies innovated with MP3 and music distribution technologies before Apple sewed up the market with the iPod and iTunes.

Venture capitalists also have a clear exit strategy. They usually withdraw after three to six years, sending out a clear message that the chosen companies have two stages in their life cycle. The first involves creating and bringing to market a successful product or service. The second is about managing that product or service as effectively and efficiently as possible. Venture capitalists separate the two. They focus on the former with their know-how and connections, while leaving the latter to someone else. Perhaps, in so doing, they provide established companies with a model for resolving the tensions we ran through above.

As we've seen, businesses find themselves in a bind. On the one hand, they want to be rational and maximize their short-term profits for the benefit of their shareholders. On the other, they know they have to innovate to compete with entrepreneurs who are working in their garages for eighteen hours a day, seven days a week with no pay but limitless motivation. The only solution seems to be to reorganize along the lines suggested by the venture capital industry, creating separate entities – some dedicated to milking existing products or services for short-term gain, and others given creative license – whilst also benefiting from the finance, expertise, and connections of the parent company.

Again this is no simple, guru-style solution. The exact distribution of resources across business units is hard to get right. Even if we could give you a magic ratio, there are by definition no formulae for innovation and success, which have a sneaky tendency to defy all rules. Yet several companies are adopting the venture capital approach. *Business Week* recently reported that Google for one is busy investing in high-tech start-ups around the world. That way, they're not only first in line for any marketable technologies developed, but also avoid paying out vast sums of money to venture capitalists who got there before them.[6] These and other innovative types of investments will have to continue if companies are going to exploit the benefits and avoid the dangers of creative destruction.

Society itself must play a part too, with governments encouraging both corporate entrepreneurs and the traditional garage or bedroom-based species with, for example, tax breaks that shift attitudes to success and failure. Heaven knows, it's hard enough to create an *internal* company culture of creativity, let alone the *external* conditions for incubating innovation. But the fact is that no successful innovation is possible without trial and error – and therefore failure.[7] Failure is thus a necessary part of our economic system, whether we like it or not. So we might as well change our attitudes to it.

## TOWARD A PERFECT WORLD OF COMPETITION

The forces of creative destruction now operate on a global scale. As managers have come to accept innovation as a critical corporate challenge, so they have sought global solutions. Many are building R&D

facilities in India and other low-cost, highly educated countries – often with financial incentives from national governments. Other solutions are to outsource innovation to universities or dedicated firms, again not necessarily around the corner from headquarters. Nowadays there are even innovation brokers who match inventors with potential funding, sometimes from large corporations which have grasped the importance of creative destruction. All in all, the rate of innovation is increasing – and with it the pace of creative destruction.

Thanks to the internet, the pace of creative destruction is accelerating yet further. Not only does global connectedness provide innovative new products and services and business models, it also provides tools for innovators. Information and even products or services are disseminated instantly at a global level, eradicating inefficiencies and wiping out any old-fashioned competitive advantages based on geography or local knowledge. Today it takes only a few minutes to compare prices from suppliers across the globe and to choose the one that offers the best value for money. The internet has transformed both markets and competition, cutting out the much-derided middle-men ... thus eliminating the necessity of a loop in the virtuous cycle of innovation.

Finally, the copper-style ascendancy of the old-school Western and Japanese multinationals is coming to an end. The fall of communism and rise of technology have enabled companies from countries in Eastern Europe, as well as from China, India, Malaysia, and Taiwan, among others, to go global. And until they start having to pay Western or Japanese wages, innovation is the only option for the rest of the world. It makes no sense that a Barbie doll or a pair of running shoes that costs less than a couple of dollars to produce in Vietnam sells for more than thirty times this amount in Europe, Japan, or the USA. Prices will be forced down in these places, while salaries in the new economies will be driven upwards – all thanks to creative destruction.

The story we have been telling in this chapter is another illustration of the paradox of control. Imagine for the moment that you are the benevolent dictator of your country and you want to make sure that the economy works both well and fairly. So – with the best of intentions – you introduce planning and control systems to make "sure" that people get what they want when they want it. The problem – and this has been illustrated again and again by the failure of centrally planned economies – is that this won't work well. There is no way that your planners will be able to forecast consumer demands nor even anticipate technological innovations or external events that can change both demands and costs. No, you are better off giving up control and letting market forces take over. The paradox of control works here too. The more you are willing to give up control and let the market forces take over the more you increase your chances of future success. This is precisely why "free markets" outperform all other economic systems and produce the greatest wealth – even though they are not without their own imperfections.

In the last two chapters we've seen that management theories are as transitory as companies themselves. There are no simple formulae for success, let alone *lasting* success. On the other hand, there are two enduring trends in the business world: exponentially decreasing prices and exponentially increasing pay. These pose long-term challenges that run contrary to most executives' short-term objectives. The only solution is to accept – and ideally exploit – the forces of creative destruction that drive the free-market system, constantly obliterating the old and replacing it with the new.

But of course, as with all advice given by well-meaning books, it's much easier said than done. Doing business is like stepping into Heraclitus's river. It's a highly complex activity, buffeted by many temporary currents. Indeed, the uncertainties that we've seen throughout the first half of this book can all sweep companies' fortunes away: terrorist attacks, tsunamis, epidemics, public health scares, rogue traders, stock market crashes, not to mention unforeseen new forces, such as the increased focus on the environment and employee rights. In the second half of the book, we'll resist the temptation to give you advice about managing your health, investments, or business, and focus instead on explanations. We'll dip into the statistics, science, and psychology of uncertainty and leave you to draw some conclusions of your own.

# Eight

# DOES GOD PLAY DICE?

*God does not play dice.*

*Albert Einstein*

*Not only does God play dice, but . . . he sometimes throws them where they cannot be seen.*

*Stephen Hawking*

The previous chapters of this book were all about dispelling your illusion of control in three specific areas: medicine, investments, and management. In each case — but in subtly different ways — we found that it's only by accepting that some things are beyond our control that we paradoxically gain *more* control over our lives.

But what's really been going on? The answer lies in a potent mix of psychology and statistics. The next six chapters are dedicated to going beyond the illusion of control to seek fundamental explanations and theories that will help us to understand uncertainty more clearly and improve our decision-making abilities in all areas of our lives. But first, here's a story that weaves together some by now familiar themes.

## THE UNFORTUNATE TWIN

The diagnosis was grave. Jules had cancer of the pancreas that had already spread to his lymph nodes and nearby organs. Although the doctors seemed hopeful about the chances of containing the spread of the cancer with chemotherapy, Jules was less optimistic. He'd read on the internet about the speed at which pancreatic cancer spreads to the liver and lungs. Maybe he had one year. Maximum. His identical twin brother Jim, who had just gone home, was still trying to persuade him otherwise. That afternoon they'd spent two hours reminiscing about growing up in a warm, middle-class home in Palo Alto, close to Stanford University. The twins had been inseparable until the age of eleven. In high school they were the best students in their class and great athletes, the stars of the school American football team. Their loving mother, who'd died four years ago, had been so proud of them both.

Then the big accident happened. In the last game of the season, against a Santa Barbara high school, Jules received a serious head injury. He spent one month in hospital then three months in bed at home, before doctors said he could resume a normal life.

But that was just it. Life was never normal again after the accident. Jules lived with constant headaches. He was unable to concentrate in class and couldn't seem to read for more than twenty minutes without feeling dizzy and exhausted. Sport – and certainly football – was too daunting a prospect. Despite all kinds of medical tests, drugs, and therapies, he simply couldn't keep up in class. After a whole year off, he managed to finish high school, then a degree at the San Jose City College. With no desire to pursue his studies any further, he found a job as a sales rep in a high-tech company and did fairly well for himself.

Meanwhile, Jim went from strength to strength. He finished high school top of his class and got into Stanford's prestigious computer science department. He was top of the class there too and during his graduate studies started a company with some friends, producing specialized graphic design chips. They sold at the height of the dotcom boom in 1999. Jim's 26% share alone was worth more than $150 million.

Then the bubble burst. Jules was fired from his high-tech sales job in 2001, but ironically Jim's personal wealth increased further. After dithering for a couple of years wondering what to do with his money, he eventually got into venture capital and struck two extremely successful deals (which had nothing to do with high-tech). And that's what he was still doing, going home every evening to his beautiful wife and their two children in their lovely home, complete with swimming pool, tennis court, and stables.

At first, Jules refused his brother's offers of financial help, but when the house was repossessed and his wife left, he had to swallow his pride. Jim ended up paying the rent on the one-bedroom flat and cleared his twin's debts. And now this: the cancer . . . and the headaches hadn't gone away either. No wonder he was consumed with jealousy of his perfect brother, who had just offered to pay for a private room in the Stanford University hospital and the best doctors in America. As evening fell, he sat in the shadows and played over the fateful events of the accident, as he had done so many times before. That crunching tackle and the juddering darkness as his skull made contact with the attacker's shoulder. Why had he gone for it? And where were the three other players – one of them Jim – who could equally have taken the tackle on? It was the most extraordinary bad fortune – followed by an incredible run of further bad luck (culminating in all likelihood with an early death).

Jim on the other hand had it all: wealth, health, and a wonderful family. He'd been in the right place at the right time – first, literally, on the football pitch, and then so many other times in his life. It was the most extraordinary run of *good* luck.

If Jules had been able to read his brother's mind, he'd have been even greener with envy. Jim was outwardly modest, but inwardly congratulated himself on having done everything just right. He'd sold at the right time, invested wisely, and all that swimming, tennis, and horse-riding kept him fit and healthy. Luck: well, you make your own, don't you? Of course, his brother had been *un*lucky, but – looking back – he'd never shown the same promise, always lacked that magic touch.

Who in this story is right? We all know by now, like Jules, that luck plays a huge role in our lives. He was clearly unlucky to get hit on the head and even unluckier to get cancer. Likewise, Jim was fortunate to avoid the dotcom crash and emerge as a multi-millionaire with a perfect family. So is life a stream of random events or do we have some control? Obviously some disasters are pure bad luck. Taking a holiday in Thailand when the tsunami struck the day after Christmas 2004, working in the Twin Towers on 9/11, getting eaten by a shark, or hit by lightning . . . these events can only be avoided by never going on holiday, never going swimming, never going to work, or never going outside. Similarly, some momentous occurrences are pure good luck: winning €1 million in a night of roulette in Monte Carlo or meeting the gaze of your future partner in life across a crowded party.

Yet, if we're more honest with ourselves than Jim and Jules were, we recognize that luck and our own actions work together to determine many of life's outcomes. If Jules hadn't been constantly competing with his own brother to prove he was the best in the team, he might not have attempted the fateful tackle. It wasn't just bad luck. And if Jim hadn't lived so close to Stanford, he might not have been accepted at the great university. Or if he hadn't met three great friends there with complementary skills and personalities, he might not have founded a successful company. Come to that, if he hadn't dithered so much after selling up, he might have reinvested in other high-tech start-ups and lost everything (exactly what happened to two of his more entrepreneurial business partners).

The conclusion is that Jim, Jules, and the less wealthy business partners all have two things in common. First, at different times they all enjoyed or suffered good or bad outcomes of what happened (for example, selling the start-up or becoming ill). Second, whereas some of these outcomes resulted from deliberate actions (for example, Jim doing well at university by working hard), others were down to sheer good or bad luck (such as the timing of the dotcom crash). But most outcomes involved both chance and design in various proportions that can't be quantified easily.

Right now, though, one thing is indisputable. Jim, Jules, and their friends have very different personal Fortunes. If you remember, we introduced this term to describe the net sums of good and bad outcomes experienced across time in terms of money, health, success, love, happiness, and much more. We hope yours is more like lucky Jim's than unlucky Jules's. Managing our Fortunes isn't easy, as we saw in the first part of this book. We'd argue that most of those who do so effectively understand the role of luck in their lives. And when we say "understand", we mean going much deeper than scratching the surface. We're talking about investigating the nature of chance events and even tackling the laws of probability that govern uncertain outcomes.

More than that, we're advocating understanding the *cumulative* effects of luck. And, although the less fortunate twin may be deluding himself that his own actions have counted for very little, he's absolutely right that the diverging Fortunes of Jules and Jim are – at least partly – down to long runs of bad and good luck. It's as if they were playing a board game where some divine power keeps on throwing sixes for Jim but only ones for Jules.

## THE FATEFUL BUTTERFLY

In the last century physicists and mathematicians came up with "chaos theory." Its central idea is often referred to as the "butterfly effect." The theory acknowledges the extraordinary power of cumulative chance and holds that the most extreme disasters can start with insignificant and benign events that occur in stable conditions. Let's imagine an innocent butterfly flying through a forest in the Bahamas in the summer of 2005. Its wings could have started a small current of air that was magnified by another chance event like the gentle flapping of a palm leaf in the breeze, then built up through other similar occurrences. With each of these, the cumulative effect could have grown bigger and bigger, gaining force and speed until it became the category five tropical hurricane, Katrina, which destroyed New Orleans and devastated much of the north-central Gulf Coast of the USA.

The same goes for manmade catastrophes. When Archduke Franz Ferdinand accepted an invitation to Bosnia-Herzegovina in 1914, against the advice of those who feared his assassination, it probably never entered his mind that he was helping to unleash the First World War. By risking his own life, he inadvertently helped to cause thirty-seven million casualties and, arguably, the train of events that led up to the Second World War. The Yom Kippur War of 1973 is another case in point. That too can be thought of as a chance event which could have been avoided or happened at a different time. But history shows that it sparked the subsequent energy crisis that multiplied oil prices several times over. The high oil prices in turn decreased rates of economic growth across the world and fueled inflation. Ever higher inflation led to ever higher interest rates, which made borrowing more expensive, thus reducing both investment and consumption. The result? A major world recession from which the global economy took eight years to recover.

Sometimes man and nature work together. The spark from a cigarette smoked during a walk in the woods falls on a particularly dry twig. It starts to smolder. A summer breeze fans some flames and soon there is a forest fire that not only destroys thousands of trees but threatens the neighboring suburbs of a major city. Further human intervention (or lack of it) might exacerbate the situation – for example, failing to alert the authorities to the strange orange glow on the horizon or poor technical decisions by the fire-fighters.

In other words, tiny chance events can have enormous cumulative effects, because the outcome of an individual occurrence doesn't disappear. Instead, the outcomes build up over time into a violent chain reaction.

## TAKE A CHANCE ON ME

Thanks to science, however, we *are* able to predict many physical phenomena with a high degree of precision. On a simple level, the law of gravity allows us to predict the trajectory of any falling object. Even before the historic apple hit Newton's head, human beings had a good intuitive grasp of the law that brings us all down to earth. On a more complex level, we still cannot predict the exact timing and location of earthquakes, but engineers are able to build bridges and skyscrapers that will stay up even when there are exceptionally strong earthquakes. Occasionally, the odd bridge falls down, but that's usually because of human error in applying the science. Most of us are so confident in the engineers' forecasting models that we entrust our lives to them every time we take a plane, get into an elevator, or drive over a bridge.

And yet we all know there are many quite mundane occurrences that we cannot predict. At all. The obvious example is the outcome of tossing a coin. On the other hand, we find it relatively easy to imagine a mental model of a "fair" coin for which coming up heads or tails is equally likely. It's also simple to take the next step and quantify this assumption, by assigning a probability of 0.5 or 50% to the event of obtaining heads. Another step is a little harder, but still accessible to most of us – if we toss two fair coins, the probability of getting two heads is 0.25 or 25%. That's because there are four possible outcomes, all equally likely: (a) heads for coin A and heads for coin B, (b) tails for coin A and tails for coin B; (c) heads for coin A and tails for coin B; and (d) tails for coin A and heads for coin B.

Despite all this clever calculation, we still can't tell whether the next coin you toss will come up heads. It's a totally chance event, unlike the forces on a bridge or a building during an earthquake. What we *can* predict, using probability theory, is the expected outcome of tossing a large number of coins. What we *can't* predict is what will happen on any one individual toss – although we can calculate the uncertainty involved and consequently the risk of winning or losing in games of chance.

Interestingly, in evolutionary terms, human beings' understanding of probability is comparatively recent. The first attempts to find regular patterns in chance events took place during the Middle Ages, but it was only in the seventeenth century that Pascal and Fermat, two French mathematicians, formulated some laws of probability (in their quest to understand gambling!). As for earlier civilizations, this is what Peter Bernstein says about the Greeks in his excellent book, *Against the Gods: The Remarkable Story of Risk.*

> Probability theory seems a subject made to order for the Greeks, given their zest for gambling, their skill as mathematicians, their mastery of logic, and their obsession with proofs. Yet, though the most civilized of all the ancients, they never ventured into that fascinating world. [. . .] Civilization as we know it may have progressed at a much faster pace if the Greeks had anticipated what their intellectual progeny – the men of the Renaissance – were to discover some thousand years later.[1]

In other words, the model of probability theory was a huge, recent intellectual advance for humankind. Indeed, there's something deeply counter-intuitive about it, particularly if we go beyond simple calculations about games of chance. There are many famous brain teasers, such as the well-known birthday conundrum. What is the probability that in a room of twenty-three randomly selected people, two of them will have the same birthday? The answer is much higher than you'd expect: 0.5 or 50%. What about a room of sixty people? Here the probability is very close to 1 or 100%, but when asked, most people say it's less than 25% (our website www. dancewithchance.com explains why these probabilities are so high). Applying probability theory is plagued with logical pitfalls and surprises. It boggles the mind. Yet probability is fundamental if we want our decisions to be rational. Remember the amniocentesis test of chapter 4. The numbers in figure 1 come from probability theory and help us make a rational decision that's consistent with our own attitude toward risk – that is, how we would feel about having a baby with Down's syndrome, a miscarriage, or a false alarm.

## SOME GAMBLING FALLACIES

To illustrate one of the difficulties of applying probability theory to cumulative chance events, here's another cautionary tale of the uncertain.

Chang was convinced he had the perfect system to beat the new Singapore super-casino. His reasoning was straightforward. He'd just read a magazine article, which pointed out that the chance of one color coming up on the roulette wheel many times in a row was very small. His resulting strategy was simple. After four consecutive results for red (or black), he'd bet $50 (Singapore dollars, that is) on the opposite color. If he lost, he'd continue betting on the same color, but double his bet to $100 to offset his previous loss. After all, the chances of it coming up six times in a row were even smaller than five times. And if the worse came to the worse, he'd just double his bet again to $200, as seven in a row, well, how likely was that? OK, it was just about possible, but in that case he'd just keep going, doubling his stake each time. Simple.

At first, all went to plan. Chang's confidence started to grow. Then, just as he was starting to feel unbeatable, black came up ten times in a row. His next bet was $3,200. Panic had already replaced euphoria, but logic was on his side, surely. His now sweaty palms dropped the chips on red . . . and he waited for the ball to trickle to a standstill. Black – for the eleventh time. Following his infallible system, he borrowed $4,200 from his pals to fund the next bet on red – now at $6,400. He lost. In fact he lost a total $12,750 that night. He couldn't even afford a bag of chips (of the potato variety) to eat on the MRT train home.

Unfortunately, this story is one that has come true many times. It's about such a common misunderstanding that it's known in psychology as the gambler's fallacy. And the mistake is as simple as Chang's false logic. While it's perfectly true that the chances of black coming up five times in a row are small – and twelve times very small indeed – it's also true that a roulette wheel has *no memory*. It can't remember what happened on its last spin, let alone the ten previous ones. In other words, for each turn, the chances of black winning are *identical*, regardless of what might have happened before. In more mathematical terms, the probability of black appearing a twelfth time, given that it has already come up eleven times, is exactly the same as on the very first attempt (and all the subsequent ones for that matter). Statistically speaking, all future outcomes are independent of the previous ones.

At least, though, gamblers who believe in the fallacy recognize that they are engaged in a chancy business, where probability theory has a place. They just apply it wrongly – and learn their lesson very quickly. You'd have to be a very, very stupid roulette player indeed to labor under the illusion of control in the long term. Or would you?

It turns out that even those who are mathematically literate can find probability theory a challenge. Take Dimitris, for example. He's a friend of one of the authors and runs a small business quite success-fully. But he's also addicted to gambling. His favorite game is roulette and he goes three or four times a week to a casino about an hour and a half from Athens, where he lives. Dimitris is the owner of a cool coffee shop in a trendy part of the city and makes a good profit every day, as the place is practically full from 11 o'clock in the morning to 3 o'clock in the early hours. He believes that, if he plays often enough, he'll get lucky and win big to compensate for his vast losses accumu-lated over the years. After a catastrophic period, when Dimitris played his way through six months' profits, losing everything in the bank plus everything he could borrow, he reached a compromise with his long-suffering wife and children. He would give himself an allowance of €3,000 a week for gambling. No more. And, well . . . in practice, no less. He's now been following this rule for five years with admirable self-control (apart from a few minor lapses, when he felt so lucky that he simply had to borrow from his friends). Things are calmer at home, anyway, since his son took over managing the shop, which means Dimitris has no direct access to the till.

But when he goes out, he's still looking for excitement. To get the biggest possible buzz, Dimitris bets only on black or red, instead of single numbers and combinations of numbers and colors, as he used to. Each stake is small, rarely going above €25 a go. That way, the weekly allowance usually lasts four days. Very occasionally, though, he loses the whole lot on the first night – and resigns himself to see-ing more of his family for the rest of the week. On the other hand, there are times when he wins big, quadrupling his money. But it still doesn't make up for the accumulated losses over the years. And it's never the jackpot Dimitris has been waiting for – the one that will break the bank and prove to his family that his passion for gambling isn't a foolish addiction. Never mind, he tells himself, the lucky break will come. It's only a question of time.

There are lots of people like Dimitris with an obsession for gambling. Do they win in the long term? Or at least break even? The answer is: almost certainly not. You see, roulette players like Dimitris have a tiny disadvantage compared to the casino. Dimitris's chance of winning is 0.4865 (not 0.5 like the fair coin we played with earlier) and the casino's is 0.5135. The explanation, for the benefit of those who have never seen a roulette wheel in action, is that there are 18 red slots, 18 black ones and one neutral space. So the probability of getting red (or black) on any given throw is 18/37 (which makes 0.4865 decimally speaking). And the probability of *not* getting red (or black) on the same throw is 19/37 (which makes 0.5135).

This tiny difference of 0.027 in the probabilities gives the casino a significant edge over a large number of spins of the wheel. In other words, the chances of Dimitris beating the casino over this large number of spins are infinitesimally small. Even more unfortunately for our friend from Athens, the 0.4865 probability is large enough to ensure that he'll win on a good few occasions – in fact, on average, *almost* half of the times – thereby reinforcing his false optimism for that jackpot in the sky. It's that potent mix of psychology and statistics again.

And the moral of the story? Perhaps Dimitris should sell the coffee shop and open a casino. It would do wonders for his monetary Fortune.

## THE LUCK OF THE DRAW

Life, unlike roulette, is not a pure game of chance. Our personal Fortunes are the cumulative results of both chance events and our own actions. But, as Jules and Jim showed us, these two elements are hard to quantify. Indeed, since we usually focus on the outcomes of events rather than their causes, we rarely stop to unravel luck from design. Consider the case of a man who won a huge prize in Spain's national lottery. Curious journalists asked him how he did it. The winner replied without any hint of shame that he had deliberately selected a ticket ending with the numbers four and eight. "But why?" pressed the reporters. "Ah," he explained. "I dreamt of the number seven for seven nights. And seven times seven is forty-eight." He may have got his multiplication tables wrong but he certainly struck it rich.

One way of figuring out the roles of chance and deliberate actions in producing outcomes is to create a baseline of Fortunes generated solely by chance processes. If we can just figure out what chance "looks like," we should get a better appreciation for what we can and cannot predict.

To do this, let's imagine the following game. Assume you're going to bet €500 on the single toss of a coin. If you bet on heads, you have a 50% chance of winning €500 and a 50% chance of losing €500. Once the coin is tossed, you either win or lose. The game is over.

So far, so simple. Now let's assume that, instead of playing once, you agree to play 100 times, betting €500 on heads each time. Then you plot your winnings and losses on a graph to see exactly what chance looks like. Having done that, you repeat the process a few times – until you have six graphs. Figures 9a–f show some that we prepared earlier, revealing some typical and not so typical patterns of outcomes. They're genuine examples of what can happen.

The trouble is, as you've probably noticed, that chance has many different faces. Each of the figures shows the cumulative effects – winning and losing – of flipping the coin 100 times and betting €500 on heads each time. In other words, the situation at any point in the graphs shows the sum of wins and losses up to that point.

Figure 9a looks a lot like what most of us would imagine. The end point is zero – the same as the starting point. And the net losses and gains jump either side of zero across the 100 tosses. In this particular case, the chance Fortune is on average a little bigger in the first fifty goes than it is for the second half of the experiment. But we know this is just due to luck.

Figures 9b, 9c, and 9d are like figure 9a, in that the net losses or gains at the end are zero, or very close to zero. Back to square one, as it were. However, the patterns across the 100 tosses are quite different. In figure 9b, things start off badly, get even worse, but somehow recover before the end. In figure 9c it's the exact opposite. If only the player had stopped after fifty-three goes! Figure 9d also shows good initial results, but then total winnings quickly turn into total losses, before recovering well for a time and then falling back to zero. Unlike figure 9a, then, the graphs in figures 9b, 9c, and 9d appear to show growth and decay, or even cycles involving both. If you didn't know better, you might think they were plotting a non-chance sequence of events with a very clear pattern.

And so to figures 9e and 9f. In figure 9e, the "Fortune" is lousy (as you might expect). It decreases and goes on sinking. Figure 9f is a much cheerier picture. Winnings just go up and up and up. It's hard to imagine that these graphs were generated by a purely chance process. Even a gambler as addicted as Dimitris would find them too good or bad to be true.

Taken together, these graphs – and our reactions to them – teach us four interesting lessons.

- First, the shape across time of net winnings – or personal Fortunes – that are entirely determined by chance can sometimes appear decidedly non-random.
- Second, we humans are very quick to see patterns in the world around us. As we saw in chapter 1, that probably makes sense from

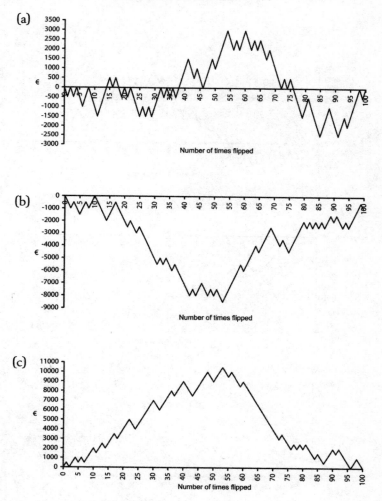

**Figure 9a, 9b, 9c** Cumulative gains/losses when a coin is flipped 100 times (each bet €500)

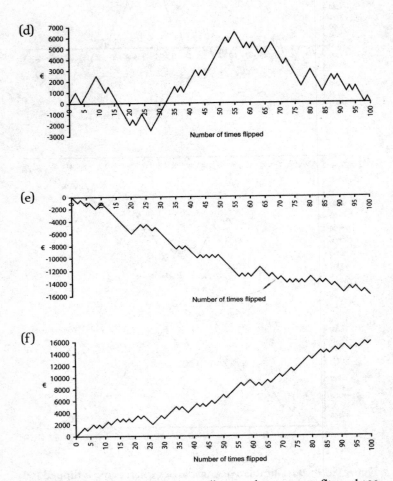

**Figure 9d, 9e, 9f** Cumulative gains/losses when a coin is flipped 100 times (each bet €500)

an evolutionary point of view. Detecting regularity in nature has brought our species many benefits: science, to name just one.

- Third, we can't always be accurate in determining whether or not such patterns really do exist. On the other hand, as we evolved, it was probably better to err on the side of seeing regularity than randomness. That may have led to a few superstitious beliefs along the evolutionary way, but the costs of everyday superstitions are typically trivial.

- Fourth, as you know from medical tests in chapter 3, there are two types of error you can make. One is to assume that a pattern is real when it isn't; the second is to dismiss a real pattern as being due to chance. When the stakes are high – €50,000, let's say – it's probably more costly to believe a pattern is there when it isn't.

Real vs Opportunity Loss

To illustrate this last point, let's look at figure 10. Given the previous six examples, it's easy to imagine that this also represents the

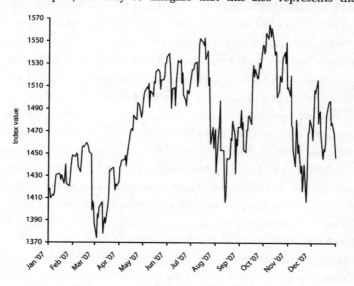

**Figure 10** S&P 500, January 2007 to January 2008

cumulative winnings from a game of chance. But no, it really shows stock market data: the daily values of the S&P 500 index from January 3, 2007 to January 2, 2008. And yes, it does look more random than some of the previous graphs! This shouldn't come as a huge surprise, given the discussion in chapters 4 and 5 about our inability to predict the stock market.

There's a simple test that can be used to figure out whether graphs such as the ones in this chapter are determined by chance. It's called the "unfolding" test and works like this. Cover up the entire diagram with piece of paper. Now, move the paper to the right to reveal the first data point. Then move it further to the right to reveal a few more. Good. Now try to predict where the next point on the graph will lie. Uncover a little more to see how accurate your prediction was. Now try again for the next point. And so on. Once you've made several predictions, you'll soon get an idea of whether there really is a discernable pattern. But you do need to be honest with yourself. If you do this exercise with all of the graphs in this chapter – even those in figures 9e and 9f – you'll find that you can't predict changes consistently. It's almost as if the line has a "mind of its own." You never know when it's going to change direction. For statisticians, these kinds of graphs represent what they call "random walks."

It turns out that the behavior of the stock markets, exchange rates, and futures prices, as well as a whole host of other economic series, all follow paths that might as well – for all practical purposes – be determined by chance. As we saw in chapter 5, in the short term, investing in the stock market is a bit like tossing a coin. But in the long term, it's more like playing with a roulette wheel where we, the investors, have the tiny winning advantage, if we avoid emotions and invest rationally. Eventually, thanks to the cumulative effects of chance and progress, our winnings will go up. Still unconvinced? You're not the only one. But the statistical evidence is indisputable. In the long run, your monetary Fortune will increase substantially if you invest by selecting stocks by chance. (On average, of course, you will do even better if your portfolio matches the index of the entire market – see chapters 4 and 5.)

## MONEY, MONEY, MONEY

Jordi is a forty-five-year-old dentist who has a very successful practice in Barcelona. As a young man, he was a bit of roulette fiend (like Dimitris), but now that he's settled down and built up some capital, his tastes are turning to the stock market. He has also read some recent works about finance and statistics and is becoming increasingly sophisticated about these topics. As he put it: "Now I know why I was wasting my time and money playing roulette. That small difference in the casino's favor really makes a big difference across many bets."

Yet Jordi is also puzzled:

I understand that the results in roulette are determined by chance. But surely there are good reasons why stock prices go up or down every day. The business pages are always talking about changes in interest rates, possible take-over bids, consumer confidence ... stuff like that. I guess there are also physical forces on a roulette wheel, but I can see that no human being is ever going to be in a position to measure them properly. Stock prices and exchange rates are different. They're reactions to specific economic factors. How can you call that chance?

Jordi is right to ask the question. In addition, he's willing to accept the *unpredictability* of the markets and even prepared to allow that the superstar investors he reads about in his favorite magazines just got lucky and that the graph we just saw (on page 179) looks like a random walk, albeit with a small uphill gradient. But, as a man of science, Jordi can't accept that *unpredictability* is the same thing as *chance*.

Nor will he concede that, just because something is unpredictable today, it will remain unpredictable for ever. After all, if mankind can solve the riddles of quantum mechanics and genetics, if human beings can build the Burj Tower in Dubai or the Millau Viaduct in France, the economic forces at play on the S&P 500 ought to be simple to unravel. "This isn't just another case of illusion of control," maintains the dentist. "I know I'm not enough statistically sophisticated myself, even if I weren't too busy looking in people's mouths. But someone out there must be."

However, there is an important theory that claims we'll never crack the conundrum of our own manmade markets. The Efficient Market Hypothesis was developed in the late 1960s by Professor Eugene Fama of the University of Chicago's Booth School of Business (whom we met briefly in chapter 5). According to the hypothesis, any new information that might have some influence on the stock market as a whole, or one company's shares in particular, has an instantaneous effect. Prices reflect that information as soon as it appears. So, if you're reading today's newspaper or even watching the news on TV, it's already too late. That's why people with inside information have such a big advantage – and why it's illegal to buy stocks based on such knowledge.

Of course, that's an oversimplification. The debate about Eugene Fama's theory continues and a few less categorical variants on the Efficient Market Hypothesis have been developed, allowing a little leeway for those who believe it's possible to beat the market. But the empirical fact remains that playing the markets is still – for all practical purposes – a game of chance. And even if Jordi's Einstein of the markets exists, why would he or she tell the rest of us the secret? It would make far more sense for this super-brain to be sitting discreetly by a pool in some tropical paradise, chuckling over a copy of this book and quietly getting rich, while sipping a cool gin and tonic.

So Jordi is right up to a point. Stock prices do react to economic factors just like roulette wheels and tossed coins react to physical forces. However, because there are so many different variables, and because they theoretically have an immediate influence on stock prices, the net effect is just like that of a game of chance. In addition, the more global the financial market, the more variables come into play. The further the internet goes, the faster the information about all these variables spreads . . . and the more unpredictable the next turning point in the stock market becomes. It is, of course, very interesting to hear expert commentators explaining specific factors that caused today's market to move. Yet those very same commentators can't predict what's going to happen tomorrow. (We'll return to the question of hindsight in the next chapter.) Sorry, Jordi, there's only one guaranteed way to make money on the stock market: buy tomorrow's newspaper *today* or watch the evening news ten hours early — just as the stock market opens.

But of course, as we saw in chapter 5, instead of accepting all the evidence, we seem to have a collective need to believe the stock market is predictable. And a whole industry of fund managers, investment advisers, and market gurus has been built on that need. But none of these abundantly paid experts predicted Black Tuesday in 1987, the technology bubble at the end of the twentieth century, the subprime and credit fiasco of 2007/8, the near collapse of the banking system in 2008, or all the similar disasters that have wrought havoc in the financial markets. We keep coming back — inevitably — to that pesky illusion of control.

*John Paulsan et al*

## THE ILLUSION OF CONTROL VERSUS FATALISM

Don't get us wrong. We know the illusion of control has its good points. Our prehistoric ancestors built houses, raised animals, and cultivated the land in order to reduce the impact of unpredictable environmental factors, such as extreme heat or cold. If the illusion of control makes such evolutionary sense, it's no wonder we took to probability theory so late in the day and that the Efficient Market Hypothesis is such a huge conceptual leap.

So psychology offers some consolation. It's only natural that we should continue to feel threatened by chance events that we cannot control. But we also have to remember that most aspects of modern life *are* governed to a great extent by chance. We've said it before and we'll say it again: eliminating uncertainty is not an option. At the same time, though, uncertainty has to be handled with care. As the famous thinker and mathematician Bertrand Russell put it: "To teach how to live with uncertainty, yet without being paralyzed by hesitation, is perhaps the chief thing that philosophy can do." Don't worry, we're not heading off into the esoteric realms of philosophy. It's enough that we've touched on psychology, mathematics, physics, and economics in this chapter. But, in our quest for deeper understanding, we will take a look at the *opposite* of the illusion of control – what psychologists call "fatalism."

Let's take a look at table 11 which contrasts beliefs versus reality.

Start with the top left box (marked OK). If we believe an outcome is due to our own abilities and this is indeed the case, well, that's fine and dandy. Better still, this situation can improve our chances of success as we're encouraged to use our abilities actively to

**Table 11** Beliefs about abilities and chance versus reality

|  | The outcome **does** depend on **our own abilities** | The outcome **does** depend on **chance** |
| --- | --- | --- |
| We **believe** the outcome depends on **our own abilities** | **OK** | **Illusion of control** |
| We **believe** the outcome depends on **chance** | **Fatalism** | **OK** |

make things happen. A good example of this is school work. If we're good at a subject and capable of hard work, then – assuming the exams are fair – we get the grades we deserve. *and we are good at taking tests !*

At the other extreme (the bottom right box), if we correctly assess that we're engaged in a chance process, we won't be surprised if things don't turn out as we wanted them to. The classic example of this is playing roulette or taking part in a lottery.

It's in the top right box that things start to go wrong. This is when people believe that a chance outcome can be influenced by their (or possibly someone else's) abilities – leading straight back to our old friend, the illusion of control. Remember the example of travelers' behavior post-9/11 from chapter 1? Many people believed they had more control over their lives when driving their own cars than when taking a plane. That sense of control was, however, illusory and resulted in many unnecessary deaths. In this particular case, the illusion was caused by a false calculation of risk, but in other contexts the motivation can be very different. When gambling, for example, it's often a matter of greed.

Incidentally, the story about the twins, with which we began our chapter, demonstrates another important feature of the illusion of control. Namely, we tend to attribute our successes to our own abilities and our failures to luck. Jim got lucky several times over, but is convinced that he engineered his Fortune with his own skill. Is this a problem? After all, it's only an interpretation of past events – and everyone likes to feel good about themselves. The trouble is that Jim's pride is precisely the kind that tends to come before a fall. Some day soon, he's likely to overestimate his ability and get a nasty surprise (see chapter 12 for more on this topic).

Yet, much as we warn against succumbing to the illusion of control, we certainly don't advocate the opposite psychological state: fatalism. This is shown in the bottom left box and refers to situations where people believe they have no control over what's happening to them. This can occur when we underestimate our own abilities or perhaps fear failure. In the tale of the unlucky twin, Jules felt helpless when he realized he couldn't compete with his brother any more – either in the classroom or on the football field. His headaches could well have been more psychological than real, giving him an excuse to avoid all competition. And he may also have believed, unconsciously, that trying too hard at school would result in the same type of catastrophe as in the football game. People who underestimate their abilities and overstate the power of chance are unlikely to succeed. They just stop trying.

Psychologist Richard Wiseman[2] explicitly investigated what distinguishes between people who believe they have been lucky in life as opposed to unlucky – just like Jim and Jules. What he found was that the Jims – or the lucky ones – tend to be more outgoing and develop a far greater network of contacts with different people and sources of ideas. Neither they nor the unlucky ones can influence chance events, but the lucky end up being exposed to many more opportunities than their unlucky counterparts. Take Jim, for example. He had many more chances to meet potential and good business partners at Stanford than Jules had at San Jose. You "make yourself lucky" (as Jim correctly spotted) by exposing yourself to more opportunities. The same is true of a start-up in the San Francisco area, which is bursting with venture capital firms. Transplant the same business idea to Greece, where venture capital is virtually non-existent in any form, and it will most likely fail.

## HOW TO PLAY THE GAME OF CONSEQUENCES

It's a shame, but reality isn't as simple as table 11. Neither our beliefs nor the actual outcomes can be classified into neat little boxes, depending on the respective roles of chance and our own abilities. It's inevitable that we'll err on the side of fatalism or labor under the illusion of control from time to time. Given that such errors are likely, we need to consider two vital factors: first, the importance of the outcome in question; and second, the emotions that are driving us.

First, imagine you're facing an outcome that only has minor consequences. Perhaps you're playing golf or trying out a new recipe. In both these activities, the outcome will reflect both luck and skill, but hey, what does it matter if you underestimate the skill required? The worst that can happen is to lose hopelessly or to have to phone for an emergency pizza. On the other hand, if you succeed, you might be encouraged to try again and so improve your skills with practice. Who knows? You might cook up something so delicious that it not only gives you and your friends immediate pleasure but, in the long term, marks the beginning of a new career as a great chef. And so, for, relatively trivial outcomes that are repeated over time, we recommend that a little bias toward the illusion of control can be in your interest. In these circumstances, even on a bad-golf day, it's probably better than fatalism.

Don't cheer up just yet! We now ask you to imagine a real-life decision involving potentially tragic consequences, such as whether to overtake that slow driver in front or when to start your new internet business. In both these situations, overestimating your skill can be disastrous, while caution would pay off. In other words, if you're risking death, bankruptcy, or a similar disaster, try a little fatalism and don't succumb to the illusion of control.

Finally, we recommend that you do something that doesn't always come naturally, especially when we're trying to make a truly logical decision. Analyze your own emotions. As we noted above, the illusion of control is often associated with greed and fatalism with fear. Rash investments on the stock market and refusal to enter into competitive situations are just two examples. One way of avoiding the paralysis of indecision described by Bertrand Russell is to use your emotions more explicitly. Neither greed nor fear are perfect guides to sorting out the relative roles of skill and chance, but by using the feelings contained in your emotions more proactively, you should be able to make better decisions. But we're getting ahead of our story. We'll return to the turbulent issue of emotions in chapter 12 when we talk about making real decisions, some of them affecting our lives in a big way.

For now it's enough to conclude that our personal Fortunes – or cumulative outcomes of good and bad in our lives up to now – reflect both skill and luck. It's important to understand both components, even if we can't hope to measure them precisely. In the next four chapters, we'll look at further theories and practices that can help you to beat the illusion of control and make good decisions. We'll start by looking at our powers of prediction. As will be seen, there is great asymmetry between the ease with which we can explain the past, on the one hand, and foretell the future, on the other.

Nine

# PAST OR FUTURE
(present)

*My interest is in the future because I am going to spend the rest of my life there*

Charles F. Kettering, inventor

The eminent Canadian psychologist Janet Bavelas once asked a group of students to imagine that one of their professors was going to take a sabbatical in Europe next year.[1] She then told them to predict in writing what the professor would do during his year abroad. A second group of students was also asked to think about the same professor. But this time, Bavelas told them he'd just returned from a sabbatical in Europe, and she instructed them to write down what they thought the professor had done during the last year.

You'd be forgiven for thinking the results would be very similar. These were two perfectly representative groups of students asked to perform more or less the same task. But it turned out that the accounts of the imaginary *past* were richly detailed, while the stories about the *future* were sketchy and vague. This experiment and many others prove that it's somehow easier to imagine what someone *has* done, as opposed to what they're *going to* do.

The case of Janet Bavelas's students captures a central theme of this chapter: the asymmetry between our ability to explain the past and our capacity for predicting the future. Once an event – even a highly unusual event – has occurred we humans find it blissfully easy to provide plausible explanations. The tragedy of 9/11 or the train bombings in Madrid and London are so well known that we're all sure we understand why they came about. And yet, even the day before these disasters occurred, we had no idea what was about to happen. If someone had come up with all the reasons we now invoke for the tragedies, we would have dismissed them as crazy. After all, there's always some screwball on a street corner announcing that the end of the world is nigh.

In psychology our know-it-all attitude to the past is known as "hindsight" bias. In the States, it's also called the "Monday morning quarterback" phenomenon, but it's pretty universal really. The financial media is rife with after-the-event experts, who are always available to explain changes in a company's stock price over the last week. Ask them to predict what will happen next week, though, and they won't sound quite as convincing. Anyone can fit past events into a rational-sounding sequence. But no one can explain, not to mention predict, the future in advance.

This chapter also has a second – more personal – theme that puzzled one of the authors from the age of nine well into his late forties. Why did his music teacher, Miss Johnstone, insist that he join the school choir, when she patently knew he was a lousy singer?

## THE FALL AND RISE OF A STATISTICIAN

Before solving the enduring mystery of Miss Johnstone's choir, let's explore the question of past–future asymmetry further, using another painfully personal example that we alluded to briefly in the preface to this book.

As an expert in statistics, working in a business school during the 1970s, one of the authors (who also, as it happens, can't sing a note) couldn't fail to notice that executives were deeply preoccupied with forecasting. Their main interest lay in various types of business and economic data: the sales of their firm, its profits, exports, exchange rates, house prices, industrial output . . . and a host of other figures. It bugged the professor greatly that practitioners were making these predictions without recourse to the latest, most theoretically sophisticated methods developed by statisticians like himself. Instead, they preferred simpler techniques which – they said – allowed them to explain their forecasts more easily to senior management. The outraged author decided to teach them a lesson. He embarked on a research project that would demonstrate the superiority of the latest statistical techniques. Even if he couldn't persuade business people to adopt such methods, at least he'd be able to prove the precise cost of their attempts to please the boss.

Every decent statistician knows the value of good research, so the professor and his research assistant collected many sets of economic and business data over time from a wide range of economic and business sources. In fact they hunted down 111 different time series which they analyzed and used to make forecasts – a pretty impressive achievement given the computational requirements of the task back in the days when computers were no faster than today's calculators. They decided to use their trawl of data to mimic, as far as possible, the real process of forecasting. To do so, each series was split into two parts: earlier data and later data. The researchers pretended that the later part hadn't happened yet and proceeded to fit various statistical techniques, both simple and statistically sophisticated, to the earlier data. Treating this earlier data as "the past," they then used each of the techniques to predict "the future," whereupon they sat back and started to compare their "predictions" with what had actually happened.

Horror of horrors, the practitioners' simple, boss-pleasing techniques turned out to be more accurate than the statisticians' clever, statistically sophisticated methods. To be honest, neither was particularly accurate, but there was no doubt that the statisticians had served themselves a large portion of humble pie.

One of the simplest methods, known as "single exponential smoothing," in fact appeared to be one of the most accurate. Indeed, for 61.8% of the time it was more accurate than the so-called Box–Jenkins technique, which represented the pinnacle of theoretically based statistical forecasting technology back in the 1970s. The academic journals of the day had proven that the Box–Jenkins method was more accurate than large econometric models where predictions were based on hundreds of equations and impressive volumes of data. So, by extension, single exponential smoothing was also more accurate than the grand-scale econometric models that cost hundreds of thousands of dollars to develop and use!

At first, the professor and his assistant were so taken aback by their results that they suspected they'd made a mistake. They made extensive checks on their own calculations but could find no errors at all. The initial shock now over, they began to cheer up. If there's one thing that makes up for an academic proving himself wrong, it's the opportunity to show that *other* eminent authorities are wrong too. So the professor submitted a paper on his surprising and important findings to a prestigious learned journal and waited for the plaudits to start rolling in. This in itself turned out to be another forecasting error. The paper was rejected on the grounds that the results didn't square with statistical theory! Fortunately, another reputable academic journal did decide to publish the paper, but they insisted on including comments from the leading statisticians of the day. The experts were not impressed. Among the many criticisms was a suggestion that the poor performance of the sophisticated methods was due to the inability of the author to apply them properly.[2]

Undaunted, the valiant statistician and his faithful assistant set out to prove their critics wrong. This time around they collected and made forecasts for even more sets of data (1,001 in total, as computers were much faster by this time), from the worlds of business, economics, and finance. As before, the series were separated into two parts: the first used to develop forecasting models and make predictions; and the second used to measure the accuracy of the various methods. But there was a new and cunning plan. Instead of doing all the work himself, the author asked the most renowned experts in their fields – both academics and practitioners – to forecast the 1,001 series. All in all, fourteen experts participated and compared the accuracy of seventeen methods.

This time, there were no bad surprises for the professor. The findings were exactly the same as in his previous research. Simpler methods were at least as accurate as their complex and statistically sophisticated cousins. The only difference was that there were no experts to criticize, as most of the world's leading authorities had taken part.

That was way back in 1982. Since then, the author has organized two further forecasting "competitions" to keep pace with new developments and eliminate the new criticisms that academics have ingeniously managed to concoct. The latest findings, published in 2000,[3] consisted of 3,003 economic series, an expanding range of statistical methods, and a growing army of experts. However, the basic conclusion – supported by many other academic studies over the past three decades – remains steadfast. That is, when forecasting, always use the KISS principle: Keep It Simple, Statistician.

## THE ACCURACY OF HUMAN JUDGMENT

Although pleased to be vindicated, the statistician couldn't help feeling a little disillusioned. If statistical forecasting models had such poor powers of prediction, maybe it would be better to rely on human intuition – the simplest method of them all. That was when he got talking to his colleague, a tone-deaf cognitive psychologist. It was the beginning of a beautiful working relationship, but the eventual co-author wasn't very encouraging at the time. "I've got bad news for you," he said. "Empirical findings in my field show that human judgment is even less accurate at predicting than statistical models."

The empirical findings he was referring to were those of the psychologist Paul Meehl and others. Meehl had applied his research to people of his own kind, turning psychology on the psychologists. He was particularly intrigued by the methods of diagnosis and decision-making used in clinical psychology. Traditionally, psychologists make their predictions about what's wrong with a patient based on a tiny sample of immediately available data, together with their own subjective judgments. Meehl asked whether they might be better off taking the time to collect quantitative data about their clients and then draw some statistically sound conclusions from it. He reviewed some twenty studies and discovered that the "statistical" method of diagnosis was superior to the traditional "clinical" approach.

When Meehl published a small book about his research in 1954,[4] it was greeted with the same kind of outrage as the statistician's paper on forecasting methods. Clinical psychologists all over the world felt professionally diminished and dismissed their colleague's findings. It didn't seem to matter that he was suggesting a way to make more accurate, more efficient, and more cost-effective clinical judgments. Although many subsequent studies have reinforced Meehl's original findings,[5] his suggestions have not yet been adopted by his own profession.

He may not have been greeted as a prophet in his own land, but Meehl's observations have been vindicated in other fields. Those in the business of lending money, for example, no longer rely on "clinical" procedures such as interviews with a bank manager to decide if you're worthy of credit. Instead, they make extensive use of computerized credit-scoring. In other words, they use simple statistical models with a select handful of variables to check whether you're a good risk. Similarly, graduate recruiters who take on fresh, young talent each year in large numbers increasingly depend on computers to profile applicants, before embarking on the expensive (and notoriously unreliable) process of face-to-face interviewing.

## THE POWER OF AVERAGING

After his brief excursion into psychology, the statistician was back to square one. As statisticians do, he sought comfort in further calculations based on his original data. He discovered that the most reliable predictions of all were achieved by taking the average of the results from a number of different forecasting methods. This worked even better than the most accurate statistical methods, including single exponential smoothing. And this incredible power of averaging has remained constant in each of the forecasting "competitions" over the years, not to mention many other areas and scientific fields.[6]

If you can improve forecasting accuracy by averaging predictions made by different models, can you do the same for predictions by people? The simple answer is "yes," a finding that has been rediscovered several times over the last century – and recently documented by James Surowiecki in his excellent book, *The Wisdom of Crowds*.[7] Surowiecki recounts the story of Francis Galton, the famous late-Victorian social scientist, who visited a county fair in Plymouth in his native England early in the twentieth century. There Galton observed a contest that involved guessing the net weight of an ox (after it was slaughtered and its skin removed). The person who provided the most accurate estimate would be declared the winner. Galton was an elitist who didn't have much time for the opinions of ordinary people, so he thought it would be interesting to investigate the levels of inaccuracy to which they would descend.

He set about obtaining all the legible predictions – 787 in total. Some of them really were way out. But the average of all the guesses was 1,197 pounds (543 kg) – and the weight of the ox, after it had been slaughtered and prepared, was 1,198 pounds. In other words, the average of all the predictions – bad and good – was almost perfect. What's more, it was much more accurate than the guess of the eventual winner. Galton, the elitist, was left to ponder his own discovery that the average prediction of few hundred ignorant yokels was highly accurate. Like the statistician some three-quarters of a century later, he'd glimpsed the incredible power of averaging.

In *The Wisdom of Crowds*, Surowiecki goes on to describe many other situations where simple averages of people's judgments provide surprisingly accurate estimates. And everyday life throws up many more examples. Internet sites like www.intrade.com, where the general public bet on who'll win the next elections, are better at predicting the winner than individual political experts with huge reputations and huge egos. This phenomenon runs contrary to the theories of statistical science, which advocate the existence of a so-called "optimal" model that, once appropriately identified and correctly used, provides more accurate predictions than alternative models. It also runs contrary to our very human need to believe in experts. Not only, it turns out, is an expert's judgment less accurate than the simple number crunching of a computer, but it's also less reliable than the average forecast of a bunch of nobodies.

## THE DISTRACTIONS OF NOISE

Why is it so easy to explain the past and yet so difficult to predict the future? Why do simple statistical methods forecast events at least as accurately as complex, sophisticated ones? Why do people make worse judgments than mechanical models based on samples of data? Why does averaging, whether of models or people, work better than anything else, including the so-called "optimal" model and the best experts, when it comes to predictions?

To answer these questions let's go back to basics. The process of forecasting, whether carried out by people or models, is to identify some pattern or relation among the relevant variables and then extrapolate from there. Identifying patterns intuitively is something that human beings do constantly and in many – but not all – cases we are quite good at it. Imagine, for example, how easy it is to predict the trajectory of a ball thrown into the air, the position of another car on the road, or the way someone else's spoken sentence will end. Most of the members of Miss Johnstone's school choir were also pretty good at predicting the last note of a good tune. Indeed, psychologists have been fascinated by the human ability to infer pattern in music and see it as a model for other kinds of reasoning. The late Herbert Simon, who was an all-round social scientist and Nobel prize-winner for economics, wrote extensively on the subject.

> Patterns, temporal as well as spatial, occur in many spheres of life besides music. People appear to have strong propensities, whether innate or learned, to discover patterns in temporal sequences presented by the environment and to use these evidences of pattern for prediction. The ability and desire to discover temporal patterns has had great value for the survival of Man: in predicting the seasons, for example, or the weather. The urge to find pattern extends even to phenomena where one may well doubt whether pattern exists (e.g. in movements of the stock market).[8]

Models do formally – and systematically – what humans do intuitively. They analyze the past and find an underlying pattern or relation between variables. Two factors, however, complicate the task of forecasting. First, the future is rarely a straightforward extrapolation of the past. That's because environmental, economic, market, and competitive conditions can change in unforeseen ways. Second, we rarely observe a pattern in its pure form. Instead, patterns are typically intermixed with "noise," that is chance fluctuations that have no discernable cause.

Let's take the slightly depressing example of climate change. Despite the slow, general trend that is global warming, the summer of 2007 brought unseasonably cold, wet weather to northern Europe and an extreme heat wave to eastern Europe. It's tempting to conclude that global warming never existed or is speeding up, depending on where you live. But the truth is that there have always been freak-weather years. More prosaically, any seasoned sales manager can recount tales of inexplicably bad or good months that stick out like a very sore thumb from the overall trend. In these and many other situations, what we observe is both the pattern and the noise together. So the first task in identifying the underlying pattern is to filter out the noise. It's a bit like having an intimate conversation in a loud, trendy restaurant, or blocking out the sound of our children fighting when we're trying to listen to a favorite CD. Of course, something unexpected could happen in the future that will defy the pattern altogether, but if we don't identify its shape correctly in the first place, we have no hope at all of making a prediction based on past events.

At this point, it's time to meet the third author of this book (who likes to sing, but only in the shower). Some people collect stamps or antiques, which is strange enough, but he collects data on the heights of male MBA students at INSEAD, the international business school with campuses in France, Singapore and Abu Dhabi. In his defense, it must be stressed that he uses this unusual collection to illustrate the notions of pattern and noise in his decision science classes. Figure 11 shows the heights of the 353 men in a recent MBA intake, displayed in random order. Each dot represents the height of a student. Clearly, there is a great deal of variation in size – between the shortest guy at

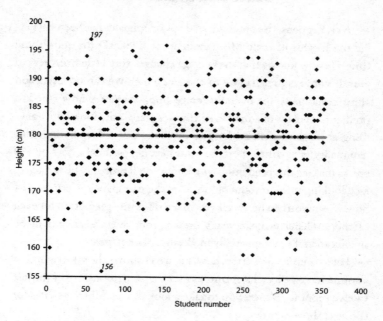

**Figure 11** Heights of 353 male MBA students

156 cm (5 feet 1 inch) and the tallest at 197 cm (6 feet 6 inches). Perhaps if we had some other information, such as the heights of each individual's parents, we could explain some of this dispersion either side of the average, which is represented by the solid line through the middle of the graph. But this is all the data we have. So, if someone asked you to predict the height of a single student from this intake (without looking at him), your best chance of getting closest would be to suggest the average: 180 cm to be precise. As it happens, not only are most of the dots on the graph close to this line, but there are more dots actually on it (49 of them) than any other horizontal line you could plot. Another way of thinking about this is that the line representing the average is the pattern, while the heights – both above and below – are the noise.

As it happens, the professor of decision sciences has been collecting the heights of male MBA students at INSEAD for quite some time. He now knows that the average changes very little from year to year. It's always pretty close to 180 cm, which we can use as a good approximation to the overall average. Suppose you're now asked to predict the height of a man in next year's class. You don't know anything about him that might possibly help you – for example, his nationality or favorite sport. So your best bet will definitely be 180 cm. In making this prediction, you know you'll probably be wrong. In fact, looking at the amount of "noise" in the past gives you an idea just how wrong you can be. But if you make this same prediction for each of the students in next year's intake, your average error will be smaller than if you repeatedly made any other estimate.

Let's complicate matters now. Figure 12 shows the sales figures of a company – we'll call it Acme, as in the best cartoons – over the last twelve months. We ask you to take a look at it and forecast sales for the next three months.

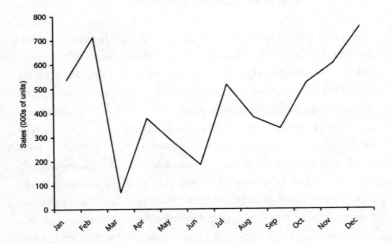

**Figure 12** Sales of Acme

What have you concluded? First of all, it's clear that this graph is very different from the previous one. Second, we have so little information that it's hard – if not impossible – to distinguish pattern from noise. Perhaps the company sells ski-wear, accounting for its increasing sales from March to December. Or maybe it launched a new gadget in September, which has had great reviews and is going to turn Acme into the next Apple. Alternatively, it's possible that Acme is in one of those niche markets, where it's quite hard to find any kind of pattern and sales tend to fluctuate radically just by chance. Third, we have no idea what's going on in Acme's market as a whole. It could be that a competitor contributed to the ups and downs on the graph or even that there was some entirely external problem beyond anyone's control, like a worldwide widget shortage. All in all, predicting Acme's sales for the next three months is nowhere near as simple as predicting the height of an INSEAD MBA student.

The problem – as Herbert Simon taught us on page 197 – is that we humans are "programmed" to see patterns and, although this is a highly functional skill, it can also be dysfunctional if we see a pattern where there isn't one. Psychologists call this "illusory correlation" and it's amplified by human frailties, such as wishful thinking (or self-promotion). Product managers, for instance, want their sales to increase, so are susceptible to seeing illusory growth trends (or pretending that they can). But – once again – there's a second kind of error too, namely, not being able to see a pattern that does exist. This can be just as serious as the first.

To illustrate, consider two purely statistical types of pattern that we could plausibly find in Acme's sales chart. The first pattern is one of continued growth in sales starting from March. The second shows a flat level of sales across time. Both patterns are shown in figure 13 – along with their implied forecasts for the next three months.

The difference between the forecasts is enormous. Predicted sales for next March are 1,296,303 units based on the exponentially

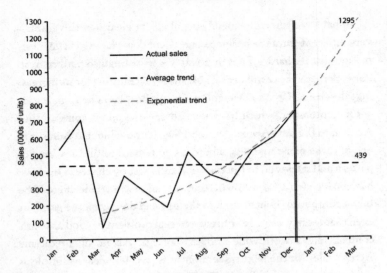

**Figure 13** Sales of Acme (with trend lines)

increasing pattern and 439,250 based on the flat, average pattern. This huge difference illustrates the significant challenges facing forecasters – and the senior executives to whom product managers report. Fortunately, in most situations there would be a few more clues than we've given you here. Meanwhile, in the case of Acme, it might be safer not to conclude anything for now.

Identifying and extrapolating a relation between two variables is much like finding patterns in sets of data. If we want to figure out the relation between the demand for a product and its price, we need to be able to observe how demand changes under different price levels. However, what we observe also includes "noise," which we have to isolate before we can identify a causal relation. For example, we might reduce the price and sales might increase for several months in a row. But how do we know this is really due to the reduction? The increased sales could be the result of seasonal fluctuations or, worse, chance factors that we can't identify at all: in other words, noise. The challenge is to isolate the noise and identify the true relation – without falling prey to false optimism.

As with predicting patterns, it turns out that simple methods of identifying and estimating relations between variables are at least as accurate as large, complex models. Indeed, extensive empirical research has shown that – just like human beings – statistically sophisticated methods find illusory patterns or relations that don't exist. Returning to Acme's sales projections for the next three months and figure 13, our more complex forecast shows phenomenal growth. The flat line of the average, however, doesn't extrapolate any pattern and just steers a non-committal conservative course. But maybe the latter is a little too simple. A slightly more elaborate method is "single exponential smoothing." (If you remember, it's the simple statistical tool that did so well in the author's forecasting competitions.) We needn't be concerned with exactly how it works, but figure 14 shows the result it gives for Acme's next three months of sales (alongside the other two forecasts).

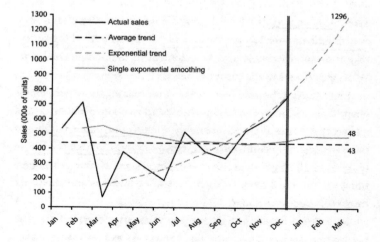

**Figure 14** Sales of Acme (with single exponential smoothing)

Although single exponential smoothing recognizes that sales vary a great deal over time, it also acknowledges that part of such variability is noise and should be ignored. Thus, the pattern it identifies is close to the average and less likely to make a large error if the increase in sales over the last few months was due to chance. On the other hand, single exponential smoothing also suggests there'll be a slow increase in the sales pattern over the next few months. So, if the last three months weren't a freak occurrence after all and sales were indeed increasing in a systematic way, the company would be prepared and have enough stock. Everyone's a winner this way. The product manager and salespeople keep their self-esteem intact and senior management can be cautiously optimistic. If the increase turns out to be greater than expected, it's a nice surprise all round. But if things take a turn for the worse and sales start to slump, at least there's not too much excess stock hanging around in the warehouse.

## THE BENEFIT OF HINDSIGHT

Søren Kierkegaard, the Danish philosopher, once wisely said, "Life can only be understood backwards; but it must be lived forwards." Like it or not, this sums up a key element of the human condition. What we achieve in the future depends on decisions that we take in the present. And the only basis we have for making those decisions is what happened in the past. This throws up two key problems – and it's worth looking at them separately. First, is our understanding of the past correct? Second, what assurance can we have that the future will be like the past? Let's use two examples to examine both questions: one fictional story from the world of business and the other from real-life meteorology.

Megabucks Retail Inc has collected a vast array of data on its past performance over many years. The company's executives have thus established three empirical regularities. One, sales are 15% higher on

Saturdays than the average weekday. Two, sales have grown at a rate of 5.5% a year for the last five years. And three, the Christmas season accounts for 18% of annual sales. It seems reasonable to assume that managers can extrapolate from these data to predict sales for next Saturday, next Christmas, and the whole of next year. As well as finding these patterns, the executives have gone one step further. They've experimented for a long time with their pricing strategies and found some interesting relations between the variables of price and demand. On one product range, for example, they've noted that if the price decreases by 5%, demand increases, on average, by 7.5%. Having established this relation, the statistically savvy execs can then manipulate demand by increasing or decreasing the price.

Has the Megabucks management understood the past correctly? Well, their accounts of the past certainly seem to make sense. Best of all, they've kept it simple (perhaps for the benefit of their bosses) and not tried to go into too much detail. However, most people prefer a story that explains 80% of what happened in the past, as opposed to 50%. The 80% version of events will be much more interesting and comprehensive as stories go, with intricate patterns of interwoven causes and effects. The problem is that the 80% will almost inevitably include noise, as well as the pattern. So the story won't be as accurate a predictor of the future as the simpler account. In other words our natural tendency to seek a "complete" explanation for past events can blind us to what's really important: namely, how well our explanation forecasts the future.

Now let's imagine that a global business magazine commissions a hot-shot financial journalist to write a feature on Megabucks. She sets to work in December, notes that sales have been falling over the last nine months, and starts to dig a little deeper. All that stuff about the Christmas period is well known, but – frankly – who wants to read about that? So instead the journalist concocts an epic saga of boardroom tensions, supply-chain fiascos, and exchange-rate time-bombs. The editor likes the piece so much that he puts it on the cover and goes to print in January trumpeting the company's impending fall from grace. Unknown to the publishers, Megabucks decides to release its final quarter's results a week early. The news of their 15% upturn in sales compared to the same period last year breaks the day before the magazine comes out. The editor loses his job and the journalist's reputation is ruined to the point that she's forced to take a job in corporate communications. It's no consolation that all the stories in the article were true and that they had indeed helped to account for lower than expected sales during much of the year. But fortunately for Megabucks, they'd sorted out the problems and got themselves back on track for a better Christmas than ever.

Statistics is strangely like story-telling. Statistical forecasting methods analyze available data to identify established patterns or relations. This is analogous to someone like a financial journalist coming up with a great story to explain past economic events. Our empirical research, which has covered thousands of data sets over the last three decades, shows that the more sophisticated the statistical method, the better it fits with past data. By contrast, simpler methods don't do so well and fail to account for up to 50% of the data. However – and here's the important point – there is no correlation between how well methods explain the past and how accurately they predict the future. Past patterns and relations change continually – sometimes temporarily, sometimes for good. In addition, new events occur and new conditions arise to shape a future that's very different from the past.

To illustrate, let's move on to our second example: weather forecasting. Thanks to satellite imaging, meteorologists can easily identify weather patterns by comparing photos taken over time. Typically they might track a low-pressure system bringing rain from, say, the south and calculate that it will arrive in your town in two days' time. So why did it turn out to be a blazing hot, sunny day? The problem is that weather systems don't always stay on the same course. A new high-pressure system can develop and stop, cancel, or modify the progress of the low-pressure one. That's why, no matter how expert they are and how many supercomputers they use, meteorologists can never be sure what the weather will do. The future isn't always a continuation of the past, no matter how well we've understood it.

To sum up, the more complicated an explanation, the less likely it is to replicate itself in the future. Simpler accounts have the advantage of staying closer to the average, underlying pattern or relation. They don't miss the wood by obsessing about the trees. Similarly, complex statistical forecasting methods "overfit" the available data and find pattern where there's actually noise. But that's not the only problem. Søren Kierkegaard and the world's best meteorologists all show us that the future is hardly ever just like the past.

## WHEN AVERAGING WORKS

As we've seen, averaging the predictions of several people or models results in more accurate forecasts than if we relied on a single person (even an expert) or method (even the most statistically dazzling). This is a well-established empirical fact.[9] And the explanation is straightforward. The data we observe consist of a combination of underlying patterns plus noise. The big contribution of averaging is to cancel out the noise. Whereas some noise distorts the pattern in one direction, other noise distorts in other directions. In the process of averaging, the distortions cancel each other out and reveal the underlying shape. Figure 11 (the graph of students' heights) is a good illustration of how averaging filters out the "noise" (that is, extreme variations in heights) to reveal the underlying "tune" (the straight horizontal line that most usefully represents the observed data).

To demonstrate further how averaging eliminates noise, imagine playing a game that involves estimating the value of a jar full of pennies. This is the modern equivalent of Galton's fairground ox, updated to avoid any cruelty to animals or messy slaughtering and skinning. It's a great favorite at school fetes, along with raffles, cake stalls, and performances of choirs like Miss Johnstone's. According to the rules of the game, you're allowed to take a good look at the jar before estimating how much money it contains. Just as in Galton's original game, the closest guess to the actual amount in the jar wins the game. Now, if each player assesses the value of the jar independently of the rest (that is, no one is influenced by anyone else's guess), it is highly likely that some will underestimate, while others will overestimate. Many of these guesses will be wildly out, and thus constitute the noise, while others will be much closer to the real amount in the jar, forming a distinct pattern either side of it. By taking the average of all the guesses we get quite close to the true value, because the wild guesses – and even some of the more reasonable ones – will cancel each other out.

Time and time again, it's the crowd who really wins guessing games like these. In fact, the average estimate is nearly always more accurate than the single guess that wins the prize. The crowd is so reliable that several companies have started to use the average opinion of their employees to predict the sales of new products and services. This innovative approach is known as "Prediction Markets" and has worked well for the likes of Google, Yahoo, and other high tech firms. The difficulty, however, is that it's difficult to keep employees' judgments independent of each other as they talk and interact with each other.

The importance of independence suddenly becomes clear when we change the rules of the pennies-in-the-jar game. If we start showing some players the results of all previous guesses, the average estimate will wander further and further from the actual sum in the jar. For averaging to retain its power, it's important that the different errors of prediction are entirely unrelated. In technical jargon, this is known as the "independence assumption." As an extreme example, imagine three financial analysts at the same investment bank, who study the same company. They base their opinions on the same information provided by the company, analyze the same data about past earnings per share, read the same industry reports, drink water from the same fountain and wine from the same bar. Given that they frequently pick each other's brains and say more than they meant to, it's highly unlikely that they'll come up with independent estimates of future earnings per share. If one of them overestimates, it's likely the others will too – which means that the average will also be an overestimate.

On the other hand, consider three doctors examining the same patient. They're all different ages, have trained in different medical schools, and use different procedures. Though they work in the same city, attend the same cocktail parties, and happen to share a passion for ballroom dancing, they're bound by an ethical code of patient confidentiality. The errors in these physicians' judgments are likely to be independent. The "average" of their opinions is likely to be close to the truth. Now you know why, in chapter 3, we were so insistent on getting a second – or even third – opinion.

Fortunately, the number of people or models required to improve a forecast doesn't have to be large. Five to seven people, and an even smaller number of between two and four models, are typically enough to block out the noise and come close to the underlying pattern or relation. Better still, it's possible to combine the forecasts of human judgment and statistical prediction, to generate a "superaverage" that exploits the advantages of both while minimizing their drawbacks. But it remains critical that the inputs of these people and models are as independent of each other as possible.

So is averaging the goose that lays the golden eggs of prediction, the fairytale ending we've been searching for? Sadly, no. Averaging improves the accuracy of forecasts but it offers no guarantees. Alas, you cannot get rid of the inherently unpredictable nature of the future. Your only option, we remind you, is to embrace the uncertainties it holds.

## THE MADNESS OF CROWDS

How much would you be willing to pay for a tulip bulb? Would you be willing to exchange a medium-sized house for one? Although the last question seems crazy, it was actually taken seriously in the Netherlands 370 years ago, during the great tulip mania. In 1636, at the height of the frenzy, some rare bulbs were valued at astronomical prices, in some cases costing more than houses in the center of Amsterdam. During the mania, many people made huge fortunes buying and selling tulip bulbs. Within a period of less than a year, bulbs originally worth only a few guilders soared in value, as demand skyrocketed and supply failed to keep up. Finally, when the bubble burst and prices returned to pre-mania levels, there were a handful of big winners – the people who had got out in time – and many, many losers. Those who'd bought bulbs, often selling or mortgaging their property in the belief that prices could only go up, found themselves financially ruined. All they had left was a worthless bunch of tulip bulbs that nobody wanted.

The tulip mania wasn't a one-off event. There have been many similar incidents throughout history and throughout the world. Nor is the phenomenon confined to the distant past. In May 1924, the value of the DJIA (Dow Jones Industrial Average) index was 90.4 points. Three months later, it had increased by 15%. From May 1924, values and yearly increases for the next five years were as shown in table 12.

These figures tell the story of a growing collective madness every bit as insane as in seventeenth-century Amsterdam. As we saw in chapter 4, the inevitable crash began in September 1929. The DJIA plunged from its peak of 362.4 to 64.1 in April 1932, less than three

**Table 12** Evolution of DJIA: May 1924 to September 1929

| Date | Index | Percentage increase |
|------|-------|---------------------|
| May 1924 | 90.4 | Base month |
| May 1925 | 125.6 | 40% |
| May 1926 | 140.3 | 55% |
| May 1927 | 168.8 | 87% |
| May 1928 | 216.3 | 140% |
| May 1929 | 310.3 | 243% |
| September 1929 | 362.4 | 301% |

years later, losing 82.3% of its value. If you'd invested $10,000 across DJIA companies in September 1929, you'd only have had $1,770 to show for it at the lowest point of the Great Depression.

If the Great Depression still seems too much like history, take note that the infant twenty-first century has blown two small bubbles that have already burst. The NASDAQ crash of early 2000 turned dotcoms into the tulip bulbs of the present day. The really spooky thing is that the rise and fall of the NASDAQ in the 1990s and 2000s followed a remarkably similar pattern, over the same number of months, to the DJIA back in the 1920s and 1930s. Using almost none of the statistical trickery at our disposal, we've plotted the two indexes very simply in figure 15.

This is one pattern that would be nice to dismiss as noise. It suggests some kind of innate tendency to self-destruction that makes human beings the financial equivalent of lemmings. Fortunately for us, however, there was a lot less of our global wealth tied up in the NASDAQ of 2000 than in Wall Street seventy years earlier. Even more fortunately, figure 15 reveals that, once the bubbles broke, both the DJIA and NASDAQ indexes returned to their previous levels – it's as if nothing had happened. Indeed, if you'd been marooned on a desert island from 1924 to 1932 or meditating in a Tibetan monastery

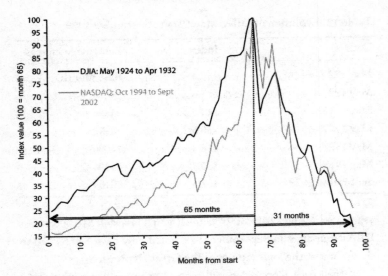

**Figure 15** DJIA and NASDAQ: relative monthly values starting May 1924 and October 1994

from 1994 to 2002, you would have noticed no great change in the various stock market values on your return to so-called civilization.

Just as we thought it was safe to go to press with our historical examples, the "subprime" and credit crisis broke and we got that *déjà vu* feeling again. A story that began with a bunch of low-earning borrowers in the US finished up rocking the entire world's financial markets. If the story has slipped your memory already, because some new investment scandal has usurped it, we'll remind you. Rising US house prices fueled a boom in "subprime" mortgage lending, which is another way of saying that high-risk borrowers started to get loans that banks should never have given them. The various financial institutions and investment banks repackaged those loans several times over and sold them on to other financial organizations and investment banks. The bonds that the dodgy loans morphed into didn't look particularly risky once the financial wizards had worked their magic – and indeed they were as safe as houses so long as property prices kept on rising and the new homeowners were making their repayments. But of course, there's no such thing as big gains without big risk. When the borrowers started to default, houses were no longer safe. Property prices plummeted, major banks and financial institutions fell, and tremors were felt all over the world as investors feared that the entire financial system was going to collapse. Another bubble had burst with catastrophic negative consequences in terms of financial and job losses. Well, the crisis will pass and calm will eventually return. The problem is that no one can tell how long it will take to return to normality. And worse, we don't know when the next financial crisis will hit, because – despite the overhaul of the financial system announced by different governments – further similar crises will still occur.

So much then for the great power of averaging. Where money is concerned, the wisdom of crowds turns into madness time and time again. But why does averaging fail in the case of bubbles? Again the answer is simple, but this time it's rooted in evolutionary psychology, rather than statistics. Of course, it's true that human beings like to be unique. Some men own drawers full of novelty ties, while many women possess hundreds of pairs of designer shoes. For these people it can be a disaster to show up at a party where some other guest is wearing the same kipper tie or identical stiletto mules (and much worse if the same person is wearing both). But even individuals who like to be different have a conformist side. Novelty-tie man wants other people to get the joke. And designer-shoe woman is determined to be in fashion. Deep down within us there is a herd instinct, based on a time when togetherness was essential for survival in an environment full of physical threats. Even today, it helps us with team work and provides a valuable sense of community.

Uniqueness boosts independence and promotes variety. Herd behavior demands conformity, generates similarity, and kills diversity. Whatever its benefits − historical or current − the pack instinct defeats the power of averaging. In the case of Galton's ox, no guess was influenced by any other. But the responses of the vast numbers of people who found out from the TV and newspapers that the NASDAQ was doubling, tripling, and then quadrupling in value were anything but independent. Many people felt left out of the big game that was making everyone else get rich quick. Finally, after the market had been increasing for many years, they felt safe to join in ... and ended up getting poor quicker.

You can't blame them, though. Such a response is part of the natural herd instinct we all share. It's when independence ends and pack behavior starts. It fuels irrational bubbles and ultimately leads to prices so unsustainable that the only rational option is to deflate them.[10] The trouble is that the herd instinct kicks in again, turning rapidly to a stampede. Rather than gently deflating, the bubble bursts with a loud pop that echoes throughout the world's economies. It's a sound as unwelcome as a certain author trying to sing.

Can you discern that precise moment when independence ends and herd thinking begins? If so, you can exploit the pros of both while steering clear of their cons. We wish we could tell you how to do it. But, to hark back to chapters 4 and 5, it's impossible to get your timing perfect and sell at the top (except by luck or illegal practices). The intellectual difficulties are compounded by the emotional. Greed may interact with the hope that the bubble can last longer and the fear of losing out by selling too early.

However, we're beginning to get ahead of ourselves here. For now, we'll go back instead to a possible course of action that we mentioned briefly in chapter 5: the "contrarian" strategy, which involves doing the exact opposite of the herd. Many stock market gurus have built their reputations in this way. They do brilliantly when bubbles burst − in fact that's when most self-styled contrarians come out of the woodwork. Assuming they were already contrarians when the bubble was building up, it's not surprising that we heard nothing from them, as they would have been losing money surely and steadily. If the strategy is applied consistently, it works well when the market is doing badly, and badly when the market is doing well. Ultimately, it's bound to lose over time, because – as we've seen before – the market is headed upwards in the long run. Worse still, there's nothing independent, big, or clever about contrarianism. Because it's all about systematically doing the exact opposite of the herd, contrarians are absolutely reliant on what everyone else is doing. Whether they like it or not, their behavior is intimately related to that of the pack – albeit in an inverse manner.

We don't deny that some people or funds that are quite contrary have gardens that grow abundantly. It's true that they do better than the market on occasion. But as a consistent, long-term solution to financial bubbles, it's definitely not an option.

## THE MUSIC OF NOISE

In this chapter, we've continued to stress how both statistical models and human judgments have limited ability to predict future events. Even when we correctly manage to discern patterns and relations in past events, there's no guarantee that the future will be the same as the past. In those cases where past and future are symmetrical, averaging and other simple kinds of modeling help – up to a point – as they cancel out "noise." But in many real-life situations (like investing) it's almost impossible to achieve the independent thinking required for averaging to work.

Having said all that, some events in the domain of social sciences are surprisingly predictable – even if they're not always the most interesting ones! For example, we can forecast with amazing accuracy how many people will travel on the London Underground during weekday rush hours, how many cars will cross the George

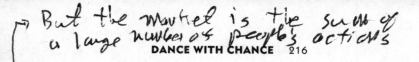
*But the market is the sum of a large number of people's actions*

Washington Bridge to enter Manhattan on a Monday morning, and how many people in France will be eligible to receive a pension five or ten years from now. In other words, when forecasting concerns a large number of events (such as people's actions) and the patterns or relations that link them don't change across time, predictions can be accurate. Under these conditions, the accuracy of socio-economic forecasting is similar to that of the "hard" sciences.

Unfortunately, the fact remains we can't predict most events of interest (and potential profit). In this book we've focused on medicine, investments, and management, but there are many other areas where accurate forecasting is nigh on impossible. Even hard science sometimes fails. Despite vast arrays of satellite images and supercomputers, meteorologists can't tell you if it's going to rain in a week's time with any certainty. The big question is therefore: how can we take important decisions when we know that we cannot forecast the future accurately?

The next chapter looks more closely at the nature of uncertainty and offers practical advice on how to assess it more realistically. We also, uncharacteristically, reveal a golden rule for predictions. Don't expect any huge surprises, however. So often in life the answers to our questions have been staring us in the face for a very long time. Indeed, several decades after being coerced into the school choir by the redoubtable Miss Johnstone, it suddenly dawned on the author who (still) can't sing why she was so keen for him to join in. As it happens, he wasn't the only kid with a lousy voice – far from it – but the choir sounded really quite good. Even he could hear that. You see, as a musician, Miss Johnstone instinctively understood the power of averaging. As long as the main tune (or pattern) was not too difficult, she knew that the bad voices (or noise) would cancel each other out. The small boy with freckles in the back row, on the other hand, would need years of study and specialization in decision sciences to discover the music of noise.

# Ten

# OF SUBWAYS AND COCONUTS: TWO TYPES OF UNCERTAINTY

*The best laid schemes o' mice an' men/Gang aft agley.*

Robert Burns, *poet*

This chapter is where we finally face up to uncertainty, only to discover that it comes in two forms: one that we can figure out reasonably well and another that defies all attempts at measurement. Our aim is to provide a practical guide for coping with your daily dose of uncertainty. If that's cheered you up no end, here's a tragic tale. It may dampen your spirits, but it will help to explain the two types of uncertainty.

## KLAUS AND THE COCONUT

Klaus Bauermeister, originally from Zurich, was working in New York for the private wealth division of a well-known Swiss investment bank, when he planned the fateful trip. In fact, he spent nearly seven months planning it. His son Frank was in his last year of high school and would turn eighteen on June 27, four days after graduation. That was when Klaus planned to hand him the surprise envelope containing the tickets and highly researched itinerary. The holiday would take the whole family (Klaus, his wife, his daughter, and Frank) from New York to Singapore, then to Thailand, where the Bauermeisters would tour the northern forests – partly by elephant – for a week. Next, they'd relax in the resort of Phuket for three days, before returning to Singapore for a weekend of pampering in the Swiss Hotel.

Klaus's passion for planning and detail was a way of life. Take going to work each morning. He lived on the Upper East Side, at 94th Street between Lexington and 3rd Avenue, and combined walking with taking the subway to his office on the corner of 51st Street and 6th Avenue. Klaus always left at exactly 8.00 am, took exactly the same route and loved recording the time it took door to door each day. The average was almost exactly forty-three minutes – and on all but the exceptional occasions he knew he'd be in the office between thirty-seven and forty-nine minutes from leaving home.

When June 27 (a good day for commuting at thirty-nine minutes) came, Frank whooped with delight, which gave Klaus all the joy he'd planned for. The birthday envelope – handed over with ceremony at the family's favorite Thai restaurant that evening – was bulging with meticulous detail. From choosing Singapore Airlines for the long-haul flights (it had the best safety record) and getting seats above the wing (in case of an emergency landing), to booking restaurants and hotels, Klaus had thought of everything. He'd spent hours and hours researching it all on the internet. Well, to tell the truth, it was his patient secretary who'd done a lot of the groundwork, but the banker prided himself on having zeroed in on the best options.

Sometimes Klaus's wife made gently affectionate comments about him being a control freak, but he didn't mind. Unlike his son, he didn't like surprises and, anyway, there weren't many downsides to over-planning. Of course, he remained blissfully unaware that his long-suffering secretary didn't share this analysis. But in this particular case – taking his precious family so far from home – even she could see that the price of planning was undoubtedly worth paying.

When the family finally arrived in Phuket on July 14, 2006, everything had gone perfectly according to plan. There were no unpleasant surprises of the kind that Klaus hated. No airplane delays, no stray luggage, no mislaid reservations, no upset stomachs. The hotels and restaurants all lived up to his expectations, with the exception of one meal, which had seemed a little over-priced given its quality. There weren't even any elephant-riding accidents, an activity which had given Klaus a few nightmares at the planning stage. (He'd only made the booking when he discovered the elephant operators adhered to the highest standards of health and safety, with harnesses and helmets for all passengers.) Singapore's cleanliness and orderliness had been a particular delight and the Swiss banker from New York was looking forward to returning there as he lay on the idyllic beach.

On the third morning in Phuket, he succumbed to the temptation of using his BlackBerry. But not for work purposes, mind you. Klaus had been pondering his pension arrangements in bed the night before and wanted to contact his financial adviser before he forgot. Having woken early so that his family wouldn't catch him in the act of emailing, he strode out onto the beach and into the brilliant sunshine . . . only to feel the hot rays of risk beating down onto his pale skin. In his enthusiasm for that pensions business, he'd forgotten to apply sun block and, with all those articles in the papers about melanomas, well, you can't be too careful, can you? So Klaus stepped into the convenient shade of a nearby palm tree, whereupon a coconut promptly dropped on to his head with a resounding thud.

By the time the hotel staff came running, he was no longer breathing. Their efforts to revive him were futile and ten minutes later a Western-trained doctor (whose presence had been one of the plus points for Klaus in choosing the resort) pronounced him dead. As the same doctor later assured Frank and his distraught mother and sister, it had all happened too quickly for Klaus to feel either pain . . . or surprise. Klaus had become one of a very small number of people who suffer death by coconut, a tragic event that even he, the master of planning, couldn't have predicted.

There is, however, a final twist in Klaus's story. It isn't quite a happy ending, but offered some solace to his grieving family. They discovered that, years earlier, Klaus had taken out a life insurance policy for 7.5 million Swiss francs. He'd also recently purchased travel insurance covering any expenses incurred by an accident during the trip, plus three million dollars for death or permanent disability. It turns out that Klaus's passion for planning had also covered the possibility of his own early death and its unexpected consequences for his family. Though he was powerless to save his own life, he had at least made sure his loved ones would suffer no financial hardship.

## A BLACK MONDAY AND A BLACK SWAN

Klaus, Frank, and their family are – we're pleased to report – entirely fictional. But our next story, that of Pierre Dufour, is tragically true, even if it relies on the same kind of awfully bad luck. Dufour, a forty-year-old Canadian, lived in Arizona with his wife and two children. His passion was investments, and he'd put practically all his money into stocks. He was extremely pleased with himself, as his portfolio had done extremely well during the five years he'd been in the USA.

Pierre Dufour died or, more precisely, committed suicide early in the morning of October 20, 1987, the day after Black Monday. The stock market had fallen by more than 22% in just one single day – and his own investments by more than 39%. His wife said that he was still worth many millions, but for Dufour losing more than $4.8 million in a single day was more than he could bear. Even if he'd been able to accept the loss of his money, he couldn't take the way his beliefs had been shaken. His portfolio consisted mainly of growth stocks and small caps, and had therefore been outperforming the Dow Jones and S&P 500 by more than 6%. Dufour had remained confident it would soon double or triple in value until less than a week before his death.

His confidence was not entirely misplaced. US stock markets had been growing nicely since the early 1980s. Then the market suddenly started falling. It fell 2.7% on October 6, 1987, and by smaller percentages over the next four days. On Tuesday, October 13 (the number 13 was always a lucky one for Pierre Dufour and Tuesday was his favorite day of the week) the decline halted, and the market grew by nearly 2%. Dufour wasn't particularly bothered by these events, as they were normal stock-market fluctuations. However, the next three days weren't at all typical. On Wednesday, October 14 the market fell 3%, on Thursday 2.3% and, worse, on Friday, October 16, an additional 5.2%. But Pierre Dufour hoped that the decline was over and that the next week would see another reversal of the downward trend. The US economy was growing strongly, corporate profits were high, and everyone was predicting they were going to increase further in 1988. So, all in all, there were no signs of any trouble and he saw the decline as a way to increase his profits. For these perfectly sound reasons, Dufour borrowed money against his existing portfolio to buy more stocks at bargain prices on the Friday afternoon.

Monday, October 19, however, turned out to be the worst day in the history of the stock market. It was even worse than October 28, 1929, which kick-started the Great Depression. By the time he tragically ended his life, Pierre Dufour had lost more than half of his money in just ten trading days. The shock was as great as if he'd been hit by a falling coconut – and his state of mind darker than the blackest Monday.

Although there have been many suggested explanations for Black Monday, none of them seems quite convincing – even with the benefit of hindsight. Today, it's only when we hear about events like Pierre Dufour's suicide that we can begin to imagine how the entire financial world was taken by total and utter surprise on that Monday. The stock-market collapse of 1987 was what former trader Nassim Nicholas Taleb calls – in his excellent book of the same name – a "Black Swan," a totally unexpected event with mammoth consequences.[1] Like the coconut that killed Klaus, no one, including all the experts whose own finances were ruined, saw it coming.

Stock markets have a mind of their own. After October 19, stock prices started rising again as if nothing had happened. Exactly twenty-one months and seven days later, the S&P 500 regained the same value as on October 6, 1987. The upward trend continued for over a decade – until the events that led up to the 2000–2003 market downturn. Today, Black Monday is no more than a blip: a small trough in a graph full of mountainous peaks and low valleys. Had Dufour been alive today, he would have seen his monetary Fortune increase many times over. It even turns out that he'd believed in the right kind of investments. His growth and small-cap stocks gained in value even more significantly than the S&P 500.

But of course, it's too late for Pierre Dufour. It's also too late for James Smith of Cedar Rapids, Iowa. He committed suicide after his broker demanded back some of the money he'd borrowed to buy stocks that were now rapidly falling in value (known in the business as a "margin call"). It's too late as well for the brokerage firm vice-president killed by George King of Durham, North Carolina, after King was asked to repay part of what he had borrowed (another margin call). And too late for King who then went on to kill himself.[2] Provided they could have stalled their creditors long enough for the markets to rise again, Smith and King would have been fabulously wealthy men today. The same would have been true of Dufour.

## TWO TYPES OF UNCERTAINTY – MADE SIMPLE

The story of Klaus illustrates the crucial difference between two types of uncertainty. In honor of our fictional friend, we call them "subway" and "coconut" uncertainty, respectively. We go into more detail below, but the main distinction is that you can quantify and model subway uncertainty, while coconuts remain totally and utterly unpredictable. Now, there's no doubt that we humans have great difficulty coping with uncertainty in any way, shape, or form. But one of our greatest difficulties, for both lay people and statisticians alike, is distinguishing between these two types. More importantly, to believe that "coconuts" can be quantified and modeled as if they were "subways" is not simply misguided. As the story of Pierre Dufour shows, it can also be tragic.

*Subway uncertainty* was what Klaus experienced each day as he commuted from his home to his office in New York. The uncertainty centered on how long the journey took. Klaus knew that it rarely took exactly the same number of minutes as on the day before. Instead, there were variations due to a whole bunch of uncontrollable factors that each had an independent effect on his travel time. These ranged from mundane train delays caused by crowding on the platforms or obstruction of the closing doors to freak weather conditions or criminal activity. But, thanks to Klaus's statistical training, he was able to map the situation very clearly. First, he knew his average (or mean) travel time was forty-three minutes. Second, he knew that a little more than two-thirds of his journeys took between forty and forty-six minutes (that is, within three minutes of the average). Third, he knew that about 95% of his journeys took between thirty-seven and forty-nine minutes (that is, within six minutes of the average). He also knew that the remaining 5% of his journeys – apart from some very rare exceptions – were in the range of thirty-four to fifty-two minutes (that is within nine minutes of the average). Finally, his travel times weren't increasing or decreasing over time: there was no trend.

In words rather than numbers, Klaus's journey to work was an event that happened very often and the time it took didn't fluctuate greatly from the average. Although the exact number of minutes remained uncertain when he set off each morning, Klaus could be confident that he would arrive before 9.00 am. In all the years he'd lived in New York, he'd only ever been late twice – and that was because of exceptionally heavy snow falls. What's more, the factors affecting his travel time were many, various, and – most of the time – independent of each other: a mechanical problem here, a crowd of Japanese tourists there, and maybe an icy patch on the not-so-sunny side of the platform. Being a meticulous kind of guy, Klaus had recorded all his travel times for the last three years and two months in an Excel spreadsheet reproduced in figure 16 with a symmetric bell-shaped curve behind it. This shows, for example, that on eighty-seven days it took him forty-three minutes while on just one day it took him thirty-four minutes and on one other day fifty-two minutes (see figure 16).

Of course, subway uncertainty applies to lots of events that have nothing to do with subways. An obvious example is the game we played in chapter 8 of flipping a coin 100 times. We can forecast the fluctuations, or uncertainty, in our expected gains or losses fairly accurately. Thanks to opinion polls, we're also pretty good at knowing who's going to win an election the day before it happens, or even more accurately on the day itself – using exit polls. And, as we saw in the previous chapter, if statistical reasoning is allowed to prevail over emotions, sales data – provided we have enough – allow companies to make reasonable projections into the future and measure the associated uncertainty. Incidentally, amongst the most expert of all forecasters are suppliers of electricity. If the average usage on July days between 11.00 am and 3.00 pm, at a temperature of 32 degrees centi-

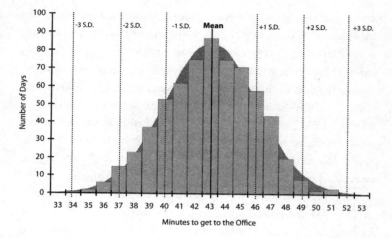

**Figure 16** Klaus's journey to work

grade, is 12,000 MW, it's highly unlikely that it will be more than 14,000 MW on such a day in the future. Electricity companies have the art of prediction down to a T – and quite literally in England, where supply is always boosted for the half-time break in national soccer games. That's when an entire country gets off the sofa and puts the kettle on for a nice, refreshing brew of their favorite beverage.

*Coconut uncertainty* is quite different from subway uncertainty. A "coconut" is the occurrence of a totally unexpected event that has important consequences. It may be something that happens so rarely that it's impossible to keep an Excel spreadsheet full of statistics. Or it may be something common enough for us to know the likelihood of such an event taking place . . . but with no idea of *when* or *where*. The classic example from the natural world is that of large earthquakes. It's well known that earthquakes tend to occur in parts of the world where there is friction between tectonic plates in the Earth's crust. In fact, in these regions (such as parts of California) small tremors are a way of life.[3] However, from time to time, there are major earthquakes that wreak death and destruction, as in San Francisco in 1906 or Chile in 1960. Today, unfortunately, science cannot tell us when or where in the tremor-prone regions of the world the next big quake will take place or how many people it will kill.[4]

Having said all that, scientists have uncovered a remarkable statistical correlation between the size of earthquakes and the frequency of their occurrence. There is, of course, a great deal of data about earthquakes and their sizes, as measured on the Richter scale. And it doesn't take a great deal of analysis to find that, as size increases, frequency decreases in a very consistent manner.

In geological terms, in any given year, there are, on average, roughly 134 earthquakes worldwide measuring 6.0 to 6.9 on the Richter scale, around 17 with a value of 7.0 to 7.9 . . . and one at 8 or above.[5] In other words, scientists are pretty sure that there'll be, on average, one huge earthquake in the world every year. The trouble is, they're completely in the dark as to when or where it will take place and whether it will occur in a populated region. The underlying reason is that the Earth's crust is in a so-called "critical state." This means that conditions are ripe for earthquakes across the globe's tremor-prone zones, but big ones only occur when there's a chain reaction of smaller events that multiply into a major natural disaster – a bit like the butterfly effect we saw in chapter 8. We can also apply this model to our lives – each of which can be considered to be in a critical state. That is, a totally unpredictable small event (such as a tropical breeze) can initiate another everyday occurrence (the falling of a coconut), which interacts with a further trivial incident (someone standing under the tree) to produce a fatal accident.

In statistical terms, there are big differences between Klaus's commuting times and the occurrence of earthquakes. The distribution of the various sizes of earthquakes isn't nicely centered around the average value with just as many big and small ones on each side (as in Klaus's commuting graph). Instead, the most frequently occurring size of earthquake is very small, and the larger the earthquake, the less likely it is to occur. On top of that, the occurrence of a destructively huge earthquake in any given tremor-prone region this year is clearly possible, while the likelihood of an extreme commuting event – such as Klaus being two hours later for work – isn't quite zero, but is astronomically small. When it comes to earthquakes, all we can really do is to wait until the coconut – or more accurately, the roof – falls on our heads. If we're lucky enough to live on a wealthy fault line, we don't have much reason to worry. Engineers will have developed building techniques to save us . . . but there's nothing they can do to stop the quake itself.

Klaus – to his eternal credit – demonstrated that he understood the difference between the two types of uncertainty. His meticulous research and planning showed that he knew how to take advantage of the regularities of subway uncertainty. And by taking out insurance to cover unforeseen disasters far from home, he also proved that he'd considered the possibility of "coconuts." That he was killed by one shouldn't diminish our respect for him. It's simply not possible to avoid coconut uncertainty in our daily lives but, as Klaus showed, it is possible to minimize their negative consequences through planning.

Coconuts, of course, come in many different shapes, sizes and textures. They can be big, red double-decker buses going too fast through the middle of London or small explosive devices on transatlantic flights. They can be as wet as a tsunami, dry as a sandstorm, hot as a volcano, or cold as an avalanche. In this book, we have emphasized coconuts with negative consequences. However, sometimes coconuts can make you jump for joy: winning the jackpot in the Spanish lottery, finding buried treasure in your back yard, getting a hole in one, or even backing a big winner on the stock market.

Although it doesn't grow on trees, money is one of the most common forms of coconut. In many ways our economy too is in a critical state. We know, for example, that in any given year, there will be many business failures. While most of these will be small firms, we can be pretty sure that there'll also be big, hairy, audacious bankruptcies on the scale of Lehman Brothers, WorldCom, Enron, or LTCM. Every so often there will be major after-shocks that ripple throughout the global financial markets. And, once in a blue moon, there'll be a Black Monday or Tuesday. We don't know when, of course, but we do know that these extreme fluctuations happen rather more often than they theoretically should – especially if we believe the models of subway uncertainty provided by conventional statistical theory. Roughly speaking, the market behaves rationally 95% of the time, under the influence of the wisdom of crowds ... but 5% of the time the crowd goes crazy. As Alan Greenspan, former Federal Reserve Chairman suggests, in his memoirs *The Age of Turbulence*, the problem is not simply that collective human nature creates and bursts bubbles. It's also that our collective memory wipes out the past. He writes: "There's a long history of forgetting bubbles. But once that memory is gone, there appears to be an aspect of human nature to get cumulative exuberance."[6] Ultimately, it's mass hysteria and collective loss of memory that transform markets from subways into coconuts.

Before braving a more complex statistical explanation of the difference between subway and coconut uncertainty, let's take a short detour into statistical history.

## A BRIEF HISTORY OF STATISTICS

As we saw in chapter 8, the human race was a late developer as far as probability and statistics are concerned. The first formal attempts to apply probabilistic reasoning to gambling date from the seventeenth century, and the use of statistics to describe characteristics of human populations only really evolved in the nineteenth century. Curiously, even though public lotteries, annuities (payments of an annual sum of money until a person's death), and insurance policies were common in the eighteenth and nineteenth centuries, it's clear that many professionals in these fields really didn't understand basic statistical concepts. The purchase price of annuities, for example, often didn't vary according to the age of the purchaser.[7] But in the twentieth century, we made significant progress. In particular, we invented computers – which made it a lot easier to use statistical models in decision making.

Even before computers, human beings made some intellectual breakthroughs of their own. Around 300 years after French mathematicians Pascal and Fermat made the first formal analysis of gambling (see chapter 8), the American economist Harry Markowitz published a ground-breaking paper on investments in the *Journal of Finance*.[8] His innovation was to introduce the concept of risk, as well as returns, into portfolio selection. He suggested that if you're unwilling to accept a larger risk, then you should also be prepared to accept lower returns. He also recommended minimizing risk by building a portfolio of securities whose returns do not co-vary (that is, don't move up and down together). It's the same as the traditional, common-sense concept of not putting all of your eggs in the same basket.

But Markowitz went one step further. He suggested using a statistical tool to measure risk. This was the "standard deviation," a term coined toward the end of the nineteenth century, but a concept that had been around for over 200 years. We won't go into how to calculate it here, but just say that it's a statistical measure that tells you how closely the various values of a dataset (for example the times it took Klaus to get to his office, or the daily prices of a given company's stock over a year) are dispersed around their average or mean. Markowitz was thus equating future risk with past dispersion or volatility, as measured by the standard deviation.

Of course, whether people use formal probabilistic models or not, uncertainty never goes away. Neither do risk or opportunities. Yet Markowitz's work started an investment revolution. It gave investors a way of quantifying risk (and opportunity) and of tackling uncertainty head-on instead of ignoring the issue. This was an incredible achievement. But was the great economist's analysis complete? The short answer is "no."

## MORE ON THE TWO TYPES OF UNCERTAINTY

The spate of statistical modeling unleashed by Markowitz's paper on the financial markets wasn't fully accurate. The experts started treating the financial markets as if the fluctuations were like the time taken by Klaus to get to work each day. But unlike Klaus's commuting times, the values of, say, the DJIA (the Dow Jones Industrial Average) aren't closely clustered around their average. There are many more big fluctuations than most people – even experts – expect. And some of those people, like Pierre Dufour, can't take the emotional impact of the biggest fluctuations.

But the road from theory to practice is full of potholes. Nobody (except for Klaus, and he's both fictional and dead) is going to draw complex graphs or identify statistical models for everyday decision making. Instead we offer you a simple rule of thumb. We could warn you about all the emotional, cognitive, and technical biases which can prevent good decision making. But we'd prefer to focus on the positive for a bit. We'll suggest following a mechanical routine for handling uncertainty that can overcome these biases. As an analogy, imagine you're a top golfer about to make a winning putt, or a star tennis player about to serve for the Wimbledon title. The outcome is both crucial and uncertain. And too much thinking, feeling, or technical analysis can be fatal. The way real professionals deal with the situation is to have a well-defined routine and to follow it every time they putt or serve. The tennis player might bounce the ball precisely five times, while the golfer follows a strict ritual of movements. It's the automated nature of the routine that leads to consistency of execution. Amidst all the pressures, in the intense heat of the moment, it's still possible to make a winning shot. And the way you handle uncertainty can be the same.

As we mentioned before, subway uncertainty is something that we can quantify or model, whereas coconut uncertainty is extremely difficult if not impossible to quantify or model. Almost all uncertain situations include elements of both subway and coconut uncertainty. Yet another way to think about this – and borrowing from a quote by Donald Rumsfeld (a former US Secretary of Defense) – is to distinguish between *known knowns*, *known unknowns*, and *unknown unknowns*. For example, the return from an insured fixed deposit in a bank is a known known – we know exactly what we will receive in the future. The outcome of a coin toss is an example of a known unknown. We know that the outcome of the coin toss will be heads or tails, but we don't know which. Similarly, we know that there will be bubbles in financial markets in the future, but we don't know when or where. Then there are the unknown unknowns, unique and rare events that are completely unexpected and unimagined. These are the *Black Swans*, so eloquently characterized by Taleb in his book. These can only be identified after their occurrence, for if we could have anticipated them before, they wouldn't be Black Swans. Looking back at history, the internet was a Black Swan, as was the Great Depression of 1929–1933.

Once we accept that there are known knowns, known unknowns, and unknown unknowns, we can set about thinking about the underlying uncertainty in a more systematic manner. There is no uncertainty associated with known knowns, as we know exactly what will happen. In the case of known unknowns, we may be able to quantify and model the uncertainty for some events but not for all. Going back to our examples above, we can model the

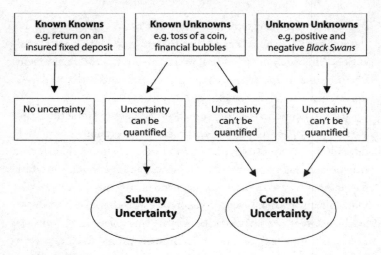

**Figure 17** Subway and coconut uncertainty

uncertainty of a coin toss, but it is impossible to quantify or model the uncertainty concerning future bubbles in the financial markets even though we can clearly expect these to occur. (A senior member of the Chinese government once aptly remarked that a financial market is like champagne – if it did not have bubbles, no one would be willing to drink it!) What this means is that some of the known unknowns involve subway uncertainty (like the coin toss) while others are part of coconut uncertainty (like bubbles in the financial markets). The unknown unknowns are necessarily part of coconut uncertainty. These distinctions are summarized in figure 17.

## THE THREE As OF HANDLING UNCERTAINTY

Our suggested routine for assessing uncertainty has three steps – all beginning with the letter A. It's the triple A approach that we mentioned briefly in chapter 1:

1.  Accept that you are operating in an uncertain world.
2.  Assess the level of uncertainty you are facing using all available inputs, models, and data, even if you're dealing with an event that seems regular as clockwork.
3.  Augment the range of uncertainty just estimated.

Here's the routine again, in a bit more detail.

## 1. Accept

Psychologically, we must first accept that uncertainty always exists, whether we like it or not. Ignoring it is not an option. This also means accepting that accurate forecasting is not an option either. Illusory forecasting practices, the extreme example being horoscopes, may be entertaining, but they're not useful. Believing that experts – from doctors and fund managers to management gurus and fairground clairvoyants – can predict the future may bring comfort in a confusing world. But, as we've illustrated many times in this book, our inability to predict the future accurately extends to practically all fields of social science. It's important to accept, once and for all, that uncertainty cannot be eliminated – even if your forecasts are reasonably accurate and your planning meticulous (think of Klaus). We have no control over a wide range of future events from earthquakes to Black Mondays or Tuesdays.

The key to handling uncertainty is finding ways to picture the range of possible outcomes. Whether your interest is in sales data, stock prices, the weather, earthquakes, or simply getting to work every day, you can't hope to be realistic about assessing the chances of anything happening, unless you at first identify all the things that could possibly go right or wrong. Once you've accepted all the possibilities, you're ready to move on to the next step.

## 2. Assess

The world of finance before and after 1952 is a good example of the importance of accepting uncertainty – and then moving on by trying to assess it. As we pointed out in chapters 4 and 5, the majority of financial professionals now realize that accurate forecasting of the markets is impossible. However, this doesn't stop them giving advice to their clients about achieving the maximum returns for a given level of risk. In some cases, they may even do so for a minimum cost, for example, by recommending index funds or similar vehicles. At the same time other professionals specialize in creating investments with different levels of risk by, for instance, diversifying between bonds and stocks of various degrees of volatility. Today there are many financial products, aimed at all sorts of investors, covering all types of needs and risk profiles: from venture capital to treasury bills and certificates of deposit. This just didn't happen before 1952, when no one explicitly considered risk.

Skeptics might argue that there's no point in attempting to control risk if your decisions about the future are based on a model that doesn't incorporate the considerable number of big fluctuations that occurred in the past. This is a valid criticism. Fortunately – for once in this book – there is a straightforward solution.

First, we suggest that you use the available models to calculate the kinds of outcomes that would be expected with subway uncertainty. Collect all the data you can to figure out as accurately as possible what mean and standard deviation best describes your data. Often people think that what they are predicting is unique, for example, the performance of a newly issued stock over the next six months, or the sales of a novel by an unknown author. Our advice in such cases is to *ignore uniqueness*. Instead, look at the track record of new issues and the sales of first-time authors *in general*. You probably have no valid reason to believe that the uncertainty surrounding your new issue or author differs from that of the wider population of new issues and authors to which they belong. What's the statistical history of the general population? Having answered this question, you're ready for the next stage.

### 3. Augment

Whatever your assessment in the previous stage, you can be sure you've just underestimated the true level of uncertainty in your situation. We'd like to suggest two ways of augmenting your previous assessment to realistic levels.

In the last chapter we demonstrated that, although people have great difficulty in predicting the future, they have little difficulty in explaining the past. So our first proposal is to exploit this hindsight bias through what we call "future-perfect thinking." To explain what we mean, here's an example. Imagine you are fifty years old and are planning investments to ensure your financial future. In particular, you want to estimate how much you'll have in the way of savings when you reach the age of sixty-five.

Now imagine that you actually *are* sixty-five – that is, we've just fast-forwarded fifteen years into the future. How big is your nest egg now? Unfortunately, it turns out that because of the great Black Friday crash of 2021, your savings – which were mainly invested in US equities – are quite small. How did this state of affairs come to pass? Over to your imagination to find a realistic-sounding story about what "happened." And most people – with the benefit of "hindsight" – really do come up with a convincing explanation. It's just a lot easier than looking forward.

Now take a different tack. Imagine once again that you are sixty-five, but this time your savings are three times greater than the amount forecast fifteen years ago when you were fifty. Time to build that swimming pool and buy the yacht! But how "did" this happen?

Once again over to you to tell the story. Chances are, it's going to make this outcome sound a whole lot more likely than it originally seemed.

If you do this kind of exercise a few times you'll start to develop a feeling for different futures and the fact that they are all plausible. Some of these futures will involve coconuts of different kinds and, though there's no formal technique for converting plausibility into probability, you can use the insights you gain to develop appropriate risk-protection strategies. This is the essence of future-perfect thinking. It involves using the fluency of hindsight to develop clearer pictures of the future. It's a way not only to augment your assessment of a coconut occurring but also to devise a plan for coping with it in advance.

The second strategy we suggest is less imaginative and a lot easier for the literal-minded to apply. Let's illustrate with an example again. As you're probably well aware by now, a common problem in assessing risk is the lack of data. Consider, for example, having to predict the sales of a brand new product. Just how low or high could the number of units sold be in the first year? One way of answering this question is to ask those involved – the product managers, technical staff, and sales team – to estimate a range of upper and lower values that would include 95% of all possible outcomes. And once they've come up with a range, double it!

The reasoning behind this rule of thumb is simple. Extensive empirical evidence shows that the range of such forecasts is typically too narrow. People underestimate uncertainty, perhaps because their powers of imagination are too small or because they don't know how to use future-perfect thinking. The trick is to use (but not believe) the numbers you're given and magnify them considerably. Doubling the range will provide a much more accurate estimate of uncertainty.

The same approach can be used when there's some, but not much, past data available. Here you can use the difference between the largest and smallest observations in the past as an initial estimate of the range . . . but then double this too. Why does this help? The main reason is that, to estimate a range accurately, you need to observe values at the two extremes. However, by definition, extreme values occur only rarely and so in small samples you're unlikely to observe them. Doubling what you've observed in a limited number of past occurrences is a crude but more realistic way of estimating the 95% range.

If, on the other hand, you've got a lot of data at hand, you may not need to double the range. Instead you can multiply it by a value ranging from, let's say, 1.5 to 2. The more data available, the closer you can go to 1.5. These values may sound arbitrary, but we assure you they're based on empirical observations. If you like, you can experiment yourself by keeping track of your estimates and then calculating the percentage of time that actual values are within your estimated ranges. It's a shame that so few professional forecasters follow this procedure. It might make them more realistic about their own abilities.

Finally, it's important to realize that the magnitude of uncertainty increases the longer we forecast into the future. Of course, this depends what your unit of future measurement is. If you're thinking in terms of sales it could be one year or just one quarter. If it's your pension you might be thinking in terms of decades.

## PROTECT YOURSELF IN A WILD WORLD

Once you've reached a realistic estimate of uncertainty, how do you go about managing the risk? If stock market investments are involved, for instance, you have to consider the possibility that your stock may fall by as much as 40% in a few days. Here the questions center on whether you'd have enough time on your side and cash in the bank, in case part of your investments are on borrowed money, to ride out the storm or whether you'd need to sell at a loss and move on. If the latter, would you still have enough money to live adequately? Have you thought through the costs and benefits of diversification – both by types of investments and geographically? What reserve funds can you create that might withstand financial earthquakes like Black Monday and Tuesday? Are there different types of insurance that you could investigate? Similarly, when developing new products, a CEO must consider whether the company can survive a complete product failure.

In the final analysis, we can't take actions to mitigate all the uncertainties we face. If a large meteorite hits the earth and causes a new ice age, there's nothing we can do – especially as most of us are preparing for the onslaught of global warming. Yet we must continue to live with the possibilities of both types of coconut. On the other hand, we should always pay attention to what we *can* do. There was nothing that Klaus could have done to avoid dying from the fallen coconut, but there was no reasonable justification for Pierre Dufour to commit suicide. In the long run, as he should have known, markets recover and continue their long-term growth. It would only have been a matter of time before he recovered his losses and saw his personal Fortune grow again. Perhaps that's what wisdom really is: knowing what our actions do and do not affect.

As so often in life, it's a writer who sums the situation up. The following quote from G.K. Chesterton explains how both subway and coconut uncertainties interact in affecting our experience of the world:

> The real trouble with this world of ours is not that it is an unreasonable world, nor even that it is a reasonable one. The commonest kind of trouble is that it is nearly reasonable, but not quite. Life is not an illogicality; yet it is a trap for logicians. It looks just a little more

mathematical and regular than it is; its exactitude is obvious, but its inexactitude is hidden; its wildness lies in wait.[9]

The quote encapsulates this chapter better than any summary we can produce, but here goes... It's tempting to see nice patterns in the past and fit them to the future. But even when we can trace the patterns, there are no guarantees for the future. All we can do is accept the uncertainty, make a reasonable assessment of our chances, and then augment that assessment, in recognition that life is rarely that simple. But enough summarizing. The wildness of the next chapter lies in wait.

# Eleven

# GENIUS OR FALLIBLE?

*It's a funny thing, the more I practice the luckier I get.*

Arnold Palmer, golfer

So far, we've been on a whirlwind journey through the worlds of health, wealth, and business – and seen the paradox of control at work wherever we go. We've also delved into the murky depths of psychology and statistics, learning how to accept, assess, and augment uncertainty along the way. But the story is far from over. And, arguably, the plot has thickened yet further. Once you've augmented the uncertainty you face, it becomes harder than ever to make a decision. In order to help you in deciding, this and the next chapter will take one final excursion into the intricate complexities of the human mind. Is it one of nature's great masterpieces or a hopeless biological lost cause?

In particular, one important topic we deal with is how to allocate our time. If – as we have maintained throughout the book – chance is so pervasive in our lives, it's tempting to conclude that there's little we can do to improve our personal Fortunes. Nothing could be further from the truth – and we hope to prove it. Practice and feedback are extremely beneficial in the acquisition of skills that influence the outcomes of our decisions. Chance, of course, is still important. But as the nineteenth-century French scientist Louis Pasteur put it a hundred years or so before Arnold Palmer coined his much-quoted witticism about practice, "Chance favors the prepared mind."

## IN TWO MINDS

Some people are undisputed geniuses. Take, for example, William Shakespeare, or two of our own personal heroes from the modern day, psychologists Daniel Kahneman and Amos Tversky. But these intellectual giants themselves offer us contrasting perspectives on the human mind.

> What a piece of work is man! How noble in reason, how infinite in faculties, in form and moving how express and admirable, in action how like an angel, in apprehension how like a god!
>
> Shakespeare[1]

> Errors of judgment are often systematic rather than random, manifesting bias rather than confusion. Thus, man suffers from mental astigmatism as well as from myopia, and any corrective prescription should fit this diagnosis.
>
> Kahneman and Tversky[2]

The rosier-tinted Shakespearean view is well documented: men on the moon, super jumbo airplanes, organ transplants, and the like. But so is the bleaker outlook. We all know from our own experience and (if we're so inclined) the extensive literature in cognitive psychology that people routinely make errors of judgment – sometimes really bad ones. Just read today's newspaper if you're in any doubt! And we've already seen together, in chapter 9, how simple, statistical models often make more accurate predictions than human beings. So the big question is: when – or under what conditions – do human beings make accurate judgments? In other words, when should you trust someone's judgment, including your own?

## BLINKING MARVELOUS

In his best-selling book *Blink*, Malcolm Gladwell tells the story of a Kouros (an ancient Greek statue of a male youth). The Kouros in question was acquired by the Getty Museum in California for some $10 million after an exhaustive fourteen-month investigation. But doubts about its authenticity lingered. After a single glance – or blink – at the statue, lasting only a few seconds, some experts in Greek art had an immediate sense of "intuitive repulsion." It just had to be a fake. In a few seconds, says Gladwell, "They were able to understand more about the essence of the statue than the team at the Getty was able to understand after fourteen months."[3]

"Blinking" isn't confined to artistic judgments either. During an exhibition tour in 1909, Capablanca, the Cuban world chess champion, played twenty-eight matches simultaneously and won them all. How did he do it? How many moves ahead did he consider when he only had a few seconds to look at each game? "I see only one move ahead," Capablanca is reported to have said, "but it is always the correct one."

As a well-structured but complex game, chess has provided a wonderful laboratory for studying the capacities of the human mind. It is to the cognitive sciences what the fruit fly is to geneticists. Initially, everyone thought that the amazing intellectual feats of chess grandmasters were due to three factors: photographic memory; high IQ; and an ability to analyze the implications of many different possibilities several moves ahead. However, scientific research has rejected these ideas – and come up with three totally different factors!

The first key requirement for a grandmaster is to focus *intuitively* on the best move. Researchers have placed cameras under chessboards to record the eye movements of great chess players. They've discovered that, once the opponent's turn is over, three out of four times a grandmaster's eyes focus on the best move available (as agreed by other grandmasters). Next, he or she examines other possible moves – often of equal quality – only to return (three out of four times) to the first move considered. Thus, grandmasters demonstrate two important abilities. One is to come up with high-quality (and often creative) moves spontaneously; the other is the analytical skill to check this move against other possibilities. It sounds as if Capablanca wasn't overstating his case after all. Genius blinks – it's official.

The second differentiating factor is pattern recognition – another blinking ability. When grandmasters are shown, for only five seconds, chess pieces on a board from an ongoing game between other grandmasters, they can reproduce what they have seen with approximately 90% accuracy. The few mistakes they do make are usually in the minor pieces, mostly involving pawns. Expert players, on the other hand, can't recall more than a few details, while novices are incapable of remembering any positions accurately. Just as importantly, no one, including grandmasters, can remember the positions on a board where the pieces have been placed by chance – that is, when they're not the result of a real game. The memories of grandmasters are highly dependent on recognizing patterns – not unlike most people's abilities to recognize a familiar tune after hearing the first few notes.

Third and perhaps most importantly, there's the "practice factor." Scientists have found that it takes years of practice to reach the level of the chess grandmaster. Not just any old practice though. Aspiring grandmasters must deliberately target continuous improvement, which means a lot of repetition, and seek constant feedback. Consistent hard work is also crucial. Great achievers – in chess as in many other fields – have been found to practice, on average, roughly the same number of hours every day, including weekends and holidays. Finally, research indicates that the more they practice in this way, the better their performance. Continuous, painstaking practice facilitates "deeper" or better information processing and helps retain, as well as develop, skills. Curiously, it seems that, to become good at blinking, there's a lot of painful thinking along the way.

Contrary to popular belief, then, it looks as if talent owes more to hard work than natural gifts.[4] Genius, in chess and elsewhere, comes from long, deliberate, thoughtful practice. Herbert Simon, whose wisdom we've drawn on several times already in this book, estimated that, through years of intensive practice, the typical grandmaster develops a long-term working memory amounting to roughly 50,000 to 100,000 "nuggets" of chess information. Because grandmasters can retrieve this information effortlessly, they're free to concentrate on evaluating the most promising moves that come spontaneously to mind. In contrast, weaker players generate and examine many alternatives without being able to focus on the essential. They lack the 50,000 to 100,000 chunks of chess information stored in the brains of grandmasters.

So it turns out that the critical skill of playing chess is not analytical. Instead, it's the capacity to focus, instantly and effortlessly, on the best move (or moves), a capacity that's developed through long, deliberate practice. The role of analysis, although indispensable, is secondary: first as part of the practicing, then to verify or reject alternative moves during the game.

The cognitive skills demonstrated by chess grandmasters stand in stark contrast with the poor judgmental abilities we've documented so far – among experts as diverse as doctors, fund managers, and management gurus. If this book were a chess match, Shakespeare would be drawing level with Kahneman and Tversky by now. Unfortunately, however, in the rest of this chapter we'll see how the human mind is both genius and fallible. Then we'll look at some of the evidence on "blinking" and contrast it with "thinking," defined as the process of reasoning our way to a decision. Finally, we'll further investigate the related issues of practice and feedback. We can't turn you into a chess grandmaster, but we may be able to help you harness the power of deliberate practice and reliable feedback.

## THE CURIOUS INCIDENCE OF AUTISTIC SAVANTS

Autistic savants (known in less politically correct times as "idiot savants") are as interesting a group as chess grandmasters. They are intellectually brilliant in some areas and completely challenged in others. Some are polyglots – they speak many languages fluently. Others can perform complex arithmetical calculations in record time. They may be able not only to tell you what the day of the week was on, say, April 23, 1981, but also to describe what the weather was like that morning. Others can estimate exact distances, measure time without a clock, memorize $\pi$ (pi) to hundreds of decimal places, or recall long sequences of football scores – even after minimal exposure. Contrary to popular mythology, there are also savants with incredible artistic and musical gifts. At the same time, many polyglots can't calculate the sum of two plus three, while the arithmetically talented savants may not be able to read or write. In general, savants are both super-gifted and super-hopeless. They're both genius and fallible in the extreme. Most cannot lead normal lives because of their autism or some other learning difficulty. Above all, they lack what the rest of us call "common sense."

It seems that some parts of the brains of savants are highly developed, while others are underdeveloped – hence their unique abilities combined with total helplessness. Perhaps it's the closest the human mind gets to a computer. Your PC performs mechanical calculations with lightning speed but it hasn't yet been programmed to exercise common sense. When computers beat grandmasters at chess, it's by brute force of mathematical computation and clever algorithms designed by humans. There's none of the creativity that we observe in human beings at the top of the game – and certainly no blinking.

So much for grandmasters and autistic savants – what about the rest of the human race? The human brain evolved to allow us to cope with a variety of tasks that require very different abilities. We have to learn at least one language, acquire common sense, and master social skills. Eventually, most of us specialize in our studies or learn the tools of a trade. Our minds are flexible. We can learn to do what may have initially seemed impossible. Think about skiing down a steep mountain, windsurfing in a force-eight gale, climbing the highest mountains, gliding high in the sky, and diving deep under the sea. The same is true of the mental processes involved in achieving break-through inventions, or coming up with highly creative ideas. This is all in addition to the activities we perform each day, the myriads of problems we solve continuously and effortlessly, and the great number of good decisions we habitually make. Humans are capable of meeting many challenges, as Shakespeare so eloquently celebrated.

Although our brain is an intricate and complex tool, the world in which we function is even more complicated. Trade-offs and mistakes are inevitable. And, given the complexity we face, our minds must frequently use mental shortcuts to take decisions, often in a split second, and using only limited information. It's inevitable that some of these decisions will be bad ones, but without them, we'd be unable to function. At the same time, as argued by the German psychologist Gerd Gigerenzer and his colleagues, shortcuts may also lead to good decisions.[5] We'll return to this issue later in the chapter.

Paradoxically, if we could evaluate all information in a super-rational way, the subsequent lack of "noise" would probably diminish opportunities for original and novel problem solving. We're not just talking about creativity in art or poetry, which often relies on irrational mechanisms, such as cubism or metaphor, but about genuine breakthroughs in science, engineering, or business. Had we always functioned rationally as a species, it's possible that today we would have no cars, personal computers, the internet, or search engines – just to mention a few – because conventional wisdom once maintained that there was no need for them. As the playwright George Bernard Shaw put it:

> The reasonable man adapts himself to the world; the unreasonable man persists in trying to adapt the world to himself. Therefore all progress depends on the unreasonable man.[6]

The challenge is to accept that, together with the genius of our minds, imperfections are also part of the human package. Once we've accepted our mental shortcomings, we must find ways to avoid or minimize their undesirable consequences. Oddly enough, it's a contemporary of Shakespeare, Francis Bacon, who best sums up our position: "while we falsely extol and admire the powers of the human mind we neglect to seek for its true helps."[7]

In what follows, we're going to distinguish between "blinking" (as coined by Malcolm Gladwell) and "thinking" (our own refinement of the everyday concept) as ways of making decisions. In blinking, we are unaware of – or *cannot* articulate – the way in which we reach decisions instantaneously. In thinking, although we may not be aware of every factor influencing us, we largely understand – or *can* articulate – our decisions.

## I BLINK THEREFORE I AM?

A tennis player in the Wimbledon final returns the serve of his opponent traveling at 130 miles an hour. His decision to stretch as far as possible and place his racket at just the right place and time to meet the ball is remarkable. This is one decision that's certainly not made by thinking through all alternative possibilities, collecting all available information, and then evaluating all the alternatives to make a choice. On the contrary, the decision is taken in a blink – subconsciously and without any analysis. For much of this book, we've been insisting on the role of luck in our lives. But the return of the Wimbledon finalist is no lucky shot. The ability to make this decision on Centre Court is honed by many years of deliberate practice, which provided objective feedback on how to return extraordinarily fast serves. Like chess grandmasters, professional tennis players apply the rule of continuous, effortful, and punishing practice. That's how they acquire the abilities necessary to return serves traveling at incredible speeds even at full stretch.

Our mind performs many blinking decisions superbly well. Consider the ability to recognize faces, even of people you don't know well and haven't seen for years – for example, an old college classmate who has mysteriously acquired wrinkles, gray hair, and a large belly. The same type of blinking occurs when you realize that the voice on the telephone belongs to Margaret, your old friend who you haven't talked to since last Christmas. Recognizing a face or voice means processing a lot of information stored deep in our minds. Somehow, the image we see or the sounds we hear must be compared with thousands of others, accumulated in our mind over a long period, in order to come up with the right answer. But this is done in nanoseconds, effortlessly and efficiently, without any conscious thinking on our part. Even today's speediest supercomputers don't come close.

Now think about the decision to make an emergency stop that halts your car a couple of feet away from a pedestrian who crossed the street against a red light. When re-playing the scene in your mind, you're amazed that you were lucky enough to avoid hitting somebody who appeared before you so unexpectedly. But again, this was skill, not luck. It was another of the many blinking decisions you take, without fully realizing what you are doing. These types of decisions happen daily and – precisely because you don't have to think about them – make life a lot easier. Yet we mustn't forget that they require high levels of cognitive skills, substantial decision-making abilities, and awe-inspiring coordination between the thinking part of our brain and that controlling our muscles.

If you wanted any further proof of your amazing blinking abilities, take what you're doing right now: the simple task of reading this page. First you recognize single letters and the shapes of whole words. Then you make sense of each sentence. And all the time you're deciding, among other things, if you like what you read as a whole or if parts of it are worth remembering for later. You're probably also judging the originality and usefulness of this book in relation to others you've already finished. These are not trivial intellectual achievements, and yet you accomplish them with ease – like a walk in the proverbial park.

There is no doubt that Shakespeare was right. Our mind is a superb instrument, capable of storing vast amounts of information that it can retrieve at will, exactly when needed, to make the perfect (blinking) decision.

On the other hand – and as we've seen over and over again – some of our decisions, both trivial and important, are terribly irrational.[8] Remember, from chapter 2, the case of Ben Kolb, the seven-year-old boy, who died in a routine ear operation at the Florida Martin Memorial Hospital. Then there was the single mother who was wrongly diagnosed with AIDS after being screened for HIV in the mid-1990s. These tragedies were the result of faulty decisions, taken by otherwise intelligent people. They're not isolated events either. As discussed in chapter 3, medical errors are the third leading cause of death in the USA. Many of our decisions are just plain wrong, and some have catastrophic consequences.

In one of his books, Gerd Gigerenzer cites the following example given by a physician speaking at a conference:

Physicians in Essen, Germany, amputated one or both breasts of some 300 women, despite most of them not having cancer. When this was proven, one physician set fire to his records and then himself. [9]

Were these doctors blinking or thinking? Why did they fail their patients so miserably? Finally, who can guarantee that future decisions in your own life, both medical and non-medical, won't be equally disastrous?

## THE TWO ROGERS

To illustrate the key to good blinking more clearly, meet the two Rogers. Roger F is a well-known tennis player. He is also rather good (in 2007 he won Wimbledon for the fifth time in a row). Roger G is an emergency-room physician who works at a large hospital in metropolitan Chicago. Contrast the quality of the feedback the two Rogers receive in the course of their work. Every time Roger F hits a tennis ball, plays a point, a game, or a match, he gets virtually perfect feedback. He has also hit a tennis ball many, many thousands of times.

Roger G works in a very different environment. His job is to decide – very rapidly – what priority to give to each patient who arrives in the emergency room. He sees people of all ages and walks of life with conditions from minor cuts to heart attacks or gunshot wounds. To complicate matters further, there are even a few patients with mysterious complaints that could be imaginary. Roger G is doing a good job if he sets his priorities such that every patient gets treated by the right doctor in time. Once he has handed over to a particular physician, it's on to the next patient with barely a moment to breathe. These emergency rooms are really busy. And the problem is this: Roger G never learns what finally happens to the patients he passes on. He hears that some get treatment in other parts of the hospital, some move to other hospitals, some go home, and others . . .

well, he just doesn't know. The only feedback he ever gets is if a receiving physician complains.

The main similarity between the two men is that they're both required to blink for a living. And the main difference isn't just one of lifestyle or earning power. Roger F lives in a world with plenty of good feedback. Roger G doesn't. Although they live and work worlds apart, it's obvious which Roger is likely to make more accurate judgments. Hint: it's not the one who has to make life-or-death decisions!

Most of us have jobs that aren't just about blinking. There's no doubt that doing business, for example, demands decisions based on thinking, but many commercial judgments have a blinking element too. Even though there's usually time for some analysis, information is often incomplete and comes with intense pressure to move fast. So recently, one of the authors did a study to assess the quality of feedback business managers receive about their daily activities. A group recruited from classes for executives agreed to complete short questionnaires when prompted by text messages on their cell phones at various unpredictable times across several days. Briefly, they were asked to describe the last decision they had taken and how they would know if they had been correct. The result: executives get little feedback and often have no idea whether the feedback they do get is accurate.[10]

There's little doubt that evolution – and our tacit learning processes – have equipped us well for performing tasks where we get both pertinent information for making decisions and regular, accurate feedback. Whereas these conditions characterize many of the physical environments we encounter in the course of our lives (like navigating through a crowded street), they're typically absent from tasks we face in the socio-economic domain (like running a company). Here, the world does not present us with the relevant information, unless we specify it, and the link between action and feedback can be missing or distorted. So it's hardly surprising that our decisions – based on imperfect information and faulty feedback – are led astray by emotional forces, such as greed, fear, and hope. At the same time, it's only natural that we should want to feel in control of our destiny. Just like when we're walking down a crowded street.

## PRACTICE, PRACTICE, THEN PRACTICE SOME MORE – FOR TEN WHOLE YEARS

Shareen, a seventeen-year-old from Lubbock, Texas, was thoroughly enjoying seeing the sights of New York for the first time, when she stopped an elderly gentleman to ask for directions. "What's the way to Carnegie Hall?" she asked. "Practice," came the response, "practice, practice, and practice!"

According to psychologist Anders Ericsson and other researchers, the process of practice extends over at least ten years. And it's not much fun either.

Individuals should attempt to maximize the amount of time they spend on deliberate practice to reach expert performance. However, maximization of deliberate practice is neither short-lived nor simple. It extends over a period of at least ten years and involves optimization within several constraints. First, deliberate practice requires available time and energy for the individual as well as access to teachers, training material, and training facilities (the resource constraint). Second, engagement in deliberate practice is not inherently motivating. Performers consider it instrumental in achieving further improvements in performance (the motivational constraint). The lack of inherent reward or enjoyment in practice as distinct from the enjoyment of the result (improvement) is consistent with the fact that individuals in a domain rarely initiate practice spontaneously. Finally, deliberate practice is an effortful activity that can be sustained only for a limited time each day during extended periods without leading to exhaustion (effort constraint).[11]

That's not all. Further research shows that it's not necessarily the smartest person who develops the most expertise and succeeds. High intelligence combined with the greatest motivation achieves more than the highest intelligence with average motivation. The implication is that it is possible to reach the expertise level of chess grandmasters, or the equivalent in other fields, as long as you are willing and able to practice, in a deliberate manner involving effective feedback, for at least ten years.

So becoming a chess grandmaster, concert pianist, or tennis champion sounds simple. Just practice for ten years! After all, experts are made, not born. As we've seen, the available scientific evidence suggests that success is not just due to natural talent or unique gifts – apart from a few basic requirements, such as above-average height for basketball players. So what's the problem: why doesn't anyone who wants to become a superstar? Unfortunately, things are not that simple.

To visualize the difficulties involved, imagine that – for ten whole years – you have to practice for five, six, or more hours every day, including weekends and holidays. And this is just the cost of entry. Moreover, it's not just any old practice. It must be *deliberate* practice, where the aim is to improve your performance continuously, to do a little better each time, and never to feel satisfied with your achievements. This requires an incredible amount of effort. The influential journalist Geoffrey Colvin, of *Fortune* magazine, has written at length about "What it takes to be great":

> Winston Churchill, one of the 20th century's greatest orators, practiced his speeches compulsively. Vladimir Horowitz supposedly said, 'If I don't practice for a day, I know it. If I don't practice for two days, my wife knows it. If I don't practice for three days, the world knows it.' [. . .] Many great athletes are legendary for the brutal discipline of their practice routines. In basketball, Michael Jordan

practiced intensely beyond the already punishing team practices. [. . .] In football, all-time-great receiver Jerry Rice – passed up by 15 teams because they considered him too slow – practiced so hard that other players would get sick trying to keep up. [. . .] Tiger Woods is a textbook example of what the research shows. Because his father introduced him to golf at an extremely early age – 18 months – and encouraged him to practice intensively, Woods had racked up at least 15 years of practice by the time he became the youngest-ever winner of the U.S. Amateur Championship, at age 18.[12]

If you're still aspiring to greatness after reading that extract, remember that the type of practice demonstrated by Churchill, Horowitz, Jordan, Rice, and Woods requires tremendous perseverance. Worse, it's monotonous and can become boring for everyone except the super-motivated.

So the good news is that real expertise is indeed available to all. The bad news is that you must be motivated and keep going despite serious obstacles and without immediate rewards. The even worse news is that nobody can tell you how to motivate yourself, or persevere in the face of tedious practice sessions. Researchers are totally unable to answer the question of why some people are motivated and others are unable (or just don't care) to practice in order to improve their performance.

On a brighter note, psychologists do know how to make deliberate practice work well. First, outstanding guidance from an accomplished teacher is essential. The value of good training can be seen from the number of top tennis players, famous musicians, or great artists who emerge from the same schools. The instructor should make the student familiar with existing knowledge in the field, teach the various methods available, and give a thorough demonstration of their advantages and drawbacks. Last but absolutely not least, the trainee should receive feedback, not only to improve performance but also to reach, as soon as possible, a level where he or she can start to give self-feedback. Only then can the long, thorough period of deliberate practice begin.

There is a great deal of evidence for the value of deliberate practice. For instance, world records in sports keep improving over time. If we take an event like the marathon, where technology has barely contributed to improving athletic performance, we see substantial progress. In the first modern Olympics held in Greece in 1896, the winner, Spyros Louis, ran the then 24.85-mile marathon in 2 hours 58 minutes and 50 seconds. If we rather generously assume that Louis could keep up the same average speed for today's 26.2-mile race, his time would be 3 hours 8 minutes and 33 seconds. At the time of writing, the world record for the official 26.2-mile marathon is over 33% better: 2 hours 4 minutes and 26 seconds. Shoes, diet, gradient, and climate notwithstanding, the biggest difference between Spyros Louis and Haile Gebrselassie, today's record holder, is the way they train. Thanks to more and better training, the same types of improvement have been reported in chess, music, and many other areas.

Deliberate practice sets objectives just beyond your existing level of competence. However, you only know that you've made it to that next level if you get relevant and, ideally, measurable feedback. In well-structured games like tennis or chess, that kind of feedback is plentiful. In other fields, as we glimpsed earlier, it starts to get more difficult. In music, for instance, feedback is subjective, but often validated by experts such as teachers or critics. By the time you reach business, politics, medicine, or economics – the world of the social sciences, where so many of life's decisions are made – getting good feedback is nigh on impossible.

Is the turnaround strategy of Dell, announced in the middle of 2007, working, for example? Clearly, bringing a company back to health may take several years. You can't give up at the first sign of difficulty. Nor, while you're waiting for concrete figures such as increased sales, profit, or share price, can you be sure the feedback you're getting is objective. INSEAD professor and leadership expert Manfred Kets de Vries likes to say that many top executives surround themselves with "liars," people who distort information to avoid being blamed for errors or to take credit for successes. This corruption of feedback occurs to a greater or lesser extent at all levels in the management hierarchy. No one likes to criticize the boss's decision and put their own promotion in jeopardy. The result is a vicious circle. The boss believes (erroneously) that he or she is right; the subordinate (untruthfully) reinforces the belief. And so it goes on.

Can we learn anything from those who have practiced their way to greatness? Is it possible to do the same in our own mundane worlds of business or the social sciences? Although far from the Olympic Stadium or Carnegie Hall, we believe there's a lot to be learned from the model of deliberate practice and, in particular, the emphasis it places on feedback. But to apply the model, you need the right culture. General Electric, for example, is known for demanding frequent, objective feedback from its executives, and many other companies are following their example. The other obvious lesson is that it's not enough just to collect feedback and file it away. It must be evaluated and used to change behavior if necessary.

One big challenge for executives is to resist the temptation to punish errors, and allow people to learn from their failures and thus improve their future performance. L'Oréal, the French cosmetics giant, is an interesting case in point. All their managers have the "right to make an error." But if they make the same mistake twice, it suggests an inability to learn – and their career is at risk.

But the biggest challenge of all is probably our old foe, the illusion of control (which we haven't seen for a little while). It can be a great impediment when we're evaluating feedback. As we saw in the story of the twins in chapter 8, most of us are guilty of attributing our success to our skills and failure to bad luck – or the fault of someone else. Many others are serial "deniers" who, despite the facts, are unwilling to accept the evidence, or incurable optimists, who always believe that success is just around the corner.

Finally, it is important to realize that expertise in one domain, say chess or entrepreneurship, does not necessarily transfer to other domains – even those that appear related. Just because someone is a great musician, it doesn't mean they can become a great actor overnight. Perhaps that's the downside of long, deliberate practice. The skills that it develops are only applicable within the specific field of training. To become an expert in another area, well, it takes another ten years – and all the motivational energy you can muster. Remember when basketball superstar Michael Jordan tried to become a top baseball player. He didn't make it.

## TIME TO DECIDE

So what should you do? We wish we could give you one of those simple recipes for success, so beloved of gurus and self-help books, but by now, you know our views on such matters. Most importantly, any such advice wouldn't be useful to you.

Having said that, there are two things that we *can* tell you. The first follows from the fact that that the road to greatness is extremely long and uncertain. Its surface is also potholed with many sacrifices. The demands of deliberate practice imply, for example, giving up many of the usual small pleasures of life. Psychologist Mihalyi Csikszentmihalyi[13] interviewed ninety-one famous people in an attempt to discover what made them "great." His conclusions were that they possessed "dialectic" personalities. In other words, a bit like the autistic savants we mentioned earlier, they are people of extremes. They are smart yet naive, extroverted yet introverted. Furthermore, Csikszentmihalyi reports that none of those he interviewed was popular during adolescence, or even more brilliant than their classmates in college. They concentrated on what interested them and focused on achieving their future objectives through their work. While their contemporaries pursued day-to-day pleasures, those destined for greatness plugged away at their practice.

Our first piece of advice therefore is as follows: carefully consider what we've just said and decide whether you have the courage, motivation, and personality to venture on to the long and arduous road that might lead to greatness. In addition, remember that, no matter how smart and motivated you are, there will always be others who are at least as intelligent and hard working as you. That is, for every great chess grandmaster, Olympic athlete, Nobel Prize winning scientist, or entrepreneur-turned-billionaire, there are probably several hundred who are equally good but don't achieve greatness. Each year there are only one or two Nobel Prize winners in each category, yet the selection committee considers many hundreds. The same is true for the Oscars and the Pulitzer Prize. Just behind the winners, there are many other hugely talented contenders, who we never hear about.

In other words, to return to our central theme, greatness is partly a game of luck. The attempt to reach the pinnacle of success is like participating in a lottery with very expensive tickets. As with any lottery, the probability of winning is very small, but the price of entry, in the form of ten long years of practice, is phenomenally high. To win a Nobel Prize or an Oscar – or equivalent – therefore requires the luck of the draw as well as intricately crafted skills acquired through at least ten years of deliberate practice.

For some perspective on this, let's go back to Nobel Prize winner Daniel Kahneman whom we cited at the beginning of this chapter. What was the source of his success? In his own words,

> Although I owe a great debt to my mother, and a great debt to my late collaborator and friend Amos Tversky, my debt to pure blind luck is surely the greatest of all.[14]

Now Kahneman is extremely intelligent and creative and has worked hard all his professional life. So was his statement just "false modesty"? No, to his credit, we believe Kahneman was being honest because we know from his work that he understands the illusion of control as well as the fact that many hard-working, creative, and intelligent scientists fail to win the Nobel Prize.

Our second piece of advice is more modest but pragmatic. Becoming great is extremely hard and, by definition, achieved by only a few. However, becoming better at what you do in any given domain is not. And gaining competence in almost any activity will do wonders for your self-esteem – and probably earning power. The principles of deliberate practice, in the form of expert training and good feedback, can be used by all of us to increase our skill levels at work or play. It's never too late to improve some of your job-related skills or to seek more accurate information about your performance. Whether you need to become a better public speaker or a more proficient sailor, water-colorist or parent, you'll add to your personal Fortune by increasing your expertise. Practice doesn't necessarily make perfect, but – with the right feedback – it can bring satisfaction . . . and better decisions.

The question remains, however, as to how to make those decisions. When is it better to blink? When should we stop and think? Actually, in many cases it's best to do neither! The plot thickens one last time . . .

# Twelve

# THE INEVITABILITY OF DECISIONS

*[M]y way is to divide half a Sheet of Paper by Line into two Columns; writing over the one Pro, and the other Con. Then, during three or four Days Consideration, I put down under the different Heads short Hints of the different Motives, that at different Times occur to me, for or against the Measure.*

*Benjamin Franklin*

In this chapter, we can't put off the inevitable any longer. We're going to get to the point about how to make decisions in our uncertain world. Now, let's talk straight. We're not about to change our spots and offer you a fail-safe method with guaranteed success. That would be dishonest as well as impossible. After all, we have been telling you throughout this book that luck nearly always plays a role in determining what happens. However, what we can promise is recommendations to increase your "batting average" of decisions. Some will be good, some will be bad, but – if you heed our advice – more of your decisions will be better than before. The chapter will be like reading a book on how to improve your skills in, say, golf or tennis. By helping you face your dilemmas consistently and methodically, as when putting in golf or serving in tennis, we'll get you in good shape. But, be warned, the actual execution and follow-through is up to you.

No one could possibly make prescriptions for all decisions. What we will do is provide a roadmap where we distinguish between two types of decision and four ways of making them. The two types are *repetitive* decisions, those that form a series of very similar judgments, and *unique* or one-off decisions. In fact, you've already come across two of the four ways of making decisions in the preceding chapter: *blinking* – or gut-level responses; and *thinking* – or making decisions through a deliberate process, much of which can be articulated. The third, which we call *sminking*, is based on using Simple Models or decision rules. (Our apologies for creating a new word, but as you will soon see, it helps to keep the concept clear.) Finally, the fourth method involves using the opinions of others – preferably "true" experts – to make the decision for you.

## FROM THE REPETITIVE TO THE UNIQUE

It's first important to distinguish between decisions that are unique, on the one hand, and repetitive, on the other hand. Let's consider an example. Top Global Management Consulting runs a highly success-ful recruitment campaign for fresh graduates each year. Many more young high-flyers apply to work for Top Global each year than their program can accept. How, then, should Top Global make decisions about who to employ?

Across all their candidates, Top Global faces a *repetitive* decision making situation. Indeed, the structure of this problem is the same as in many other contexts – doctors admitting patients to hospitals, firms granting credit to customers, supermarket managers ordering stocks, universities accepting students, and so on. The same decision is taken over and over again in a relatively unchanging environment.

Now let's look at Top Global's recruitment decision from a different viewpoint. Alex, a twenty-one-year old student, soon to graduate from Prestigious University, has just been offered a job with Top Global. But there's also an offer on the table from Pain & Co., while McFlimsey made very positive noises at the final interview last week. To complicate matters further, there's a good chance of a place on a highly respected graduate program in journalism at an Ivy League university, while Alex's gorgeous girlfriend is pressing to go traveling round Europe and Asia for six months. To many people Alex seems annoyingly perfect, but for once this brilliant student is faced with an impossible task – to make a one-off, life-changing decision. It really doesn't help that all of the options seem too good to be true.

Before we try to help Alex out by considering the issues involved in unique decisions, let's deal with the straightforward matter facing the recruitment partner at Top Global. Yes, it really is quite uncomplicated. Repetitive decisions, as we'll see, lend themselves to what we call "sminking": the use of simple models or decision rules. We'll explain how it works through three different examples.

## SMINKING 1: PREDICTING MARITAL HAPPINESS?

George and Jill are a nice young couple. He's thirty and works at the local hospital; she's twenty-eight and is just finishing her Ph.D. in molecular biology. Are they happily married? Their families think so but then they don't really see them very often. You could interview them at great length and try to form an impression through a combination of "blinking" and "thinking." That's what marriage counselors do – but here's an alternative method.

Psychologists John Howard and Robyn Dawes trained one partner from each of twenty-seven couples just like George and Jill to monitor their own behavior for thirty-five consecutive days. The monitors counted two types of behavior and also rated the couples on a seven-point scale of marital happiness. Howard and Dawes used a simple decision rule to predict marital happiness: the difference between the frequencies of the two types of behaviors across the thirty-five days.[1] The result: the simple decision rule they discovered was a valid albeit imperfect predictor of marital happiness.

The point here is that, in a domain as complex as marital happiness, predictions based on elaborate theories typically miss the mark (remember chapter 9 and the problem of noise) – although, in hindsight, they can make great stories! On the other hand, simple decision rules can have better – even though limited – predictive validity. As Robyn Dawes and another of his research partners, Bernard Corrigan, put it: "The whole trick is to know what variables to look at and then to know how to add."[2] You do need judgment for the first task, but you can delegate the second to a calculator.

Can you guess what those two variables in the case of marital happiness were? The simple decision rule was the number of times the couple made love less the number of times they argued. Now you know what to do (?).

Given that knowledge, let's move on to our next example, which is a multi-million dollar business decision.

## SMINKING 2: CREDIT SCORING

The Bell System, the giant former monopoly US telephone company, had a problem with bad debts back in the 1980s. The obvious solution was to demand a deposit from each new customer, but unfortunately, state laws prohibited this. To ask any individual for a deposit, Bell executives needed to come up with a good reason.

So the company conducted an experiment. They randomly selected over 80,000 new customers and gave them access to phones without demanding a deposit. After a while, they followed up to see who – from this large sample – wasn't paying their bills. They had only a limited amount of information about each customer, of course, but they were able to identify a few yes-or-no factors that did a good job at distinguishing between those who did and did not pay. Company executives then developed a simple decision rule to predict who in future should have to pay a deposit.

At the time of the study, the company had twelve million new residential customers each year. They estimated that the new rule would result in an annual reduction of $137 million in bad debts.[3]

Bell's innovation was a forerunner of today's credit-scoring practices. These days the variables tend to be weighted, but it's rare even now to need more than a few of them. They can be specified judgmentally through observation, as in our example of marital happiness, or identified through statistical analysis, as carried out by Bell. In credit decisions, it's typically factors like how long people have lived in the same home, whether or not they own it, how long they've held their current job, and how much the household earns in total. Applicants are awarded points for each variable – for example, the longer you've owned your house, the more points you get. The points are then summed and weighted to create a total score, which determines your credit-worthiness. The lesson is that repetitive decision making *is* straightforward. Identify the right variables (usually only a few of them) and use a simple decision rule. Or – in one word – smink! It may not be a real word, but it's a concept that's of very real value. Sminking involves accepting error to make less error.[4] It's the ultimate example of the paradox of control. You know it's impossible to predict accurately, so don't even try. Instead, be content to identify and use only the most important predictors and live with the wrong decisions, comforted by the knowledge that there'll be a lot more right decisions. It's like playing baseball or cricket. You can't expect to score each time you swing your bat. But your strategy should be to achieve the highest possible batting average.

Many people resist these suggestions. There are three main reasons for this. The first is that they don't fully understand the rationale. The sminking-skeptics argue that humans are capable of considering much more information than a few basic variables and can also cope with unusual cases. And they're right. The problem is they're also downplaying the fundamental inconsistency of the way we think and the fact that people's reasoning can be wrong. Confronted with identical cases, but at different times, the same human being is liable to make different decisions, perhaps because of tiredness or mood swings. There are also cognitive biases to take into account, such as overconfidence or misplaced beliefs. It's true that simple models can't handle some important information in a few rare cases, but they're perfectly consistent and immune to emotional or cognitive biases. In a nutshell, there's a trade-off: the ability of the human mind to process additional information versus the consistency of decision rules. Time and time again, empirical evidence, as we saw in chapter 9, favors the simple models.[5] Sminking outperforms human judgment in the case of repetitive decision making, such as mass recruiting, reducing bad debts, or lending money to lots of people.

The second objection is even more tempting. Despite all the empirical evidence, some people worry that the use of decision rules for recruiting, reducing bad debt, or granting mortgages might be discriminatory in some way. Could it be unfair toward certain minorities? Well, simple models can be wrong, but they tend to be less discriminatory than human beings. Even if there is a tenuous correlation between bad debts and a given group of people, the simple modeling process can ensure that it's not a factor in granting a loan or giving a job. What's more the decision rule can be adjusted to take into account special treatment for selected minorities. Affirmative action may be illegal for Top Global's London or Paris recruitment team, for instance, but the firm is allowed to build quotas for women and ethnic groups into its US decision-making process.

The third major objection to sminking comes from blinking fans. They say that a simple model takes away power from the people whose intuitions it replaces: bank managers and job interviewers, for example. Again, this may be true. But why should people do routine jobs that a calculator or computer can do just as well? After all, we trust the judgments of computers for all kinds of other important calculations, such as working out our tax bills or the forces on a motorway bridge.

More and more organizations are beginning to follow the sminking principle for their repetitive decisions, but it's hard to see why it's not taken up more widely – in medical diagnosis for example or in admitting students to universities. It's that illusion of control again. People want to predict every case for themselves and are unwilling to give up control to a rule, even though it would lead to better decisions on the whole. This is illustrated nicely by our third example, a classic experiment in psychology.

## SMINKING 3: FLASHING LIGHTS

Imagine you have just agreed to participate in an experiment at your local university. You are seated at a desk with two buttons in front of you: A and B. The researcher tells you that on each of many trials your task is simply to press A or B. After you press a button, a light goes on. If the light is green you win a small cash reward. If it's red, you win nothing. Got it? OK, start.

You begin by experimenting and soon find that buttons A and B can both result in red and green lights. But you soon notice that there's a green light with A rather more often than with B. So what do you do? As this experiment has been conducted many, many times, we can tell you *exactly* what most people do. They decide to keep on pushing both buttons, but rely a little more on A than B.

What you – and they – don't know is that the scheming scientist behind the scenes has programmed the system so that the green light flashes on average 60% of the time for button A, but only 40% of the time with button B. In other words, what most people observe is correct. But their decisions are not. Having noticed that the chances are better with A, they should have pushed it every single time – which would have been sminking at its very simplest. But why don't they do this?

As further research shows, one of the main reasons is greed. Participants can't resist trying to out-predict the system. If the financial stakes are increased, participants are more likely to stick to A. Fear of losing the greater sums on offer overcomes greed. It's the classic illusion of control, exaggerated by emotions.

We see the same behavior outside the laboratory. When ignorant of the implications, people are reluctant to gain control by ceding control to a simple decision rule. Many recruiters still prefer to rely on gut instinct, rather than sminking. While the smart recruiters use a combination of data about qualifications, university attended, experience, test scores, and psychological questionnaires . . . and only after all that more subjective criteria, others stubbornly insist that they know best and keep blinking. Meanwhile when large financial gains are more directly at stake, as in the laboratory, behavior changes. Large banks don't bother to interview potential credit-card customers. They just ask a few indicative questions and check all available databases for past bad-debt. Sminking has saved so many billions of dollars that it just isn't questioned.

We're not claiming that simple models are always easy to build. The main challenge lies in selecting the right variables. And to do that, most of the difficulties are usually emotional rather than cognitive. What's more, you can only hope to achieve what the level of inherent uncertainty will allow. In the laboratory experiment, the green light was set to flash only 60% of the times you pushed button

A – so on average you're not going to do any better than that. But, when all that's said and done, you're going to make better decisions by using a simple model. It's exactly what Top Global did when they offered Alex a job – although they did give him a final interview just to check he'd fit in.

## UNIQUE DECISIONS: EFFECTIVE THINKING

Alex is still pondering his own big decision. And he's absolutely right to do so. A unique decision with little time pressure requires a great deal of thinking. But any decision method can be applied effectively or ineffectively. This is particularly the case for thinking, because it's open to so many different possible influences. How can Alex think *effectively*, then? Should he follow his father's sensible advice and accept the offer from Top Global? Should he follow his heart to Europe and Asia – and hang the career consequences? Or should he take the financially risky option of journalism, his secret ambition ever since he can remember? Alex is finding out that unique decisions are hard – both cognitively and emotionally. There are no simple models to smink with. What we can do, however, is help Alex to *think* through his problem. To do so, we suggest that he systematically consider three basic questions. First, what's at stake? Second, what are the uncertainties (time to deploy the triple A approach)? Third, what is his personal attitude toward risk?

Taking each question one by one, what exactly *is* at stake? Here the focus is on the different alternatives and their consequences. Alex may think he's already got too many options, but it's time to think out of that clichéd box and see if there are any others he's missed. Could he, for example, get some experience in business and save up for journalism school later? Does one of the three consultancies he's considering publish a journal that he could write for? Finally, if his relationship is really so great, surely it can survive a few months of separation?

Smart Alex knows that he can't expect a flash of inspiration, a eureka moment, or a genie. Innovative thinking requires great concentration. In addition, he recognizes the need to discuss the situation with trusted friends who – unlike his father and girlfriend – can be entirely objective. What can they suggest? Do they know other people who have direct experience of the various alternatives? Can they put him in touch with them? Alex realizes that the more alternatives he generates, the more likely he is to find good ones. He also knows that he shouldn't discard some options too quickly because, with a little elaboration, they might become attractive. Finally, he recognizes that he has to figure out how each alternative will help him reach his overall life goals. It's all too easy just to accept the offer from Top Global, just because everyone else graduating from his program is boasting about their starting salaries. It may be a job to die for, but he's got his whole life ahead of him.

Having generated further alternatives, Alex now has to consider the uncertainties. More precisely, he has to accept, assess, and augment them, as we described in chapter 10. The key here is to inject a healthy dose of realism into proceedings. At once, this allows him to *accept* that there's uncertainty involved in each of the alternatives. To will it away – or hope for the best – is to fall prey to the illusion of control.

Now for the *assessment* bit. For example, one of the advantages he sees in doing the journalism program is to get a good job with a top magazine or newspaper when he graduates from it. But recruitment in the media is much more ad hoc than in big firms like Top Global. What if they aren't hiring when the time comes? Or just as bad, what if he can only get an unpaid internship – not an uncommon first step in the competitive world of journalism? By this time next year, Alex will be heavily in debt. He won't be able to afford an unpaid job and his chances of a well-paid consultancy post will have evaporated. Alex continues in this vein, through each of the options, finding more and more uncertainty wherever he goes. But, luckily for him, he also finds that one of his Prestigious University colleagues' father is a journalist with a major international business magazine and another's mother is a partner with Top Global. He makes appointments to talk to them on the phone. Clearly, this involves a lot of work, but it is necessary if Alex wants to cover all possible angles and avoid future surprises.

In the meantime, as the uncertainty increases, so does Alex's anxiety. That's when he needs to be at his most careful. When uncertainty becomes too threatening, there's often an unwillingness to consider its consequences. Instead, people adopt optimistic attitudes that make light of potential downsides. For this reason, we recommend that Alex adopt what is called an "outside view". That is, instead of working on the decision for himself, he should imagine that he is a consultant with Top Global, hired to analyze the problem and make recommendations. How would the consultant go about assessing uncertainty? He figures that they'd start with some benchmarks. As one of the best students in his undergraduate class at Prestigious, he stands a good chance of doing well as a management consultant. As a highly numerate economics major and active member of many student societies with good interpersonal skills, he has the classic profile. But journalism is a harder case to call. Success is much more about flair, networking, and pushiness, not to mention plain luck. As for love, is it even appropriate to seek benchmarks at the age of twenty-one?

Next, as specified in chapter 10, Alex must *augment* the uncertainty he's just assessed to make sure that it is as reasonable and pragmatic as possible. Moreover, the longer into the future he looks, the larger the upward adjustment for uncertainty should be. Will the demand for consultants and journalists, for example, be higher or lower in the longer-term future? Furthermore, Alex should think about the possibility of personal "coconuts." What if he gets sick or has an accident, and can't finish the journalism program, but still has to pay the tuition while not having any income from a job? An alternative would be to buy insurance to cover such eventualities. But how much would that cost on an already tight budget?

Augmenting is critical to assessing uncertainty in a more realistic manner. Many businesses suffer the negative consequences of what is sometimes called the "optimism bias" in planning activities. IT projects are the classic example. They typically take much longer to develop than engineers' first estimates. Underestimates also plague the construction industry not to mention intellectual projects such as writing books or, in the political domain, attempts to bring about social change. Interestingly, the UK government requires planners to augment their estimates for budgets associated with large transport projects by a factor known as the "optimism bias uplift."[6] And they still regularly go over budget, over deadline, or both.

Finally, having adjusted for his own optimism bias, Alex has to set his personal risk levels. Whereas different people could agree as to whether, given his goals, he's structured the alternatives well and assessed the uncertainties realistically, only Alex can decide how much risk he should face. The best advice we can give is to be *active* in setting his risk level. There's a plethora of scientific literature to prove that people's decisions in the face of risk can be influenced by either greed or fear, depending on just how the situation is presented to them. Patients, for example, are more likely to opt for a medical procedure if their doctors present the outcomes in terms of the survival rate rather than the proportion of people who don't make it![7] So it's important for Alex to see the glass as both half empty and half full and to consider the consequences of both.

We also suggest that Alex consider his possible decisions from different emotional perspectives. This can help diminish the negative effects of hope (mentioned above). One view should emphasize what he can gain from taking the actions and will appeal to greed. The other should emphasize what he could lose, and will appeal to fear. By considering *both* perspectives, Alex will better understand how he feels about his decisions, the risk involved, and where the balance lies between fear and greed.

In the end, there's clearly no right answer and Alex will never know whether his decision was the best one. But – by thinking through the procedure we've outlined in the past few pages – Alex stands a better chance of determining what is right for him than by "blinking," "sminking," or simply tossing a coin.

## USING EXPERTS

However, Alex is tempted by one further course of action that we haven't really explored yet. He's been using the university's career services office ever since he arrived at Prestigious, and is extremely impressed by the expertise of its staff. He sets off for one last visit, in the hope that someone there can tell him exactly what to do. Alex reasons to himself that Top Global has built an international business on making companies' decisions for them, so it's not unreasonable for him to delegate his decision to the equivalent expert for his own situation – a careers advisor.

Alex isn't unusual in taking this step. Because decision making can involve a lot of work and is so fraught with the uncertainties that this book is all about, many people prefer to outsource their decisions to "experts." It's a strategy that's very popular and, as we saw in the first part of this book, common practice in health, investment, and business decisions as well as many other domains. After all, if the expert turns out to be wrong, it's not your fault – you've controlled the situation as much as you could.

We take issue with this viewpoint. It's that dastardly illusion of control all over again. The ultimate decision is still your responsibility. And the expert can't get rid of all uncertainty. Nobody can. On the other hand, if you ask the expert the right questions, you can make a much more informed decision. In the next few pages, therefore, we consider what we should be asking experts if we want to improve our decisions.

The most important point about using experts is something we call the Harry Potter Rule in honor of J. K. Rowling's fictional boy magician. And fiction is the point. The rule is: there is no magic in our world – we are all "muggles." You should therefore be highly suspicious of advice that seems magical. For example, there are several "One Minute" books and some have sold millions of copies. They provide advice on a range of issues: how to become an effective manager, a millionaire, a great mother or father, and so on. The titles of a few are: *The One Minute Manager*, *The One Minute Millionaire*, *The One Minute Father* and *The One Minute Mother*, even *The One Minute Entrepreneur*.[8] But no. You cannot achieve any of these goals by reading a book – let alone in a minute!

The same applies to many other forms of advice, as we saw in chapter 6, including books on how to achieve success in life or business. An excerpt from one of these books, *The Science of Success: How to Attract Prosperity and Create Harmonic Wealth® Through Proven Principles*, is typical of the kinds of promises made:

> The Science of Success makes universal principles of success available and practical. Anyone on Earth can apply this science, and it will make them successful every time. That's because the Science of Success works with universal laws, laws as fundamental and unbending as the law of gravity. If you follow these laws, I guarantee that you will succeed – every time, and in whatever endeavor you undertake – just as surely as a pencil will fall down instead of up when you drop it.[9]

This statement clearly appeals to and feeds on the unsuspecting person's (or should we say "victim's"?) illusion of control. But remember, we don't live in one of J. K. Rowling's novels.

Strangely, while there are many books about fantasy and success, there are few books about failure and how to avoid it. Those that do make it into publication rarely become bestsellers. Yet, it's obvious that dealing with failure and avoiding common mistakes is very important and much more common.[10] A recent book by R. J. Herbold goes so far as to say that "success is a huge business vulnerability," preventing people from seeing the need for change and diminishing their motivation.[11] Easy success – particularly if we don't understand what lies behind it – may not be so advantageous if we really want to do well in the longer term.

In short, we need to question the role of experts and their advice, whether provided in books, or in person. At the risk of sounding repetitive, we emphasize that there are limits to what experts can predict, and no one, including the best and most expensive expert, can reduce future uncertainty. Yet this is exactly what people expect from experts. They want experts to predict the future and absorb their uncertainty – an impossible dream and a classic case of the illusion of control.

On the other hand, it is important to realize that true experts, such as doctors, lawyers, psychologists, and accountants, possess state-of-the-art knowledge in their fields. We can and should use them to access this knowledge and inform our judgments. But that's not the same as outsourcing our decisions. Instead, we recommend using expert advice as just one of many inputs in our own decision making. The process that we described for consulting doctors in chapter 3 can be generalized to other fields. This means:

- Finding as much information as possible in the area of expertise, including the extent to which opinions are divided – and, ideally, some hard, preferably empirical data about the past in order to estimate future uncertainty.

- Asking the expert what type of advice they would give if, instead of one of us, it was their father, mother, child, or spouse who was involved.
- Seeking help to identify any available options that you might not have thought of, then getting ideas about how to evaluate different options and the costs and benefits of each.
- Requesting objective advice about the urgency of the situation – or the option of further consideration if there is no time pressure.
- Getting suggestions about *other* experts and sources (including websites) for obtaining additional, independent advice or information.
- Posing direct questions about possible conflicts of interest that the expert may have in providing information or advice.

We don't often have the time or the resources to consult experts at this level of detail. However, the internet is changing our ability to canvas expert opinion. It allows us to answer questions we would like to have asked experts, quite often free of charge. But in no case should we expect experts or the internet to make infallible forecasts, eliminate future uncertainty, or decide for us. Trusting experts blindly is another way of becoming a victim of the illusion of control – enough said!

That's exactly what the Prestigious University careers advisor told Alex – if in slightly different words. He gave him lots of useful information about the three strategy consulting firms, about careers in journalism, and about the potential drawbacks of taking six months off to travel. But, as an expert with a reputation for being very good indeed at his job, he sent Alex on his way to make the final decision for himself.

## BLINKING, THINKING, SMINKING, AND USING
## EXPERTS: THE PROS AND CONS

In this and the previous chapter we've shown that a decision can be taken in one of four ways – or a combination of them. The important thing to remember is that each has its pros and cons.

Starting with blinking, it's the only way of making decisions in practically all tasks that involve muscular reactions, such as returning a serve in tennis or stopping a car in an emergency. When there's only a split second, there's no time to make conscious effort.

But apart from muscular reactions, blinking doesn't always work. Worse, we typically have little insight into when it's been effective or not. There are good reasons for this. Yes, some of the experts described by Malcolm Gladwell in *Blink* claim that the Getty Kouros was a fake the moment they saw it.[12] But there is still no agreement that their intuition was correct. In talking about the still-unresolved question of the Kouros' authenticity, John Walsh, director of the J. Paul Getty Museum concluded: "After years of intensive research, we recognize that the puzzle may not be solved in our time." In fact, the same opinion is shared by the great majority of the nineteen eminent art historians summoned to Athens to decide on the authenticity of the Getty Kouros. After considerable debate, five of the nineteen concluded that the Kouros was fake, three that it was genuine, while the remaining eleven agreed with Walsh and stated that they could not express a definite opinion.[13] Thus, even in Gladwell's celebrated illustration of blinking, there is no agreement that it works.

But even if it was agreed by everyone that the Getty Kouros was fake this would not have proven that blinking always works. Experts, like most people, typically don't advertise their mistakes so we have limited chances of uncovering cases where experts blinked wrongly. Conversely, how many fakes exist, including those exhibited in the world's great museums, which experts have so far failed to recognize? An especially infamous case is that of the Dutch painter Han van Meegeren who, before and during the Second World War, produced several widely acknowledged Vermeer masterpieces that were exhibited in great European galleries for many years. They were eventually revealed as forgeries by the painter himself.

Outside the realm of muscular reactions, one of the few areas where blinking produces consistently outstanding results is grandmaster-level chess. But, as we saw in the last chapter, there are two important factors at work. The first is that grandmasters are only able to blink after ten years or more of extensive practice with consistent, accurate feedback. The second is that the grandmasters employ a combination of blinking and thinking – in fact they think to verify each and every blink. In 75% of cases, systematic analysis confirms that the initial intuition (blink) was right. But in a significant 25% of moves, the hunch is corrected on further reflection. In other words, thinking is critical to a grandmaster's success and a prerequisite to successful blinking.

If time allows, our advice is to follow the practice of grandmasters every time you're tempted to make a blinking decision – and particularly when the stakes are high. This is the only way of avoiding possible mistakes. It may even be wise to involve a third party in the post-blink thinking in order to gain a little objectivity and to overcome the influence of emotions. This is how Alex was very quickly able to overcome his initial instinct to rush out and buy a round-the-world ticket to go traveling with the love of his life.

Now for sminking, or simple modeling in the form of a decision rule. When it comes to repetitive decisions, we have little hesitation in advocating this course of action. All the available evidence points to the same conclusion, namely, sminking offers considerable improvements over intricate thinking – and with substantially lower costs. Top Global, the management consultancy that offered Alex his job, only recruits actively at the world's best universities, for example. They used to spend time and money doing presentations at second-tier institutions, but soon realized that more than 80% of their most successful employees (and an even higher percentage of their executives) came from further up the educational hierarchy. So they simplified matters and saved money at the same time (whilst marketing their special internship programs for women, people from ethnic minorities, and disabled students at all universities). The only real danger with sminking is that the decision rules involved can become obsolete when the environment changes. So it's always advisable to put your thinking cap on from time to time in order to recognize such changes and modify the rules appropriately. And it's worth remembering as well that sminking relies on a considerable amount of thinking to choose the right variables and develop the simple model, or decision rule, in the first place.

Next, consider using experts. There's an ongoing debate about the role and value of experts, not least because there's big money in expertise. In a recent book, Philip Tetlock, a professor at Berkeley's Haas School of Business, explored these issues using information from a mammoth study analyzing more than 82,000 decisions from experts in the field of political science.[14] His findings – which echo our own and those of previous research – are quite stark. Simple models turn out to be more accurate than human forecasters. And if you really must rely on human beings, experts are rarely more accurate in predicting than informed individuals. Indeed, Tetlock's political experts weren't as good as non-experts at modifying their forecasts in the light of new information, as they felt they knew all the relevant facts. They were also overconfident about the accuracy of their predictions. Having said all that, as we saw earlier, good expert advice can be very valuable in helping people arrive at their own decisions – provided they handle both the experts and the advice carefully.

Last, but certainly not least, we come to thinking. This is the default option, so long as the decision in question is neither repetitive nor muscular. Thinking is also vital in confirming blinking decisions, as in the case of chess grandmasters, and in formulating sminking rules. In this chapter, we illustrated some principles of *effective* thinking in discussing Alex's big career decision. We warned that thinking can be derailed by a combination of cognitive and emotional factors. However, we hope we also showed that, by setting up the problem carefully and following clear principles and procedures, it is possible to think your way to good decisions.

And Alex? Well, his conversations with his fellow students' parents revealed that there was a shortage of journalists with a solid grounding in business. In fact, the magazine editor even went so far as to say that he was fed up with journalism grads with neither experience nor interest in their subject matter. And the Top Global partner revealed that the firm was soon to announce a new division specializing in advice for media companies. This was all just as well, as – in the course of all that reflection – Alex had realized he was extremely risk averse and couldn't justify a further year of expensive studying. He accepted the job with Top Global and managed to get assigned to the new division, where he made lots of good contacts and met a tall, slim, attractive Associate called Ellen who quickly made him realize that his own girlfriend had not been so "gorgeous" after all.

## AND WHAT ABOUT EMOTIONS?

Over the years, social scientists have typically followed the tradition of the ancient Greek philosophers who placed reason on a pedestal and denigrated the role of emotions in decision making. Yet it's significant that later philosophers specifically recognized the importance of emotions. In the seventeenth century, Blaise Pascal famously observed that "the heart has reasons that reason does not know" and in the eighteenth century David Hume pointed out that reason was subservient to emotions. More recently, neuroscientists have demonstrated that emotions can often play an important, positive role in decision making.[15] How then should we treat our emotions when making decisions?

We believe it is important to recognize that our Bermuda triangle of emotions – greed, fear, and hope – can also serve important, useful functions. In taking risks, for example, fear can protect us from excesses and hope is an important motivating force for many activities. Indeed, our emotions constitute what might be called a "primitive" decision making system. However, except for certain activities, we maintain that these need to be complemented by other considerations. In particular, we need to know when and how much attention to pay to our emotions.

We argue that the wise use of emotions depends heavily on the kind of decision being taken and the method you are using.

First, in the context of repetitive decisions, emotional influences are likely to add noise to the process – that is, sometimes an emotion may suggest one action (a job candidate is selected because you take a liking to what she said in the interview) or the opposite (if she'd caught you in a bad mood, her humorous aside would have meant instant rejection). One of the many advantages of sminking is that it explicitly avoids any distortions due to your mood or emotions. As we've said before, repetitive decision making becomes simpler provided you have the courage to smink.

Second, if you are blinking, you may often depend entirely on emotions. For example, if you are suddenly aware that an object is about to land on your head (perhaps a coconut), fear will automatically lead you to take protective action – get out of the way in a hurry. Here, of course, you don't even think about emotions – the process is automatic. And a good job too.

Third, and more problematic, is how to handle emotions when taking a decision by thinking. There are two main points to consider. The first is that you cannot avoid having emotions about the decision. That's human nature. However, as discussed earlier in this chapter, it isn't always appropriate to rely on your first blinks. The second point is that different emotions can be triggered by different stimuli. At one moment, a proposed course of action might seem quite risky, while at other times, it might seem too safe. Our proposal is to recognize both aspects of emotions by, first, thinking of emotional reactions as "data" or information that you can include with other information in analyzing your decision.[16] In other words, list and think carefully about both the emotional *and* other considerations of your decision. Second, make a point of deferring your decision – like Alex in our example above – until you have had time to consider it on more occasions. In this way, you'll profit from seeing how sensitive your decision is to variations in the strength of your feelings. The strategy of deliberately "sleeping on a decision" before taking action isn't a cliché for nothing.

Finally, when using experts you would be less than human if your emotional feelings about experts did not affect how you react to their advice. Our recommendation: recognize that this happens and try and put yourself in somebody else's shoes. How would you feel if the expert had given the same advice to a rival?

## TOWARD BETTER DECISIONS

The idea we'd most like you to remember is that of simple models or decision rules. Our advice about thinking is sound, but it's a tad too sensible to be exciting. We confess that we get more of an intellectual kick out of sminking than thinking, because it doesn't simply acknowledge the *illusion* of control. It involves going one step further and embracing the *paradox* of control: by relinquishing control to a simple model, rather than your own thought processes, you actually stand to gain *more* control over the outcome.

That's not to say that there are any easy answers to good decision making. No recipes. Nothing's changed. And sminking only works for genuinely repetitive decisions. But there's no doubt that it's under-used. Simple models are common in credit scoring or recruitment, but could be much more widely deployed in medicine, business in general, and not-for-profit organizations. Individuals can also benefit from sminking, though most of our non-work-related decisions tend to be either unique or too unimportant to merit developing simple models.

By separating decisions between repetitive and unique, we've done a little simple modeling of our own. We've presented two endpoints of what is really a continuum. Many decisions have elements of both the repetitive and the unique. So, even if they're not the sole basis of a final decision, simple models or decision rules can – like experts – be used as benchmarks to calibrate our judgments or forecasts. But to do so means recording our decisions and their outcomes, which is always going to be problematic. The reason? Fear of being held accountable. The cost of this fear, however, is that it prevents you from obtaining the feedback necessary for learning.

Clearly, not all decisions have repetitive elements, so thinking and blinking will also be required. You've seen our recommendations about these two forms of making decisions in the last two chapters, so we won't dwell on them further. But once again, we emphasize the need to supplement blinking with thinking. And we also insist on repeating that outsourcing decisions to experts should generally be avoided, even if experts' opinions can help us to make our own decisions.

In evolutionary terms, the development of our higher level thinking processes is quite recent. Until the last few decades, they were restricted to a tiny minority of people. For most of its existence, the human race has had to spend practically all its time worrying about food and safety. There's been little or no time left to pursue arts and sciences, to play chess, or to get involved in intellectual endeavors of any kind. There was, of course, the morally dubious exception of Ancient Greece, where slaves did most of the manual work, freeing up a large proportion of the population to pursue intellectual activities. But in the Western world, it was generally only after the Industrial Revolution and the rise of automation that ordinary people had the opportunity to study and to work with their brains instead of their muscles.

So it shouldn't come as any surprise that we humans are ill-equipped to grasp probabilities, comprehend future uncertainty, or face its implications rationally. This is one reason why our decisions are often inferior to those of simple statistical models. At the same time, the products of our ever-developing brains have, in a short time, created a complex world in which we must make decisions and for which physical evolution hasn't prepared us.

The good news is that we do have the intellectual ability to appreciate the full extent of future uncertainty, understand the illusion of control, and figure out their implications for decision making. The bad news is that we often fail to do so for psychological reasons and pay a high price accordingly. In our world, governed by both chance and skill, we must first penetrate the illusion of control and, where appropriate, exploit the paradox of control. In other words, by giving up control, we sometimes gain more of it. This long story, cut short to a single sentence, is the story of the last twelve chapters.

# Thirteen

# HAPPINESS, HAPPINESS, HAPPINESS

*Money doesn't buy happiness.*

*Traditional saying*

*Those who say that money can't buy happiness don't know where to shop.*

*Anonymous*

At the beginning of this book, we rashly promised you happiness. Well, a final chapter on the subject at any rate. If you remember the genie of chapter 1, his most popular request was for happiness – along with health and longevity, wealth, and professional success. In the first part of this book, we focused on the role of luck in these three areas of life. And in the second part, we gave you the underlying practical and theoretical understanding to grow your personal Fortune in all fields. So, assuming you've followed our advice already, are you happy? You should have amassed a big personal Fortune by now, but is that the same thing as greater happiness? You may even have been blessed with unrelenting luck. But that doesn't necessarily mean you're happier either. Happiness is as slippery a concept as it is a highly subjective feeling. In short, it seems impossible to predict our future happiness, or to control it, as pure chance plays a huge role. Unlike love, however, (another wish of those in possession of genies), there is a surprising amount of information on the subject. It *is* possible to draw some firm conclusions about the pursuit of happiness. And that's what we'll endeavor to do for you in this chapter.

Of course, even by imparting all our knowledge on the topic, we can't promise you happiness itself. But if you press on with this chapter, we can at least guarantee a heady mix of celebrities, fast cars, sex, and nuns . . .

## A PROBLEM LIKE MARIA?

One of the authors knows a girl named Maria. Now, if anyone merits the description of "happy," it's Maria. And she's got plenty to be glad about. She's just turned eleven and lives with her loving parents and brother in Sarrià, a well-to-do neighborhood of Barcelona. But that's where her luck seems to end. Maria is disabled and will always need to wear leg braces. Doctors aren't sure why her legs don't work properly – perhaps it's something to do with lack of oxygen at birth or an obscure genetic defect. It doesn't seem important, anyway, as Maria is always smiling. She never asks for help going up or down the stairs and never falls, even though she always looks as if she's about to. The little Spanish girl seems to get so much pleasure out of life that her happiness is infectious – for her family and those around her.

Maria goes to the local school, but has few friends. It's not just that her classmates don't want to play with her. They tease her too, constantly reminding her of her disability. But somehow, Maria behaves as if she hasn't heard their comments and enjoys being surrounded by able-bodied kids, who never hear her complaining about her disability or her bad luck. She's also a good student: top of the class in mathematics and computers. And she never gives up trying to make friends – even with Pilar.

Pilar lives across the road from Maria, in an even bigger house. The two girls are in the same class. Pretty, smart, healthy, loved, and pampered, Pilar ought to be the happiest kid on the block. But she isn't. For a start, she complains about everything – from the color of her shoes to getting up early to go to school. Once there, she gets on OK with her work and the other children. Not that she's top of the class in any subject, but then she rarely does her homework or any extra studying. Back at home, she's most commonly to be found fighting with Anna, her younger sister. The rest of the time Pilar is generally sulking or declaring that she hates her family, her home, and her life. Even as a baby, she rarely smiled and cried when no one was entertaining her. Fortunately, Anna is of a cheerier disposition, but the atmosphere in the house is undoubtedly poisoned by Pilar's presence. Their mother cannot understand how her two daughters can be so different, as she believes that she raised them in the exact same way.

It's not obvious why Maria seems to be happier than Pilar, or why Anna is a sunnier child than her sister (their mother reluctantly puts it down to fate). Similarly, it's not clear why some countries or cultures are happier than others. But research has repeatedly shown that the differences themselves are big and indisputable. Compare and contrast Japan with Bhutan, which in 1999 became the last country in the world to introduce television.

Bhutan is a small Buddhist kingdom, sandwiched between China and India, with an area of about 47,000 square kilometers (that's 18,000 square miles, which makes it a bit bigger than both Switzerland and Maryland). The population is about 672,000 according to the government's own census, and 60% of the people make their living from subsistence-level farming. The World Bank estimates GNP per capita at only $1,400, giving its people a fairly low purchasing power by global standards. Yet Bhutan is a beautiful, unspoiled land with mountains, dense forests, and picturesque monasteries. And its people always score highly in international surveys on happiness.

Japan too is a Buddhist country in Asia. Living standards are high and, as we saw in chapter 2, life expectancy is the highest of all countries, with the exception of some tiny ones like Andorra. But according to surveys, the Japanese are a miserable lot. In 2006, Adrian White, a psychologist from the University of Leicester in the UK, produced a meta-analysis of major satisfaction studies, resulting in a world map of happiness.[1] Bhutan comes out in eighth position, mingling with some of Europe's richest countries, while Japan ranks only ninetieth – lower than Uzbekistan, where GNP per capita is about eighteen times smaller. Just as there seems to be no good reason why Maria is so much happier than Pilar, so there's no obvious explanation as to why the Bhutanese are so much more content than those from the land of the rising sun.

Happiness is our friend the genie's most popular request, but some nations and people seem to be naturally happier than others for no obvious reason at all. This is not the only puzzle involving happiness as we will see below.

## THE TRICKY QUESTION OF MONEY

Are we to assume from the examples so far that money can't buy you happiness any more than it can buy you love? It's a question that has intrigued philosophers, poets, and pop stars over the years. And recently, two psychologists, Ed Diener and Martin Seligman,[2] set out to answer it once and for all. They carried out a survey of various groups of people, ranging from the tycoons and heiresses on *Forbes* magazine's billionaires list to Calcutta's pavement dwellers. The respondents were asked to indicate their agreement with the statement, "You are satisfied with your life," using a scale from 1 (complete disagreement) to 7 (complete agreement), with 4 suggesting a neutral attitude.

> How much do you agree with the statement? _____
> (According to the survey, if your answer is above 5.8, you're happier than a billionaire.)

Mind you, apart from among homeless people, the research found no huge differences in happiness between the different groups. The Inughuit natives of glacial northern Greenland and the Pennsylvania Amish expressed the same levels of satisfaction with their lives as the very richest Americans. The semi-nomadic Maasai of Africa may be fractionally less content than the billionaires, but they score higher than a random selection of Swedish people. Even the satisfaction rates of Indian slum dwellers are not much worse than an international sample of college students, a privileged group. Intriguingly, one of the biggest differences in satisfaction rates is between the Pennsylvania Amish (scoring the same as the billionaires) and the Illinois Amish (scoring a little better than the Calcutta slum dwellers). But the most striking result is that that none of Diener and Seligman's groups – including the super-rich list – came close to the perfect 7. (You can compare your own answer with the results of Diener and Seligman shown in table 13.)

This and other studies point to the same conclusion: life satisfaction doesn't increase once people reach a certain minimum level of income.[3] Some researchers have even expressed this threshold in dollars: per capita GDP, in purchasing power parities of around $16,000.[4] In one particular survey, inhabitants of different countries were asked the following question: "On a scale of 1 (dissatisfied) to 10 (satisfied), how satisfied are you with your life as a whole these days?"[5] This time, the researchers plotted the country's average satisfaction rating against its per capita GDP. This enabled them to distinguish

**Table 13** Average life satisfaction for various groups

| | |
|---|---|
| *Forbes* magazine's "Richest Americans" | 5.8 |
| Pennsylvania Amish | 5.8 |
| Inughuit (Inuit people from northern Greenland) | 5.8 |
| African Maasai (semi-nomadic tribes from Kenya and Tanzania) | 5.7 |
| Swedish sample | 5.6 |
| International college-student sample (47 nations in 2000) | 4.9 |
| Illinois Amish | 4.9 |
| Calcutta slum dwellers | 4.6 |
| Fresno, California, homeless | 2.9 |
| Calcutta pavement dwellers (also homeless) | 2.9 |

two distinct groups – countries with per capita GDP of more than $16,000 and those with lower levels of income. The two groups are shown in the rectangular and oval shapes in figure 18.

This mapping of international happiness reveals one very strong message. Within each of the two groups of countries, there is no obvious relation between wealth and life satisfaction, but the average level of satisfaction is higher in richer countries. There are, however, some notable exceptions. Bhutan, which we already know about, is joined by Costa Rica in reporting higher satisfaction than the USA. Similarly, Indians are more satisfied than Russians, despite lower GDP per capita, and communist Cuba seems happier than capitalist Japan. The comparison between Hong Kong and China is particularly interesting. People in Hong Kong are on average much better off than those from mainland China, but their levels of satisfaction with life aren't that different.

What happens to happiness in countries which experience rapid economic growth? To return to Japan once again, real income increased fivefold between 1958 and 1987. But self-reported satisfaction levels remained constant across this period.[6] And the London School of Economics professor Richard Layard reports that the

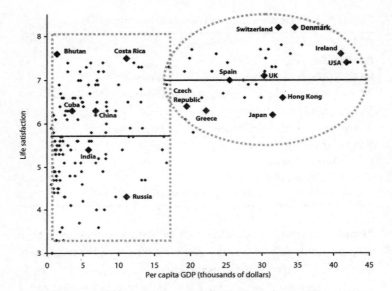

**Figure 18** Life satisfaction vs. per capita gross domestic product (GDP)

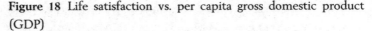

percentage of people in Britain and the USA describing themselves as "very happy," "quite happy," or "not happy at all" has remained the same for five decades, despite the fact that they were getting steadily richer all this time.[7]

In some ways, this is hardly surprising, as researchers have documented the same phenomenon on an individual level, notably with lottery winners. As you might expect, winning the jackpot does make people happy. But not for long. After a year, or at most four or five, they revert to their previous levels of satisfaction. They just get used to being rich and stop being happier than before they won the lottery. So does it really make sense that many of us toil for long hours under constant stress to raise our income to a level far below that of a lottery win? Are we any happier as a result?

The Oxford economic historian Avner Offer goes one step further than asking such questions. He argues that increased wealth has actually undermined human well-being. According to his book _The Challenge of Affluence_, a rise in psychological distress, together with increased crime, drug dependency, and obesity, are all correlated with economic growth and added wealth.[8] Will we be able to reverse this situation in the future and learn to be happier?[9] In that case, is there anything that will bring us _lasting_ happiness?

## IT'S THE LITTLE THINGS THAT COUNT?

Daniel Kahneman (see chapter 11) recently took a new approach to understanding happiness, which he named the Daily Reconstruction Method.[10] His project involved research participants filling out a detailed diary. They had to list everything they'd done during the day, then rate – on a seven-point scale, from 0 (= "not at all") to 6 (= "very much") – a number of feelings for each event (for example, pleased, happy, depressed, tired, concerned). The researchers then worked out a "net" satisfaction rating for each activity and took the average across the entire population surveyed. They also calculated the average number of hours spent on each of the activities per day.

Why not try a simplified version yourself? Kahneman's list of activities is given in table 14, arranged in alphabetical order. We suggest that you just give each of them a score between 0 and 6, where 0 means "doesn't give me any pleasure whatsoever" and 6 means "makes me very happy." If you want to go one step further, you can also estimate the number of hours you spend on each activity on an average day.

Kahneman's happiness guinea pigs consisted of a large sample of Texan women – 909 of them to be precise. They were a pretty representative bunch: 24% African American, 22% Hispanic, 49%

**Table 14** List of daily activities

| | Level of satisfaction | Number of hours |
|---|---|---|
| Commuting | _____ | _____ |
| Eating | _____ | _____ |
| Exercising | _____ | _____ |
| Housework | _____ | _____ |
| Intimate relationships (sex) | _____ | _____ |
| Napping | _____ | _____ |
| Praying/worshipping/ meditating | _____ | _____ |
| Preparing food | _____ | _____ |
| Relaxing | _____ | _____ |
| Shopping | _____ | _____ |
| Socializing | _____ | _____ |
| Taking care of your children | _____ | _____ |
| Talking on the phone | _____ | _____ |
| Using the computer, e-mail, or internet | _____ | _____ |
| Watching TV | _____ | _____ |
| Working | _____ | _____ |

white, and 5% other, with an average age of thirty-eight and a mean household income of about $55,000. As experts in statistics, we know you're probably not a woman in Texas, but as keen observers of human nature, we reckon you probably want to compare their results with yours. So don't look at table 15,[11] unless you're ready.

We don't know how these figures compare with your own answers, but some of the data are intriguing. It's not surprising that sex and socializing are the most satisfying activities or that working and commuting are the least appreciated. But it's curious that taking care of children comes so low on the list – even lower than doing

Table 15 Average "net" satisfaction and average hours of daily activities

| Activity | Average "net" satisfaction | Average hours per day |
|---|---|---|
| Intimate relationships (sex) | 4.74 | 0.2 |
| Socializing | 4.02 | 2.3 |
| Relaxing | 3.91 | 2.2 |
| Exercising | 3.81 | 0.2 |
| Praying/worshipping/meditating | 3.76 | 0.4 |
| Eating | 3.75 | 2.2 |
| Watching TV | 3.61 | 2.2 |
| Napping | 3.27 | 0.9 |
| Preparing food | 3.24 | 1.1 |
| Shopping | 3.21 | 0.4 |
| Talking on the phone | 3.07 | 2.5 |
| Using the computer, e-mail, or the internet | 3.01 | 1.9 |
| Housework | 2.96 | 1.1 |
| Taking care of my children | 2.95 | 1.1 |
| Working | 2.65 | 6.9 |
| Commuting | 2.56 | 1.6 |

housework. Are Texan kids really that bad? Or is childcare a universal disappointment?

Data in the social sciences should never be taken at face value, however. Note that the 0.2 hours spent on sex is an average – no one is suggesting that twelve minutes is enough for a 4.74 satisfaction rate! Sex is always a problematic issue in surveys, anyway. It's hard to get people to be really truthful about it: some people exaggerate, while others come over all coy. In this particular study only 11% of respondents listed sex as an activity, so sweeping generalizations aren't possible. Instead, the researchers turned their particular attentions to the second activity on the list: socializing. They collected data on

**Table 16** Satisfaction from different kinds of social interactions

| Interacting with: | Average "net" satisfaction | Average hours per day |
|---|---|---|
| Friends | 3.69 | 2.6 |
| Relatives | 3.37 | 1.0 |
| Spouse/partner | 3.32 | 2.7 |
| My own children | 3.29 | 2.3 |
| Clients/customers | 2.84 | 4.5 |
| Co-workers | 2.84 | 5.7 |
| Boss | 2.43 | 2.4 |
| *Overall average* | *3.11* | |
| Being alone | 2.72 | 3.4 |

different types of social interaction and came up with the results shown in table 16 (using the same scale of satisfaction).[12] Unsurprisingly, spending time with friends is most satisfying, while being with the boss is about as miserable as it gets. The respondents clearly don't enjoy being alone either, but even that's better than suffering the presence of the big bad boss.

After analyzing all the data, Kahneman and his colleagues concluded that people's happiness with daily life is strongly influenced by personality characteristics, situational conditions, and mental health. If you're prone to depression, it's obvious that you're not going to find routine activities very uplifting. More significantly, the researchers found that factors such as education or income had little impact on the Texan women's satisfaction. However, the better they slept, the happier they became the next day. So even if you can't buy happiness, perhaps you can at least sleep your way to satisfaction.

## INCREASING THE SUM OF HUMAN HAPPINESS

Sleep isn't the only solution. The newish field of positive psychology aims to help people improve their satisfaction with life and develop a more optimistic outlook. Its basic thesis is that Freud was wrong to characterize the human condition by its different neuroses. Instead, they cite evidence that smiling people are not only healthier and live longer, but also work harder, are more productive, more socially engaged, and generally more successful in life. Miserable souls, they argue, are self-obsessed and pessimistic, which gives others a low opinion of them too. As a result, things get even worse for them . . . and they get even unhappier. The most important teaching of the positive psychologists, however, is that absolutely anyone – even the grumpiest people – can take specific actions to increase their happiness in the long term.

This is where the nuns we promised you come in. Now nuns provide great opportunities for psychologists – positive or not. That's because they all follow routine lives with similar activities and comparable diets. What's more, they don't get married or have children. In short, nuns constitute a homogeneous population.

One of the positive psychologists' favorite studies concerns 180 nuns in Milwaukee.[13] Back in 1932, the then novices were asked to write short sketches of their lives. One wrote: "God started my life off well by bestowing upon me grace of inestimable value. The past year has been a very happy one." She recently died, aged ninety-eight, after a lifetime of extraordinarily good health. By way of contrast, one of her sisters painted a neutral-to-sad picture of her own life, concluding, "With God's grace, I intend to do my best for our Order." She died of a stroke at the age of fifty-nine.

OK, so two nuns from Milwaukee don't prove much. But experienced researchers studied all 180 of the sketches and ranked them according to their net satisfaction with life. Then they looked at how long the nuns lived. It turns out that nearly 90% of the "happiest" quartile made it to eighty-five or more and 54% of them were still alive at ninety-four! By then, there weren't many of the "saddest" quartile left. Less than a third of them reached the age of eighty-five and only 11% survived to ninety-four. As well as the nuns, Martin Seligman of the University of Pennsylvania, one of the leading lights in positive psychology, cites another survey, this time of 839 patients at the Mayo Clinic in Minnesota. It was found that "optimists" from this sample lived 19% longer than "pessimists."[14] But that's all you can conclude. Who's to say that the main reason for being an optimist wasn't better health in the first place?

There are many further studies linking life satisfaction with health, long life, and success in general from all over the world. In the UK, researchers took blood samples from 216 middle-aged civil servants and found that the happiest people had the lowest levels of cortisol (a hormone that can be harmful in excess) and plasma fibrinogen (a chemical linked with heart disease).[15] And in Holland, a large-scale study of 3,149 elderly people concluded that happiness – or at least satisfaction with various aspects of life – was closely correlated with longevity.[16] Curiously, too, some researchers have even seen fit to investigate the difference in life expectancy between those who won major awards and those who were simply nominated (although it may be going one logical step too far to assume that the former are happier than the latter). Nobel Prize winners between 1901 and 1950 lived on average two years longer than mere nominees. Winning an Oscar is even better! Out of 1,649 nominees studied, the ones with Academy Awards on their mantelpieces lived 3.6 years longer than the rest.[17] Don't say we didn't warn you that social sciences data have to be handled with caution, as another study, never mentioned by positive psychologists, found that Oscar winning screenwriters lived 3.6 years shorter on average than those merely nominated for the prize.[18]

But by far the most controversial claim of the positive psychologists is that they know how to increase and sustain your happiness.[19] Some of them recommend exercises such as keeping a daily diary for six weeks to "count your blessings" or "writing a letter of gratitude" once a week for two months. Other suggestions include: building optimism by visualizing the best possible future for yourself once a week for eight weeks; practicing altruism and routinely committing kindness for six to ten weeks; and spending fifteen minutes a day reflecting, writing, and talking about the happiest and unhappiest events in your life. Dr. Seligman's own website – one of many internet projects devoted to boosting your spirits – isn't exactly modest about its own achievements.[20]

> Early results from the Reflective Happiness website of Dr. Seligman demonstrate that after taking the first Happiness Building Exercise, 94% of members had a decrease in depression (some greater than a 50% reduction) and 92% increased their happiness. These results are comparable to the beneficial effects of antidepressant medications and cognitive therapy.

Positive psychology is common sense – up to a point. Of course people can shift their mindsets temporarily to focus on the upsides of life. It also stands to reason that happy people are likely to attract more friends, have fewer divorces, exude more confidence, and exhibit less stress. But this is a bit of a chicken-and-egg situation. And as for happiness making you live longer, who are you going to believe? One hundred and eighty nuns from Milwaukee or the entire nation of Japan who score so low in "happiness" surveys but live the longest of practically all countries? (Actually, the correlation between satisfaction with life and life expectancy among countries with more than $16,000 per capita GDP is zero.)

Fortunately for those cynical souls who come over all queasy when counting blessings or visualizing beautiful futures, there's a simple alternative to positive psychology. It's called golf. A recent study found that 300,818 golfers from Sweden lived, on average, five years longer than non-golfers, regardless of sex, age, and social group.[21] Assuming these calculations are correct, this is a huge increase in life expectancy. But before you rush out to buy a new set of clubs, take a common-sense check again. Does the increase in life expectancy come from regularly spending four or five hours in the fresh air, walking briskly for six to seven kilometers, and flexing a few other muscles along the way, while at the same time socializing with other like-minded golfers? If so, then there are many other ways to improve your health and life expectancy. Golf and positive psychology are just two of the options.

It's no wonder that so many psychologists are skeptical about the claims of Dr. Seligman and his followers. They question whether someone's basic personality can change, whether you can turn a Pilar (from the beginning of this chapter) into a Maria (from over the road). Julie Norem, a psychology professor from Wellesley College and author of *The Positive Power of Negative Thinking*, says, "If you're a pessimist who really thinks through in detail what might go wrong, that's a strategy that's likely to work very well for you. In fact, you may be messed up if you try to substitute a positive attitude."[22] She's concerned that the messages of positive psychology may reinforce the naive belief, so prevalent in the US, that individual initiative and a positive attitude can solve all problems.

In particular, the critics of positive psychology question the link between happiness and success. History is littered with tales of tortured geniuses after all. The psychologist Mihaly Csikszentmihalyi's research, which we mentioned in chapter 11, confirms that celebrity at least doesn't go hand in hand with happiness.[23] He found that none of the ninety-one famous people he interviewed had been popular during adolescence. Instead, their great strength was the ability to focus on the skill that eventually made their name. Success, it seems, typically requires a level of dedication that's incompatible with a healthy social life. Perhaps, in old age, as they look back at their lives, successful people *are* happy. But the converse is certainly not true. In fact, most of us tend to stop trying, as soon as we're happy with our performance, leaving little room for further success.

Csikszentmihalyi is himself something of a celebrity in psychological circles. He's most well known for an earlier piece of research, which seemed to prove – unlike the survey of Texan woman we reported earlier – that people are happiest at work (or at least, under certain circumstances)![24] Rather than getting his subjects to fill in exhaustive diaries of their activities and states of mind, he sent them messages at random moments in the day using an electronic beeper. They had to report exactly what they were doing at that precise time . . . and how happy they felt. According to Csikszentmihalyi, his respondents were happiest when in a "state of flow." By this he meant that they were absorbed in a precise activity that is intrinsically rewarding, difficult but not impossible, and has clear goals that allow for frequent feedback on progress. In states of flow, people have a sense that they're in control, yet lose all track of time and feelings of self-consciousness. A good example – take it from us – might be writing a book when it's going well. As it happens, most cases of this heightened state occur at work rather than at play.

Positive psychology is all very well, but perhaps the answer lies in the Far East. Meditation, as practiced by religions such as Hinduism and Buddhism for thousands of years, seems to combine Csikszentmihalyi's state of flow with the relaxation prized by the Texan women. However, it requires considerable effort and the mastery of some pretty difficult techniques. Attaining deep spiritual fulfillment is much harder than visiting a "happiness" website and carrying out some positive-thinking exercises. Beware of gurus bearing easy recipes, as we said before. And to reprise another recurring theme of this book, *predicting* happiness – even our own – is also pretty difficult, or even pointless. Let's explain . . .

## WHOA-OA-OA! I FEEL GOOD, I KNEW
## THAT I WOULD, NOW

So far we've ticked off sex, celebrities, and nuns. Now for the fast cars. Daydream for a moment that you're making a choice between a sleek sports car (perhaps a Porsche convertible), and a nice, reliable, but rather dull, saloon (let's say a Volvo). Implausibly, in our hypothetical world there are no major financial or practical obstacles to either option. But there is a fairy godmother who makes one stipulation. Before making your decision, you have to envisage how happy you'll be as a Porsche-owner. Then you must do the same for the Volvo. In fact, even in the real world, where there are no fairy godmothers, this is a good strategy for many of life's decisions.

So which car did you go for? For most of us, even with the happiness-predicting condition, the Porsche wins every time. It's a no-brainer. But that's the crux of the problem. We ought to be better at applying our rationality to the slippery concept of happiness.

Harvard psychology professor Daniel Gilbert has made extensive studies of people's ability to predict their future states of happiness. His book, *Stumbling on Happiness*, makes entertaining but depressing reading.[25] As a species, he claims, we are truly rubbish at predicting our satisfaction levels. And the main reason is our intrinsic adaptability. The new Porsche may indeed give us a first rush of pleasure, but we soon get used to it (like the lottery winners we mentioned earlier) . . . and move on to the next desire – a fabulous house or stunning spouse maybe. Of course, we make a similar prediction error about that, before getting our fix of joy and then coming down from the initial high. And so it goes on. And on and on. It's almost as if we're too adaptable for our own good. We rapidly get used to even the most luxurious material possessions or outstanding achievements that subsequently have little or no affect on our happiness.

Collectively, however, the constant renewal of discontent helps the human race to progress. It's part of the creative-destructive process we saw in chapter 7. And our surfeit of adaptability also has its plus points for the individual. We all have an amazing ability to bounce back – after disasters, as well as triumphs. People who discover they're HIV-positive are devastated to start with. But as the weeks go by, they learn to live with their condition and the emotional distress subsides. The same goes for those suddenly afflicted with severe disabilities.[26] Human beings somehow adjust their sights. Some are just grateful to be alive, while others find new pleasures in the capacities they formerly took for granted: seeing, hearing, smelling, talking. Divorce, bereavement, bankruptcy, loss of a limb, you name it, the pain eventually fades and we rebuild our lives. Sadly for us, though, intense pleasure fades in exactly the same way. Euphoria, by definition, is short-lived – even more so for a non-golfer or a miserable nun.

In short, our adaptability extends to both the good and the bad events that chance brings our way, and we tend to overestimate the long-term impact of both the good and bad outcomes in our lives. What's more, our inability to forecast our future happiness leads us to make bad decisions over and over again. But – as we've seen with health, investments, and management – it's important to *recognize* our poor powers of prediction and to take this into account when we make our decisions. As the empirical research shows, we can't expect our recently sought happiness to continue indefinitely. At the other extreme, the influence on our happiness of even highly negative outcomes fades with the proverbial healer that is time.

According to Gilbert, the main issue we have to confront is the limitations of our own imagination. We tend to exaggerate certain details and conveniently overlook others. For example, we have a vivid image of driving our Porsche with the roof down on a sunny day. We don't glimpse the possibility of sudden rainstorms, high insurance premiums, expensive repairs, careless speeding fines, spoiled hair-dos, three six-foot passengers . . . or any of the other annoyances associated with owning a cool convertible.

Gilbert's solution is to consult people who have been there, done that, and got the T-shirt. Rather than relying on our incomplete imaginations, he argues, we should consult people who have owned both Porsches and Volvos for a while. We should ask them to tell us what they like and dislike in the most precise detail. Experiments performed by Gilbert and his colleagues show that we can figure out our happiness more accurately if we consult just one, randomly selected person who's already had the same experience. This is "future perfect" thinking of the kind we described in chapter 10 taken to its logical extreme. As well as *imagining* what a future experience was like in the past, we find someone for whom it's already done and dusted. Decisions affecting our happiness can be, therefore, dealt with in a more rational manner than naive belief in its predictability. As for all the other areas of life we've considered in this book, we can safely conclude that predicting our future happiness is not possible.

## MEASURING HAPPINESS

By now, you're probably wondering how much all this research into happiness is really worth. After all, there's no convenient unit for measuring happiness. It's all very well to ask people to rate their satisfaction on scales of 1 to 5 or 1 to 7, but the answers surely depend on their cultures, their ages, their moods, how well they slept the night before, and all manner of subjective and objective factors. Indeed, there's a great deal of controversy in psychology about the measurement of happiness.

On the one hand, there are academics who point out that their so-called subjective measures are remarkably consistent. On the other hand, some psychologists have gone to amusing lengths to prove that happiness levels fluctuate according to the weather or what you had for lunch. Professor Norbert Schwarz of the University of Michigan, for instance, asked people to fill out a questionnaire on life satisfaction. The catch was that they had to photocopy the questionnaire before filling it out. The further twist was that some subjects found a dime on the photocopier (planted by the experimenters), while others didn't. And yes, you guessed it, those who found the dime were upbeat about their lives as a whole as well as the economy.[27]

Another experiment used students as its subjects. One group was asked, first, "How happy are you with life in general?" and then, "How many dates did you have last month?"[28] There was practically zero correlation between the answers to the two questions. However, the order of the questions was reversed for the second group of students. This time there was a clear link between the number of dates and the level of their happiness. Of course, the groups were large enough and representative enough for their real differences in happiness to be negligible. It just goes to show that a satisfying month of love can cast a rose-tinted glow over every other aspect of life.

Obviously, the same question asked in different contexts yields very different answers. Remember the Texan women, who rated "taking care of my children" as less fun than "housework"? Their attitude contradicts the findings of the academic literature and the popular press alike. People questioned by the University of Uppsala in Sweden ranked interacting with their children the most enjoyable activity of all, followed by going on trips and being with friends.[29] And when *TIME* magazine asked its readers, "What one thing in life has brought you the greatest happiness?" 35% said it was their children, grandchildren, or both.[30] We shouldn't jump to the conclusion that the children of Sweden or *TIME* readers are little angels, but focus instead on the way the question is asked. Clearly, there's a big difference between childcare as a day-to-day activity and as a lifetime's achievement. Raising kids is a time-consuming and exhausting task, especially when you're a working mother. But look back on the experience (even when your children are still quite young) – and it takes on a whole new light.

The difference between the pain involved in completing a task and the pleasure of the outcome is not only significant but complex. It's not a gap that can be measured with a single question about how happy you feel. Imagine you're in a small sailing boat, crossing the Atlantic single-handed. It's midnight and there's a storm raging. You're wet, cold, and physically exhausted. If ever there was a zero on the happy-ometer, this is it. In fact, you mutter to yourself between chattering teeth: "I will *never* do this ever again. If I survive, that is." But a week later, as you sail into harbor in the sunshine, your view has changed. The sense of achievement and joy at seeing your family smiling and waving on the waterfront is overwhelming. And a month later you're planning your next big trip, this time across the Pacific.

The same is true of writing a book. It's time consuming, mentally draining, and makes your family complain. But once it's published and your readers are enjoying it, somehow it all seems worthwhile. And if it makes it onto the bestseller lists then it all the negatives are forgotten. Even the grumpiest family members encourage the author to start writing the sequel.

## THE PRICE OF HAPPINESS

All in all then, it's difficult to measure happiness. But that doesn't mean to say we should give up. The American Declaration of Independence famously holds that "Life, Liberty, and the pursuit of Happiness" are among man's unalienable rights. And the eighteenth-century Enlightenment thinker Jeremy Bentham went so far as to propose that the purpose of public policy was to maximize happiness. Today, "Happiness Economics" has entered the mainstream and some academics are even putting dollar values to different aspects of life. Using a long-term survey sample in the UK, one researcher matched up answers to life-satisfaction questions, various socio-economic data, and income figures to come up with the happiness price list shown as table 17.[31]

Unsurprisingly, good health has by far the highest value, while unemployment and disability have the highest costs. Good relationships – whether with a spouse, partner, friends, neighbors, or

**Table 17** Valuations of social network status and other life events

|  | Value (in $) |
|---|---|
| Meet friends and relatives | |
|    On most days | 85,750 |
|    Once or twice a week | 75,750 |
|    Once or twice a month | 52,500 |
| Talk to neighbors | |
|    On most days | 59,000 |
|    Once or twice a week | 35,501 |
| Socioeconomic variables | |
|    Health: excellent | 456,000 |
|    Health: good | 376,500 |
|    Married | 96,000 |
|    Living as couple | 80,750 |
|    Divorced | −36,750 |
|    Separated | −86,501 |
|    Disabled | −108,000 |
|    Unemployed | −111,251 |

relatives – are clearly very important to a happy life. And interestingly, divorce is about $50,000 less painful than separation. It seems that the initial separation is the hardest part of the process and that the final divorce brings an almost beneficial sense of closure.[32]

So we're back to where we started our journey toward understanding happiness with the thorny issue of money. Money may not automatically *bring* happiness, but some people are using it to measure happiness. Such studies as these have their limitations, but provide an interesting if rough guide not only to what makes us happy but also to what's possible in the study of happiness. Neuroscience is adding to the debate, as researchers start to measure activity in the parts of the brain where happiness resides. Nutritionists have joined the fray, suggesting that certain foods – among them turkey, tomatoes, and chocolate – can make you happy thanks to their high levels of serotonin. And of course, drugs that cheer people up have long been of great interest and profit to the pharmaceuticals industry, not to mention illicit dealers.

Meanwhile, countries as diverse as Bhutan, Australia, China, Thailand, and the UK are working on "happiness indices" to be used alongside GNP to evaluate socio-economic progress. In the UK, even the Bank of England – a national symbol of the importance of money – is looking for ways to measure happiness. But the greatest challenge is perhaps to *use* wealth in such a way that it generates happiness – without in turn compromising prosperity. Most people think, for example, that a good work–life balance makes you happy. And everyone knows that losing your job makes you unhappy, at least in the short term. However, countries such as France, which have legislated for greater job security and a shorter working week with long paid vacations, have felt the economic pinch. Rightly or wrongly, in 2007 the French population elected a new president on a ticket of employment reform in the belief that the economy would benefit. Happiness isn't necessarily a vote-winner.

## A HAPPY ENDING

Curiously, several languages, including French, German, and Spanish, don't fully distinguish between luck and happiness. The adjectives *heureux, glücklich,* and *feliz* can all be used to denote both *luck* and *happiness.* Yet the two concepts are very different in one fundamental way: although no one can change their luck, some people may be able to influence their happiness. Quite how to do so is not clear but some psychologists suggest that we're getting there, slowly.

What we do know is that the quest for happiness drives many of our actions. Although money isn't the answer, we're not yet sure what *is* – even if sleep and chocolate both help. And despite the fact that we're hopeless at predicting our own feel-good factors, we can take heart. Innate human adaptability usually reduces fluctuations in our happiness, at least in the longer term. Although happiness is, according to Aristotle, the most important human pursuit, "something complete and self-sufficient," even he – in all his classical wisdom – couldn't tell us how to achieve it. And we can't either, except by suggesting that you spend more time playing golf (or any other similarly healthy activity that you enjoy) and less time making money. Apart from that, try to base decisions that will affect your future happiness on the experiences of others who have been in similar situations.

But we still can't understand why some people, like Maria, are content while others, like Pilar, aren't, or why the Bhutanese are so much happier than the Japanese. Is it the luck of the genetic draw or there are some deeper reasons that we'll never fathom?

Throughout this book, we've had tantalizing glimpses of the power of the human mind: placebos that suppress acute pain; self-rated health questionnaires that are more accurate than doctors; years of dedication to attain grand-master status; how the destructive forces of creativity can be beneficial to our societies. At the same time we've presented the biases and limitations of our minds and their negative consequences on the way we make decisions and face future uncertainty, including the infamous illusion of control. These phenomena may be little understood and accepted, but they're all part of our mental inheritance. Unfortunately, we can't ignore them just because we can't understand them or predict their consequences.

So it is with happiness. If it were straightforward, we'd be one hell of a lot better at managing it. But, as with our health and longevity, wealth and professional success, happiness is complex to the point of unpredictability. One fact about happiness is simple, though: as the old Scottish proverb goes, be happy while you're alive for you will be dead for a long time.

# CONCLUSION

## Thirty years later

It would be nice to conclude that all who have read (and written) this book will live happily ever after – by putting the knowledge from chapters 1 to 7 together with the insights from chapters 8 to 12 and the glimpses of happiness in chapter 13. To maximize the chances of this happening, here's a brief recap . . .

First and foremost, accept the empirical evidence. This shows that – in many circumstances – it's best to dispel the illusion of control and dance instead with chance. Paradoxically, in so doing, we gain more control over many aspects of our lives.

One such area is health and longevity. Medicine, it turns out, is an inexact science. It cannot predict what will make individuals live longer or more healthily. Neither can doctors. So the best course of action is to stay away from them, until we feel unwell (or become pregnant). Consulting doctors, taking precautionary tests, or having regular check-ups does not increase life expectancy. Instead, these activities can lead to further expensive and unpleasant tests and treatment, possibly even unnecessary surgery. On a cheerier note, we can take heart from the power of the human mind to heal the body, as demonstrated by the placebo effect and self-rated health. Best of all, by taking a statistical, evidence-based approach to our own healthcare, rather than placing blind faith in physicians, we stand a better chance of getting the right treatment.

Now for this book's second area of interest: wealth. Economics and finance are even more inexact sciences than medicine. Experts from these fields are good at explaining past performance but no better at predicting which securities will bring the best returns than a monkey with a dartboard. Rather than seeking expert advice, then, we're better off investing our savings by selecting stocks at random or by buying into an index fund which tracks a reputable selection of securities. Not only does this reduce long-term risk, it also saves paying fees to fund managers with seven-figure salaries and Ferraris. It's also important to realize that short- and medium-term stock market uncertainty can be huge. In the twentieth century, the record fall of the Dow Jones Industrial Average index in a single day was 22.6% and in two weeks 38.4% (the corresponding records for increases were 15.3% and 31.5% respectively). The models of mainstream financial theory, most of which rely on "normal" distributions, simply cannot capture such huge rises and falls. All the more reason to trust luck or monkeys rather than self-appointed experts.

Third, what about success in management? Well here, we're no longer in the realms of science at all – exact or inexact. It's not clear that management gurus can explain the past let alone predict the future. Averaging the opinions of knowledgeable individuals or using simple statistical models is often more accurate. But frankly, business forecasts usually serve to diminish executive anxieties about future uncertainty – and reinforce the illusion of control. In addition, we must all accept that creative destruction is an integral part of the free-market system, destroying the old and creating the new. Although some individuals and even whole industries may get hurt in this tsunami of progress, society as a whole is a winner. Creative destruction, like evolution, can only be explained after the event rather than predicted in advance, adding an extra level of uncertainty to managerial decision making and strategic planning. The only solution is for managers to embrace the unpredictability of the business environment and to operate a little more like venture capitalists – "investing", at least for the long term, in a few well-chosen ideas. The trick is to be in with a good chance of at least one brilliant (and lucky) idea more than making up for the inevitable failures.

The principles behind the stories in the first part of the book are explained in the second:

1. The future is never exactly like the past.
2. "Complex" statistical models fit past data well but don't necessarily predict the future accurately.
3. "Simple" models don't necessarily fit past data well but predict the future better than complex models.
4. Both statistical models and people have been unable to capture the full extent of future uncertainty and been surprised by large forecasting errors and events they did not consider.
5. Expert judgment is typically inferior to simple statistical models, at least for repetitive decisions.
6. Averaging (whether of models or judgment) usually improves forecasting accuracy.

In addition, there are two different types of uncertainty (called *subway* and *coconut* for the purposes of this book), which add a whole new dimension to the task of forecasting.

When it comes to making decisions, the importance of taking full account of uncertainty is paramount. One method is to use the three As: first accept, second assess, and third augment the uncertainty of the situation. Unfortunately, too many people fail to augment and end up having to deal with surprising outcomes. Another strategy is to support intuitive decisions (or "blinking") by analytic thinking wherever possible – remember the chess grandmasters and their years of painstaking practice. As for the remarkable properties of simple modeling (or "sminking"), decision makers tend to under-exploit them, while relying excessively on the opinions of experts who are immune to the consequences of their expertise.

Finally, to return to happiness, chance seems to play a significant role here too. And there's yet another bunch of experts to fend off – the "positive psychologists" who claim they have prescriptions to make us happier and thus live longer. Once again, empirical evidence proves that the self-styled experts may be wrong. Golf seems to work just as well as their recipes for happiness. What's more, the Japanese, who regularly rank among the most miserable people on earth, are one of the longest-lived nations of all. The same goes for the Greeks, who are well known for their inclination to tragedy yet enjoy one of the world's highest life expectancies. The paradox of control implies that it's by coming to terms with the way we are and the culture we're from, however negative or melancholy, that we create our best chance of happiness. And that's as happy as this ending gets. $H = R - E$

As the final words of this book are typed in August 2009, it is some thirty years since the chance encounter in a business school of the two professors who cannot sing.

During these three decades, their lives have taken many unpredictable twists and turns. There have been new jobs and new countries, new wives, and new children. Fortunately for these patient and forgiving wives and children there has been very little singing. But there has been a great deal of talking – which is something that professors do almost as well as thinking. The talking now tends to take place via the medium of technologies that could not have been imagined thirty years ago: huge networks of fiber optics, mobile phones, video conferencing, and most importantly Skype with its free conference calls.

However, during these thirty years not everything has been a surprise. The professors' conclusions about our inability to predict have been confirmed by a great number of empirical research findings and their classification of two types of uncertainty is increasingly widely recognized.

As for the third professor, he may not have been around for quite such a long time, but he has been making up for it by spending longer and longer in the shower, where – when not singing – he likes to think. Together with his tone-deaf friends, he has tried to come up with some practical advice to deal with the big challenges facing forecasters, decision makers, and ordinary people alike. Hence this book that is so very nearly finished.

The big question that originally brought the three professors together was what to do about the limited accuracy of forecasting. How can we make decisions, plan, and formulate strategies, given the low levels of predictability and high levels of uncertainty in our lives? But our three wise men would be the first to recognize that luck played as important a part as the big question in bringing them together. How else could three such different people – one Greek, one Scottish, and one Indian – have met in France, after Ph.D.s from top US universities, then have written this book together while living in three cities so far apart: Athens, Barcelona, and Singapore?

Will the book, this tale of three cities, be a success? Will readers enjoy it? Will it sell well? Who knows? Least of all the three professors, who are sticking to their story right up to the paradoxical last line. Indeed, if you have any lingering doubts about the story of the dance with chance, take a look at figures 19a–19d. They were drawn at the beginning of the twentieth century by Parisian futurologists who were trying to predict what life would look like at the beginning of the next century. Draw your own conclusions, but it's safe to predict that life 100 years from now will be as unpredictable as it always has been.

**Figure 19a** A busy street in central Paris

**Figure 19b** A restaurant kitchen

**Figure 19c** Relaxing at home

**Figure 19d** Technology on the farm

# POSTSCRIPT: HOW DO YOU
# PREDICT THE UNPREDICTABLE?

We have argued throughout *Dance with Chance* that it is easy to explain the past but much more difficult and challenging to predict the future. We would now like to consider this statement in light of how well our book predicted events after it was first published.[1] In addition, we focus on a question frequently posed by readers and people attending presentations about our book, namely: what can be done to face financial crises and similar high impact events if we are unable to predict their occurrence? But first, we summarize our claim that we face serious limits to predictability in practically all areas of social sciences.

In the late 1960s, and most of the 1970s, social scientists – including business professors – hoped that computing technology and sophisticated mathematical models would lead to the same level of success in forecasting in the social sciences as that achieved in the physical sciences and engineering. For a variety of reasons, it is now clear that these hopes were unfounded. Instead, empirical evidence has shown:

- The future is never exactly the same as the past. This means that extrapolating patterns and relationships from the past to the future cannot provide accurate predictions.
- There are plenty of statistically sophisticated models that can fit (explain) past data almost perfectly. However, these complex models do not necessarily predict the future so well.
- Conversely, whereas simple statistical models do not fit the past very well, they generally do better at predicting the future than their complex counterparts.
- Empirical evidence has also shown that human judgment is even worse at predicting the future than statistical models.
- Both statistical models and human judgment have been unable to capture the full extent of future uncertainty. People have been often surprised by large forecasting errors and events (both negative and positive) they did not even consider.
- Experts do not predict more accurately than moderately well-informed, intelligent people in the street.
- On a brighter note, averaging the independent predictions of several individuals (whether experts or not) generally improves forecasting accuracy.
- What's more, averaging forecasts based on more than one model also improves accuracy and reduces the size of errors.

Let's look at some new developments in the areas of medicine, economics, business, and happiness that occurred after our book was first published that further underline the serious limits to predictability that we face in these domains.

## MEDICINE

In Chapters 2 and 3 we stressed that medicine is an inexact and evolving science, and that claims to the contrary exist not just because of our susceptibility to the illusion of control but also because of vested interests. Below we discuss cases involving "swine flu" and preventive medical tests to verify in an ex-post manner our claims of inexact science and vested interests.

**Swine flu:** The origin of swine flu has been traced to Veracruz, Mexico, at the end of March 2009. Not long after that time, there were concerns that a new flu virus had appeared that could lead to a pandemic with grave consequences involving many deaths (some estimates were in the millions). A heated discussion took place as to whether widespread vaccination of the general population was necessary. This continued for several months with many people advocating the pros and cons of large scale vaccination but with no consensus among the experts. At the same time, newspapers carried reports of the number of swine flu deaths and the dangers of not being vaccinated. On June 11, 2009 the World Health Organization (WHO) raised the influenza pandemic alert level from phase 5 to phase 6 (its most severe phase) and declared that "the virus was contagious, spreading easily from one person to another, and from one country to another." WHO's concerns were echoed by many medical experts who recommended vaccination to minimize the risk of the flu spreading at a fast pace throughout the world. Pharmaceutical firms rushed to produce large quantities of vaccines and a large number of countries ordered them by the millions to prepare for the pandemic's arrival.

In early March 2010, the National Pandemic Flu Service was closed in the UK and countries that had bought millions of vaccines were trying to get rid of them (but they could not find any buyers). The number of confirmed world-wide deaths from the pandemic has been estimated at around 15,000. To put this figure in perspective, about 36,000 people die in a "normal" flu season in the USA alone according to the Centers for Disease Control and Prevention (CDC).

As expected the swine flu became a cash cow of the pharmaceutical industry with a handful of companies generating millions of dollars in revenue and making huge profits. But this was not the first time. In 1976 there were predictions of a flu pandemic and 46 million Americans were vaccinated. This pandemic also never happened. There was only one confirmed death but up to 4,000 people who had been inoculated fell seriously ill by contracting Guillain-Barre paralysis and some even died.[2] In 2010, the Guillain-Barre paralysis of Alyson Dygnas was reported in the UK after she received a swine flu vaccine.[3] Curiously, there was little mention of the possibility of side effects or of the 4,000 Americans who fell seriously ill or died during the long debate about the advantages and disadvantages of vaccination.

**Preventive medical tests:** In Chapters 2 and 3 we discussed the uncertain benefits of periodic tests for prostate, breast and other forms of cancer and the possible negative consequences of such tests. The debate about their value is still continuing among physicians and medical experts. In a recent blog in NBC,[4] Shannon Brownlee explains screening as follows:

> Screening allows us to look under the water, at the tumors that haven't yet become symptomatic. We assume they will eventually cause symptoms, but increasing evidence suggests that's not always the case. Evidence from autopsies, for instance: In one study, post-mortem exams showed that nearly 9 percent of women of all ages who died of any cause other than breast cancer had undiagnosed DCIS (Ductal Carcinoma In Situ, the most common type of non-invasive breast cancer). Among women from Denmark, where mammography is not as common as it is here, a whopping 39 percent of middle-aged women who died of other causes had undetected

breast cancers. Similarly, says outcomes researcher Dr. Welch, a 1989 study found that 60 percent of men over age 60 have undetected prostate cancer – yet only about 3 percent of deaths in men are due to prostate cancer.

Brownlee then refers to the case of Dennis Fryback, Ph.D., a former member of the US Preventive Services Task Force, a group of experts convened by the federal government to make recommendations about screening. The task force recommends colonoscopy every ten years for people between the ages of 50 and 75, yet the 61-year-old Fryback concluded it did not make sense for him to get screened. He explains that he came to that decision in part because he has no family history of colon cancer. If he did, his chances of getting it would increase, and so would the odds he'd benefit from the test. He also knows that getting the exam requires at least a day of taking laxatives to clean out the colon and then facing the possibility of a perforation from the procedure, a risk that goes up with age. He balanced the possible reduction in his chances of dying of colon cancer against his other health problems. He had a heart attack in the previous year and suspects he will die of heart disease before a colon polyp has a chance to kill him. Clearly, even for experts the decision whether or not to screen is not straightforward, though for self-serving interests many doctors recommend screening for all.

As the arguments for and against testing continue, they leave many confused.[5] As a compromise, the new recommendation is to test later (e.g., for breast cancer after 50 instead of 40 years of age) and less often (i.e., every two years instead of annually). Clearly the vested interests are huge. Sharon Begley in a *Newsweek* article entitled "This won't hurt a bit: How we can save billions by cutting out unnecessary procedures that kill tens of thousands a year"[6] references several studies showing that the huge cost of unnecessary treatment totals hundreds of billions and provides no benefits for patients but brings riches to doctors, hospitals, and pharmaceutical firms.

Given the huge and rising cost of medical treatment and the unsustainable financial burden on individuals and nations, the time has come to re-examine the costs and benefits of different medical practices in a realistic and objective way.

## WEALTH

Global wealth fell considerably between October 2007 and March 2009 when the world was hit by the most severe recession since the 1930s. In addition to huge stock market losses, the number of bankruptcies increased exponentially, the real estate market disintegrated and the unemployment rate reached double digits in many countries. Interestingly, practically no one predicted the financial tsunami that hit almost all nations of the world with great force. Even today, when the worst of the financial crisis is over, there are no convincing explanations of the underlying causes, who should be blamed, and the effectiveness of the measures taken by governments and central banks to deal with the catastrophic consequences.

Then, in the midst of the gloom when many economists, including the head of the IMF, were predicting a forthcoming depression, things suddenly started to improve. Within fourteen months from March 2009 when the market was falling rapidly, instead of the Dow Jones Industrial Average (DJIA) dropping to 5,000 as had been predicted by some, it increased to above 11,000. As with the strong fall in the market, few predicted the even stronger recovery that increased stock market valuations more than 100% in many emerging markets (e.g., the Russian stock market increased more than 150%). This means that those who stayed out of the stock market missed the greatest boom in history as, even in advanced economies, the values of the stock markets grew between 60% and 80% from

March 9, 2009 to a little more than that a year later. The prophets of doom who had been hailed for predicting the recession were unable to explain how they lost their prophetic powers and completely missed the recovery. Lately, Bloomberg and the other financial networks have stopped asking the opinions of those predicting catastrophe for the economic system while the bulls have taken a more prominent role.

The unpredictability of both the fall and subsequent rise of the stock market prove, one more time, our inability to forecast and our overreaction to both negative and positive developments. Has such overreaction ended? What will be the effects of sovereign debt, in particular among European countries? Will the market increase or decrease in the rest of 2010? Should an investor be buying or selling stocks? That nobody can answer these questions, and that leading experts can have diametrically opposing views, is illustrated by a recent debate in the pages of the *Wall Street Journal* (*WSJ*).[7]

*Shiller vs. Siegel:* Professors Shiller and Siegel are two prominent economists we referred to in Chapter 4 and, as noted there, authors of two best selling books about stock market prices. A summary of their views is given in the *WSJ* as follows:

> Mr. Shiller worries that the housing market could be turning down after a brief recovery, which could contribute to a decline in U.S. stocks, which already look expensive to him. "I wonder about a return to another break in the market," he says, though he notes the market is far less expensive today than when he wrote his book.

> Mr. Siegel scoffs at his friend's concerns – and at his numbers. "This is an extremely cheap market," he says, and its future is bright . . .

> The way Mr. Shiller sees it, the problem today isn't just that the current P/E is above 20. It is that since 1991 it has spent only seven months, in late 2008 and early 2009, below the average level of 16. At the start of 2000, it was above 40. No one can say how much longer

the P/E can keep rising or when the past year's bull market might end, especially with the government providing heavy stimulus. But past trends, and the law of averages, suggest that at some point the P/E is likely to fall below 16, pulling stocks with it. Mr. Siegel, for his part, strongly disagrees with this kind of analysis. He argues that his friend's use of 10-year average profits works poorly in the current environment, because big financial companies took such heavy write-offs in 2008 and 2009. Such write-offs, he argues, won't be repeated, so earnings including them shouldn't be used for forecasting. . . . "My research shows that the common P/E is 18.5" when the economy is coming out of a recession, he says. The way he looks at it, the market now is trading at about 14.5 times forecast 2010 profits, making it cheap compared with the typical P/E of 18.5. If stocks rise to 18.5 times profits, the S&P 500 could rise to 1400 this year, a 23% gain from today's level, he notes. "We could easily see 10% to 12% stock returns with low inflation" in future years, he says.

What can a layman say when two of the best world experts, without vested interests, disagree about the direction of the stock market in the USA, the biggest and the most stable in the world? Is there any point in trying to forecast the direction of the market? In addition to whether stocks in the USA are overvalued or not, what about valuations in emerging markets where some have experienced triple digit growth in less than a year? Will advanced countries be able to reduce their huge government debt without halting economic growth? What will be the effects of possible double digit inflation similar to that of the late 1970s and early 1980s? What about stagflation? What about the dangers of a real estate bubble in China where properties values have been increasing at a fast pace? What about a "W" recession? Equally important, what is the value of experts when they provide diametrically opposing advice? Whatever the answer to these questions, one thing is clear: the uncertainty in forecasting is huge and we must not fall prey to the illusion of control that fosters predictability and certainty. Perhaps in the long run the market will increase substantially, but this may take a decade or two. So, as we stated in Chapters 4 and 5, it is up to the individual investor to consider the pros and cons of investing in today's market and the specific types of securities and risk he or she is willing to assume. But remember, there is no such a thing as a free lunch, and no one can accurately forecast the future.

## SUCCESS

On July 6, 2009, after many years of financial and other troubles, GM was finally officially placed under bankruptcy protection. It would have been inconceivable 40 years ago that the icon of American business would be overcome by what was at the time a small local firm, Toyota Motors, and that it would eventually end in bankruptcy. Yet, one more time, the inconceivable happened: GM went under chapter 11 protection and Toyota became the undisputable world automobile leader. Its rise to fame was further sealed in 2009 when it was ranked number 3, just behind Apple and Berkshire Finance, in *Fortune*'s annual survey of the most admired companies in the world.

Toyota has been legendary for its perfect quality, attention to detail and for building a culture among its workforce to assure buyers that its cars will be trouble free. Toyota's manufacturing has been the benchmark to follow while the "Toyota Way" of management has been the source of many cases written and taught in business schools and innumerable articles and books. For example, a search in Amazon for books about "Toyota" lists 4,000 while a similar search for "Toyota Way" shows 249 books (the corresponding number of entries in a Google search is 153 and 48 million). Toyota was until recently the modern icon of the super successful global firm unsurpassed in quality and service for its customers.

Yet during the last two years, Toyota has fallen from grace. It has suffered a large reduction in its market share and a loss of $5.5 billion for the fiscal year ending in March 2010. Uncontrollable acceleration in some of its cars, problems with the brakes of others, some design faults and defects in construction have allegedly caused deaths and serious injuries to drivers and passengers. At present, there are thousands of individual and class action law suits against Toyota that threaten its financial stability. (Moody's cited litigation risks when it warned in February 2010 that it might downgrade Toyota's credit ratings.) Worst still, its reputation with consumers has been seriously damaged as up to ten million vehicles have or will be recalled worldwide. No more can its cars be considered of the best quality vis-à-vis those of its competitors.

In *Fortune's* 2010 list of the most admired companies, Toyota fell to the seventh position from third in 2009. In all likelihood, it will not be part of the top ten in 2011. Once again, we observe that outstanding firms of the past can fall into serious financial and operational problems. In fact, Toyota reminds us of Dell mentioned in Chapter 6. Dell was the most admired company in *Fortune's* ranking in 2005, fell to the eighth position in 2006 and then it slid out of the 2007, 2008, and 2009 surveys altogether. A massive battery recall in its laptop computers tarnished its high quality reputation, making it just another computer company. By the middle of 2010, Dell has still not recovered. It seems that a first rate reputation built over decades can be lost overnight. This fact should be taken seriously by business school professors and business gurus praising certain companies for their unique achievements and recommending that others should imitate them in order to succeed. Past success is no guarantee for the future.

Does success breed its own failure? The answer according to Toyota's critics is yes. The firm's managing team started believing their own PR slogans. They were the best, superior to all others, and nothing they did could be wrong. They never accepted, for instance, that the unrelenting cost reduction demanded of their suppliers could affect the quality of their vehicles or that other car manufacturers would catch up with them in terms of quality and manufacturing performance. Their verdict is that Toyota's problems were inevitable. Others criticize Toyota's management for its unwillingness to accept that there were problems with its cars although some of these problems had been known to them for more than a decade.

Our purpose here is not to analyze how Toyota fell from grace but to re-emphasize that it is difficult to predict the future. As we showed in Chapters 6 and 7, Toyota is not an exception and the Toyota Way is just another "method" that may have been useful in the past but carries no guarantee of success in the light of changing environmental, business and management conditions. Will Toyota follow the path of GM? Well, whereas we are the first to say that accurate forecasting is not possible, the possibility always exists because success breeds its own failure and creative destruction never ends.

## HAPPINESS

The financial crisis has created a phenomenal degree of hardship. In addition to those who lost huge amounts of money in stock markets, large numbers of people defaulted on their homes, many more were fired from their jobs and have remained unemployed for long periods of time, and still others saw their incomes falling substantially. Under these circumstances the dissatisfaction, if not unhappiness among those affected increased. As we saw in Chapter 13, once people pass a certain level of income, they soon get used to extra money with no corresponding increase in their happiness. However, it probably takes much longer to get used to income decreases and more so when such decreases bring people's income to levels below the minimum required for life's necessities. There are interesting implications in the asymmetry between income increases/decreases and life satisfaction or happiness that needs to be further explored.

Recent research has shown that more important than money is the ranked position of people's income within a comparison group.[8] Such position predicts general life satisfaction much better than absolute income and reference income which have no effect. At the same time, individuals weight upward comparisons more heavily than downward comparisons. Thus, increases in individuals' incomes will increase their utility only if their ranked positions also increase. However, this will reduce the utility of others who will lose rank. This explains (partially) why people are outraged at the huge salaries and bonuses of the golden boys (and women) in banks and financial institutions who make millions at a time when the income of most people is reduced. This is especially the case when these people believe that the banks are responsible for the financial crisis.

All this suggests that it is worth exploring alternate models of "well being" and progress in societies rather than those which are primarily anchored on economic numbers like GDP.

## WHAT CAN WE DO?

The serious limits to predictability in all the important areas of our lives raise vital issues for anyone making decisions. What is the best way of taking care of your health, wealth, and career, not to mention your happiness in a context of high uncertainty and possible futures that you cannot even imagine?

Physical scientists are generally very good at making predictions. But the scientific community is equally good at knowing its own limits. And earthquakes are a good example. Scientists accept that it's impossible to predict the timing and location of earthquakes. Indeed, current understanding of the processes that produce them leaves no doubt that no one is able to pinpoint their occurrence or exact location in advance. Yet, the intensity and frequency of earthquakes exhibits a remarkably consistent pattern in the long run.

The point we'd like to make is that statistical regularity does not equal predictability. For example by studying the occurrences of past earthquakes statistically, we can predict that during the next 35 years they will be roughly 44 earthquakes with an intensity of 7.5 to 7.599 on the Richter scale. But seismologists have no clue as to when or where they'll occur – apart from being in one of the world's earthquake-prone zones and that they will be accompanied by aftershocks. Will these zones be populated or unpopulated? Will there be a tsunami after the earthquake? Will they cause large-scale death and destruction? No serious scientist pretends that he or she can answer these questions.

How, then, does the world cope with earthquakes? The answer is simple. Instead of relying on prediction, the strategy focuses on preparation. For example, engineers can and do construct buildings capable of withstanding very strong tremors, and quick-response emergency services are considered crucial. The recent earthquakes in Haiti and Chile underline this point. The earthquake in Haiti measured 7.0 on the Richter Scale, while the earthquake in Chile was significantly more powerful and measured 8.8 on the Richter Scale. Yet, the number of deaths in Haiti has been estimated to be as high as 230,000 while those in Chile has been estimated around 700. Both these earthquakes were unpredictable but two factors distinguish the situations. First, the earthquake in Haiti struck an area with a much higher population density than that in Chile. But, second, in Chile there was much greater awareness of the possibility of earthquakes and hence greater preparedness in terms of building codes and emergency services (and this despite accepting the inability to predict the timing and exact locations of earthquakes). Of course, the fact that Haiti is one of the poorest nations on earth made it difficult if not impossible to be well prepared. Nonetheless, the point remains that a strategy focused on preparation rather than prediction is key.

Hurricanes such as Katrina can wreak just as much devastation as big earthquakes. But even ordinary storms can cause significant damage. From a statistical point of view the number and intensity of hurricanes is pretty much constant over the long run. Like earthquakes, the number of storms and hurricanes in a given period decreases exponentially, the higher the wind speed. Yet unlike seismologists, meteorologists can usually predict where hurricanes will strike a few days in advance. Once they start developing, they can be tracked and their path forecast. If you're out at sea with a safe harbor within easy reach, this is extremely useful. On land, however, it's more like coping with an earthquake. The key is to be prepared: stay home, cover your windows, and fasten down. In some cases, there may be time and resources for a mass evacuation, as occurred in August 2008, when 1.8 million people were moved from the coast areas of South Louisiana. But Gustav only changed its course, thus once again highlighting the inaccuracy of predictions even when hurricanes can be monitored with computer age technology and high definition satellite images.

By analogy with natural disasters, think of the enormous number of small businesses or new ventures that start or fail worldwide. The precise figures vary from year to year, but there is a continual process of businesses entering and leaving the market – with some regions of the world more prone to both start-up and failure than others. Those companies that don't depart early in their existence may go on to be hugely successful, while many more simply survive for decades. Sticking with the earthquake analogy, the small-business failures can be seen as minor movements of financial tectonics, while the Lehman Brothers, Enrons, and WorldComs are larger tremors. Clearly, the large 2007–2009 recession is the equivalent of a major earthquake or a catastrophic hurricane, shaking the global economy to its core and sending huge aftershocks rippling across the world as well as towering ruinous economic tsunamis. Yet we must be prepared to face the next financial crisis, or other unpredictable events that will certainly hit us again some time in the future, although when and with what intensity, we don't know.

In terms of what to do, we remind readers of the "triple-A" approach (accept, assess, augment) presented in Chapter 10 as a way to help us never to forget that we live in an uncertain world and that we must take steps to face its uncertainties as realistically and effectively as possible.

### 1. Accept that you're operating in an uncertain world.

This is the first and crucial step. Psychologically it's tough, we know, but ignoring uncertainty is not an option. In fact, whether your interest is in tomorrow's oil price, next quarter's sales data, next year's stock price, earthquakes, or simply getting to work on time, you can't be realistic about assessing the chances of a given event occurring unless you first confront all the other possibilities that might come true instead.

Unlike in the physical sciences, where the scientists focus on "nature" minus the human beings, social scientists must necessarily include human beings in their models. And it is not difficult to imagine that reducing the possible behavior of human beings to some few universal laws as in Physics is simply too much of a blind leap of faith. In Chapter 10, we discussed two types of uncertainty: *subway* and *coconut*. Subway uncertainty is what we can model and hence assess fairly well. Payoff on a roulette wheel in a casino, demand for electricity in a given period of time in a major city, and number of phone calls in a given period of time in a network, are examples of uncertainty we can model from fairly well to extremely well. On the other hand, coconut uncertainty is something which is difficult if not impossible to model and hence difficult to assess accurately. One source of coconut uncertainty are the "unknown unknowns," or what might be called Black Swans, which by definition are extremely rare events with disproportionately large consequences and are events that we can't even imagine beforehand. However, a much more common source of coconut uncertainty is the class of events that are "known unknowns," events we know can happen and will happen, events that are much more frequent than Black Swans, but which we can't model or predict with any degree of accuracy. For example, will there be another asset bubble in the financial markets that will subsequently burst at some point? The answer is "almost surely yes" but we don't know when this will happen and in what form. All we can predict is that it will happen fairly frequently and to different degrees. In fact, Alan Greenspan, who was the Chairman of the Federal Reserve of the United States from 1987 to 2006, remarked in the *Financial Times* on March 27, 2009 that "we have never been able to model successfully the transition from euphoria to fear," highlighting the difficulty of predicting when a bubble in the financial markets forms and then bursts.

The overall uncertainty in most real life situations is a mixture of subway and coconut uncertainties. And in the socio-economic domains, compared to most physical sciences, the coconut uncertainty is a much greater proportion of the overall uncertainty, thus making predictions much more difficult. This is what we have to accept.

## 2. Assess the level of uncertainty you're facing realistically.

In the assessment of uncertainty in a given situation, first deal with the subway uncertainty which can be measured. Evidence has shown that in such an effort simple statistical models can be very beneficial and do much better than human judgment. This brings out another point that might be misunderstood in some of our discussions. All models are not incorrect or useless, but are very often incomplete, as these tackle only the subway uncertainty in a given situation. The models then have to be complemented by the possibility of coconuts in order to get a more realistic level of overall uncertainty, by using judgments.

Consider the staffing decision for an emergency ward at a hospital. It is fairly easy to model the uncertainty regarding the number of incoming patients on a "normal day", without any extreme events. This would be subway uncertainty. This however must be complemented by the possibility of coconuts, such as a big traffic accident, a major fire or an earthquake, a start of an epidemic, and the like, which can't be predicted accurately but which can't be ignored either. The best response to such uncertainty is not building huge amounts of overcapacity, but includes taking steps to create contingent staff who can be called to duty in a short time, creating pools of multi-skilled staff who can perform emergency procedures in addition to their normal tasks, increasing staff during the snow seasons when more accidents are likely, and so on.

Take the sales of a first novel by an unknown author. It sounds like a unique case. But our suggestion to publishers is to ignore the uniqueness. Instead, look at the track record of the sales of first-time authors *in general*. You have no valid reason to believe that the uncertainty surrounding your new author differs from the wider population of new authors to which he or she belongs – especially if you've used an industry-standard process for collecting reader feedback (also known as human judgment). By now, you should have a reasonable estimate of just how low or high the sales might go. This range probably covers 95% of all possible outcomes. Done that? Well now take the estimated range ... and increase it! Hence the next step: augment.

### 3. Augment the range of uncertainty you've realistically assessed.

You can be sure that you've just underestimated the range of uncertainty you estimated, no matter how realistic you thought you were when you assessed the uncertainty. Extensive empirical evidence shows that people consistently underestimate uncertainty – perhaps because their powers of imagination are usually less than their powers of mathematics. As a rule of thumb, we suggest that you double the range of uncertainty estimated at the second stage above. If this seems excessive to you, we suggest that you collect data about forecasts made in your own organization. We think you will be quite surprised!

## IN CONCLUSION

To sum up, we must learn to live with uncertainty in most domains of our lives. Falling into the trap of the illusion of control and underestimating uncertainty has very high potential costs. Of course, we must continue efforts in trying to predict the future more accurately, as this will always be an integral part of human nature. However, in doing so, we should not lose sight of the fact that we can never eliminate the uncertainty completely and in fact in most socio-economic domains the level of uncertainty will remain persistently high. The implication is that we should shift resources from being focused on prediction to being prepared for the unexpected, building resilience to live through negative events, and at the same time being nimble enough to leverage unexpected good luck.

# ENDNOTES

## PREFACE

1 Makridakis, S. and Hibon, M. (1979). The accuracy of forecasts: An empirical investigation, *Journal of the Royal Statistical Society*, Series A, *142*, 97–145 (with discussion).

2 See also Sawyer, J. (1966). Measurement and prediction, clinical and statistical, *Psychological Bulletin*, *66(3)*, 178–200.

3 The concept of "illusion of control" is central to this book and owes much to the work of psychologist Ellen Langer. See Langer, E. J. (1975). The illusion of control. *Journal of Personality and Social Psychology*, *32* (2), 311–328.

4 BBC news, China's "lucky" phone number, Tuesday, 19 August, 2003.

5 Sagan, C. (1996). *The Demon-Haunted World: Science as a Candle in the Dark*. New York, NY: Ballantine Books.

## CHAPTER 1

1 See, for example, Gigerenzer, G. (2006). Out of the frying pan into the fire: Behavioral reactions to terrorist attacks, *Risk Analysis*, *26* (2), 347–351. But see also Su, J. C., et al. (2009). Evidence of a regional increase in impaired driving and traffic fatalities after the September 11 terrorist attacks. *Psychological Science*, 20(1), 59–65.

2 On average, fewer than 200 people die each year in airplane accidents in the USA compared to more than 40,000 in cars. This makes the life-long odds of dying in a car in the USA approximately 1 in 100, while those of dying in an airplane are around 1 in 20,000. *~~miles travelled~~*

3 In two books, Nassim Nicholas Taleb discusses at length our inability to make accurate forecasts of the important events that affect our lives. See Taleb, N. N. (2004). *Fooled by Randomness: The Hidden Role of Chance in Life and in the Markets.* New York, NY: Random House, and Taleb, N. N. (2007). *The Black Swan: The Impact of the Highly Improbable.* New York, NY: Random House.

4 For more information about our inability to predict accurately in the social domains, see Makridakis, S., Hogarth, R., and Gaba, A. (2010). Why forecasts fail. What to do instead. *Sloan Management Review, 51(2),* 83–91.

5 See Fenton-O'Creevy, M. et al. (2003). Trading on illusions: Unrealistic perceptions of control and trading performance, *Journal of Occupational and Organizational Psychology,* 76, 53–68.

## CHAPTER 2

1 Kolata, G., Live long? Die young? Answer isn't just in genes, *New York Times,* August 31, 2006.

2 Haggard, H. W. (1934). *The Doctor in History.* New Haven, CT: Yale University Press.

3 See seroxatsecrets.wordpress.com/2008/02, and Bass, A. (2008). *Side Effects: A Prosecutor, a Whistleblower, and a Bestselling Antidepressant on Trial.* Chapel Hill, NC: Algonquin Books.

4 Starfield, B. (2000). Is US health really the best in the world? *The Journal of the American Medical Association, 284 (4),* 483–485.

5 For further analysis of these stories, see Gigerenzer, G. (2002). *Calculated Risks: How to Know When Numbers Deceive You.* New York, NY: Simon and Schuster.

6 Ibid.

7 For all life expectancy figures, see www.nationmaster.com/graph/ hea_lif_exp_at_bir_tot_pop-life-expectancy-birth-total-population

8   Ezzati, M. et al. (2003). Estimates of global and regional potential health gains from reducing multiple major risk factors, *The Lancet, 362 (9380)*, 271–280.

9   Wright, J. C. et al. (1998). Gains in life expectancy from medical interventions – Standardizing data on outcomes, *The New England Journal of Medicine, 339*, 380–386.

10  Stamler, J. et al. (2000). Relationship of baseline serum cholesterol levels in 3 large cohorts of younger men to long-term coronary, cardiovascular, and all-cause mortality and to longevity, *The Journal of the American Medical Association, 284*, 311–318.

11  Taubes, G., What's cholesterol got to do with it? *New York Times*, January 27, 2008. See also Taubes, G. (2007). *Good Calories, Bad Calories: Challenging the Conventional Wisdom on Diet, Weight Control, and Disease.* New York, NY: Alfred A. Knopf.

12  Cover story, Do cholesterol drugs do any good? *Business Week*, January 17, 2008

13  Rubenstein, S. New York probes vytorin study, *Wall Street Journal*, January 26, 2008

14  Doll, R. et al. (2004). Mortality in relation to smoking: 50 years' observations on male British doctors, *British Medical Journal, 328*, 313–316.

15  Franco, O. H. et al. (2005). Effects of physical activity on life expectancy with cardiovascular disease, *Archives of Internal Medicine, 165*, 2355–2360.

16  Peeters, A. et al. (2003). Obesity in adulthood and its consequences for life expectancy: A life-table analysis, *Annals of Internal Medicine, 138*, 24–32.

17  Franco, O. H. et al. (2005). Blood pressure in adulthood and life expectancy with cardiovascular disease in men and women life course analysis, *Hypertension, 46*, 280–286.

18  Tworoger, S. S. et al. (2008). Caffeine, alcohol, smoking, and the risk of incident epithelial ovarian cancer, *Cancer, 112 (5)*, 1169–1177.

19  Graudal, N. A. et al. (1998). Effects of sodium restriction on blood pressure, renin, aldosterone, catecholamines, cholesterols, and triglyceride: A

meta-analysis, *Journal of the American Medical Association*, *279*, 1383–1391.

20 A recently published study shows the positive effects of reduced salt intake on cardiovascular health. But the controversy continues. See Cook, N. R. et al. (2007). Long term effects of dietary sodium reduction on cardiovascular disease outcomes: observational follow-up of the trials of hypertension prevention (TOHP), *British Medical Journal* (April 28), *334 (7599)*, 885.

21 Van Den Akker, E. H. et al. (2004). Large international differences in (adeno)tonsillectomy rates, *Clinical Otolaryngology & Allied Sciences*, *29 (2)*, 161–164.

22 See Bjelakovic, G. et al. (2007). Mortality in randomized trials of antioxidant supplements for primary and secondary prevention: Systematic review and meta-analysis, *The Journal of the American Medical Association*, 297, 842–857.

23 Lawson, K. A. et al. (2007). Multivitamin use and risk of prostate cancer in the National Institutes of Health–AARP diet and health study, *Journal of the National Cancer Institute*, *99 (10)*, 754–764. Liz Baker, science information officer at Cancer Research UK, said: "It's still not entirely clear what factors can affect a man's risk of developing prostate cancer while there is conflicting evidence on the pros and cons of vitamin supplements these products don't seem to give us the same benefits as vitamins that naturally occur in our food."

24 See Hellmich, N. Obesity on track as No. 1 killer. *USA Today*, March 9, 2004. The underlying study was by Mokland, A. H. et al. (2004). Actual causes of death in the United States, 2000, *Journal of the American Medical Association*, *291 (10)*, 1283–1245.

25 See Flegal, K. M. et al. (2005). Excess deaths associated with underweight, overweight, and obesity. *Journal of the American Medical Association*, *293 (15)*, 1861–1867.

26 For a timeline on this whole controversry see 'History of a great unraveling' at www.consumerfreedom.org/article_detail.cfm?article=162

27 You can be too thin, after all. *The New York Times*, April 22, 2005.

28 Gronniger, J. T. (2006). A semiparametric analysis of the relationship of body mass index to mortality, *American Journal of Public Health, 96,* 173–178

29 Flegal, K. et al. (2007). Cause-specific excess deaths associated with underweight, overweight, and obesity, *The Journal of the American Medical Association, 298 (17),* 2028–2037.

30 Sui, X. et al. (2007). Cardiorespiratory fitness and adiposity as mortality predictors in older adults, *The Journal of the American Medical Association, 298 (21),* 2507–2516.

31 Tatsioni, A. et al. (2007). Persistence of contradicted claims in the literature, *The Journal of the American Medical Association, 298 (21),* 2517–2526.

32 Gilbert, H. G. (2004). *Should I be Tested for Cancer? Maybe Not and Here's Why.* Berkeley, CA: University of California Press, pp. 154–155. This cites Shapiro S. et al. *Periodic Screening for Breast Cancer: The Health Insurance Plan Project and Its Sequelae, 1963-1986* (Johns Hopkins Series in Contemporary Medicine and Public Health).

33 Miller, A. B. et al. (1992). Canadian National Breast Screening Study: 1. Breast cancer detection and death rates among women aged 40 to 49 years, *Canadian Medical Association Journal* (November 15), *147 (10),* 1459–1476.

34 Welch, H. G. (2004). *Should I Be Tested for Cancer? Maybe Not and Here's Why.* Berkeley, CA: University of California Press, pp. 153–162. Even after five decades of testing, there is much debate about the value of mammography testing. See ije.oxfordjournals.org/cgi/content/ abstract/33/1/43, as well as Olsen, O. et al. (2001). Cochrane review on screening for breast cancer with mammography, *Lancet,* 358, 1340–1342.

35 Adriole, G. L., et al. (2009). Mortality results from a randomized prostate-cancer screening trial, *New England Journal of Medicine,* 360 (13), 1310–1319.

36 Schröder, F. H., et al. (2009). Screening and prostate-cancer mortality in a randomized European study, *New England Journal of Medicine,* 360 (13), 1320–1328.

37 This is calculated as $(112/162,837) \times 1,000 = 0.7$.

38 Franco, O. H. et al. (2005). Blood pressure in adulthood and life expectancy with cardiovascular disease in men and women life course analysis, *Hypertension, 46*, 284.

# CHAPTER 3

1 Linde, C. et al. (1999). Placebo effect of pacemaker implantation in obstructive hypertrophic cardiomyopathy. PIC study group. Pacing in cardiomyopathy, *American Journal of Cardiology, 83 (6)*, 903–907.

2 Coronary Drug Project Research Group. (1980). Influence of adherence to treatment and response of cholesterol on mortality in the coronary drug project, *New England Journal of Medicine, 303 (18)*, 1038–1041.

3 In Spiro, H. M (ed.) (1986). *Doctors, Patients, and Placebos.* New Haven, CT: Yale University Press.

4 Mossey, J. M. and Shapiro, E. (2005). Self-rated health: a predictor of mortality among the elderly, *Journal of Epidemiology and Community Health, 59*, 794–798.

5 See, e.g., Chacko, K. M. and Anderson, R. J. (2007). The annual physical examination: important or time to abandon? *American Journal of Medicine, 120(7)*, 581–583. In addition see the article "The Annual Rip-Off" in *Time Magazine* (Monday July 26, 1976) that provides strong evidence from more than thirty years ago showing that there is little value in annual check-ups.

6 Rabin, R., New screening advice for pregnant women, *International Herald Tribune*, January 10, 2007

7 Gigerenzer, G. (2002). *Calculated Risks: How to Know when Numbers Deceive You.* New York, NY: Simon & Schuster, p. 103.

8 Black, W. C. and Baron, J. (2007). CT screening for lung cancer; spiraling into confusion? *The Journal of the American Medical Association, 297*, 995–997.

9 Welch, H. G. (2004). *Should I Be Tested for Cancer? Maybe Not and Here's Why.* Berkeley, CA: University of California Press.

10 Hadler, N. M. (2004). *The Last Well Person: How to Stay Well Despite the*

*Health-care System.* Quebec City, Canada: McGill-Queens University Press.

11 Quoted by Carey, J. and Barrett, A. Is heart surgery worth it? *Business Week*, July 18, 2005.

12 Lemonick, M. D., Medicine's secret stat, *Time*, Tuesday, Feb. 15, 2007.

13 Kennare, R. et al. (2007). Risks of adverse outcomes in the next birth after a first Cesarean delivery, *Obstetrics & Gynecology, 109*, 270–276.

14 "The preliminary rate of Cesarean delivery rose 4 percent in 2005 to 30.2 percent of all births, another record high for the Nation . . . The Cesarean rate declined somewhat during the early and mid-1990s, but has risen 46 percent since 1996 (from 20.7 percent)." (www.cdc.gov/nchs/data/nvsr/nvsr55//nvsr55_11.pdf)

15 www.nationmaster.com/graph/hea_bir_by_cae_sec-health-births-by-caesarean-section

16 As a matter of fact, the correlation between rates of Cesarians and infant mortality is 0.57 (and is statistically significant).

17 Mossialos, E. et al. (2005). An investigation of Cesarean sections in three Greek hospitals: The impact of financial incentives and convenience, *European Journal of Public Health, 15*, 288–295.

18 Weintraub, A. Physician, reveal thyself, *Business Week*, May 12, 2008.

19 News, *Business Week on Line*, July 18, 2005, www.businessweek.com/magazine/content/05_29/b3943037_mz011.htm

20 Fisher, E. S. et al. (2003). The implications of regional variations in medicare spending. Part 1: The content, quality, and accessibility of care, *Annals of Internal Medicine, 138 ( 4)*, 273–287.

21 Romains, J. (1923). *Knock, ou, Le triomphe de la medicine.* Paris, France : Gallimard.

22 Welch, H. G. et al. What's making us sick is an epidemic of diagnoses, *The New York Times*, January 2, 2007.

23 Foundation for Informed Medical Decision Making (www.fimdm.org).

24 Groopman, J. (2007). *How Doctors Think.* Boston, MA: Houghton Mifflin Company.

25 Wurzbacher, T. (2007). *Your Doctor Said What? Exposing the Communication Gap.* Ontario, Canada: LifeSuccess Publishing,

## CHAPTER 4

1 Batra, R. (1988). *The Great Depression of 1990.* New York, NY: Simon & Schuster.

2 Glassman, J. K. and Hassett, K. A. (1999). *Dow 36,000: The New Strategy for Profiting from the Coming Rise in the Stock Market.* New York, NY: Random House.

3 Elias, D. (1999). *Dow 40,000: Strategies for Profiting from the Greatest Bull Market in History.* New York, NY: McGraw Hill.

4 Kadlec, C. W. (1999). *Dow 100,000: Fact of Fiction.* New York, NY: Prentice-Hall.

5 We note that by June 24, 2008 the DJIA had fallen to 11453, that is less than the high of 11722 it had reached almost eight and a half years earlier on January 14, 2000. So much for predicting a high of 36,000!

6 Shiller, R. J. (2000). *Irrational Exuberance.* Princeton, NJ: Princeton University Press.

7 For more information on the predictability of economic forecasters, see Makridakis, S., Hogarth, R., and Gaba, A. (2009). Forecasting and uncertainty in the economic and business world. *International Journal of Forecasting, 25*, 794–812.

8 Shiller, R. J. (2005). *Irrational Exuberance* (2nd ed.). Princeton, NJ: Princeton University Press.

9 Hamel, G. (2000). *Leading the Revolution.* Boston, MA: Harvard Business School Press, p. 212.

10 Figure 3 shows a much higher value than $675 because it depicts gold prices in constant 2006 dollars.

11 At the beginning of July 2008, the price of gold was about $935 per ounce.

12 Siegel, J. J. (2002). *Stocks for the Long Run* (3rd ed.). New York, NY: McGraw-Hill.

13 Dimson, E., Marsh, P., and Staunton, M. (2002). *Triumph of the Optimists: 101 Years of Global Investment Returns.* Princeton, NJ: Princeton University Press.

14 Again, note that we're not reinvesting dividends and we're assuming we can buy into funds that "track" both the DJIA index and the NASDAQ "composite" index of all its shares.

## CHAPTER 5

1 Malkiel, B. G. and Saha A. (2005). Hedge funds: Risk and returns, *Financial Analysts Journal, 61 (6)*, 80–88.

2 Kaplan, S. N. and Schoar, A.(2005). Private equity performance: Returns, persistence, and capital flows, *The Journal of Finance, 60 (4)*, 1791–1823.

3 Bird, S. The future of venture capital: Private equity gets more private, *Focus Venture*, January 6, 2004.

4 Malkiel, B. G. (1995). Returns from investing in equity mutual funds 1971 to 1991, *The Journal of Finance, 50 (2)*, 549–572.

5 Kosowski, R. et al. (2006). Can mutual fund "stars" really pick stocks? New evidence from a bootstrap analysis, *The Journal of Finance, 61 (6)*, 2551–2595.

6 Nitzsche, D. et al. (2006). *Mutual fund performance*, Working Paper, University of London, Cass Business School.

7 Graham, J. R. and Harvey, C. R. (1997). Market timing ability and volatility implied in investment newsletters' asset allocation recommendations, Working Paper 4890, National Bureau of Economic Research.

8 Jensen, M. (1967). The performance of mutual funds in the period 1945–1964, *The Journal of Finance, 23 (2)*, 389–416. See also Carhart, M. R. (1997). On persistence in mutual fund performance, *The Journal of Finance, 52 (1)*, 57–82.

9 Blake, C. R. et al. (1993). The performance of bond mutual funds, *The Journal of Business, 66 (3)*, 371–403.

## CHAPTER 6

1 Hammer, M. and Champy, J. (1993). *Reengineering the Corporation: A Manifesto for Business Revolution*. New York, NY: Harper Business.

2 Abrahamson, E. and Fairchild, G. (1999). Management fashion: Lifecycles, triggers, and collective learning processes, *Administrative Science Quarterly, 44*, 708–740.

3 Peters, T. and Waterman, R. H. Jr. (1982). *In Search of Excellence: Lessons from America's Best-Known Companies*. New York, NY: Harper & Row.

4  Collins, J. and Porras, J. (1994). *Built to Last: Successful Habits of Visionary Companies*. New York, NY: HarperBusiness.

5  The survey started in 1983.

6  Popper, K. R. (1989). *Objective Knowledge: An Evolutionary Approach* (rev. ed.). Oxford, UK: Clarendon Press.

7  Kim, C. and Mauborgne, R. (2005). *Blue Ocean Strategy: How to Create Uncontested Market Space and Make the Competition Irrelevant*. Boston, MA: Harvard Business School Press.

8  Foster, R. and Kaplan, S. (2002). *Creative Destruction: Why Companies that Are Built to Last Underperform the Market – and How to Successfully Transform Them*. New York, NY: Currency.

9  De Geus, A. (2002). *The Living Company: Habits for Survival in a Turbulent Business Environment*. Boston, MA: Longview Publishing.

10  Foster, R. and Kaplan, S. (2002). *Creative Destruction*. p. 9.

11  Collins, J. (2001). *Good to Great: Why Some Companies Make the Leap... and Others Don't*. New York, NY: HarperCollins.

12  Joyce, W., Nohria, N., and Roberson, B. (2003). *What Really Works: The 4+2 Formula for Sustained Business Success*. New York, NY: HarperCollins.

13  Marcus, A. (2006). *Big Winners and Big Losers: The 4 Secrets of Long-Term Business Success and Failure*. Philadelphia, PA: Wharton School Publishing.

## CHAPTER 7

1  Schumpeter, J. (1942). *Capitalism, Socialism and Democracy*. New York, NY: Harper & Row, p. 83.

2  Quoted by Battelle, J. (2005). *The Search: How Google and Its Rivals Rewrote the Rules of Business and Transformed Our Culture*. New York, NY: Penguin.

3  Nayak, P. R. and Ketteringham, J. M. (1986). *Break-Throughs*. New York, NY: Rawson Associates.

4  Colvin, G. Steve Jobs' bad bet: The visionary CEO didn't have enough faith in Apple's future, *Fortune*, March 5, 2007.

5 Foster, R. and Kaplan, S. (2002). *Creative Destruction: Why Companies that Are Built to Last Underperform the Market – and How to Successfully Transform Them.* New York, NY: Currency.

6 Ricadela, A. Google's newest role: Venture capitalist, *Business Week*, September 4, 2007.

7 Komisar, R. (2000). *The Monk and the Riddle: The Education of a Silicon Valley Entrepreneur.* Boston, MA: Harvard Business School Press.

## CHAPTER 8

1 Bernstein, P. L. (1996). *Against the Gods: The Remarkable Story of Risk.* New York, NY: John Wiley & Sons, pp. 15–16.

2 Wiseman, R. (2004). *The Luck Factor.* London, UK: Arrow Books.

## CHAPTER 9

1 Bavelas, J. B. (1973). Effects of the temporal context of information, *Psychological Reports, 32*, 695–698.

2 Makridakis, S. and Hibon, M. (1979). The accuracy of forecasts: An empirical investigation, *Journal of the Royal Statistical Society, Series A, 142*, 97–145 (with discussion).

3 Makridakis, S. and Hibon, M. (2000). The M3-competition: Results, conclusions and implications, *International Journal of Forecasting, 16 (4)*, 451–476.

4 Meehl, P. (1954). *Clinical versus statistical prediction: a theoretical analysis and a review of the evidence.* Minneapolis, MN: The University of Minnesota Press.

5 See also Sawyer, J. (1966). Measurement and prediction, clinical and statistical, *Psychological Bulletin, 66 (3)*, 178–200, and Kleinmuntz, B. (1990). Why we still use our heads instead of formulas: Toward an integrative approach, *Psychological Bulletin, 107 (3)*, 295–310. Most recently Grove, W. M. et al. (2000). Clinical versus mechanical prediction: A meta-analysis, *Psychological Assessment, 12 (1)*, 19–30, summarized the results of 136 studies comparing clinical and statistical judgments across

a wide range of environments. They concluded by stating: "We identified no systematic exceptions to the general superiority (or at least material equivalence) of mechanical prediction. It holds in general medicine, in mental health, in personality, and in education and training settings. It holds for medically trained judges and for psychologists. It holds for inexperienced and seasoned judges."

6 Clemen, R. T. (1989). Combining forecasts: A review and annotated bibliography, *International Journal of Forecasting, (5)*, 559–583.

7 Surowiecki, J. (2005). *The Wisdom of Crowds*. New York, NY: Anchor Books.

8 Simon, H. A. and Sumner, R. K. (1968). Patterns in music. In B. Kleinmuntz (ed.), *Formal Representation of Human Judgment*. New York, NY: Wiley, p. 220.

9 For instructive examples of this principle, consider the many betting sites where one can place wagers on many different future events including sports and elections. The odds offered reflect the opinions of many people and, on average, are quite accurate.

10 For an interesting analysis of herd behavior, see Prechter, R. R., Jr. and Parker, W. D. (2007). The financial/economic dichotomy in social behavioral dynamics: The socionomic perspective. *Journal of Behavioral Finance, 8(2)*, 84–108.

## CHAPTER 10

1 Taleb, N. N. (2007). *The Black Swan: The Impact of the Highly Improbable*. New York, NY: Random House.

2 These stock market stories are based on reports in the public domain. We have, however, disguised names and places.

3 For the latest earthquakes in California and Nevada see, for example, the website http://quake.usgs.gov/recenteqs/

4 See Buchanan, M. (2001). *Ubiquity: The Science of History or Why the World is Simpler than We Think*. London UK: Phoenix.

5 See http://neic.usgs.gov/neis/eqlists/eqstats.html

6 Greenspan, A. (2007). *The Age of Turbulence: Adventures in a New World*. New York, NY: The Penguin Press.

7 See Daston, L. (1988).*Classical Probability in the Enlightenment.* Princeton, NJ: Princeton University Press.

8 Markowitz, H. (1952). Portfolio selection, *The Journal of Finance*, 7 *(1)*, 77–91. Bruno De Finetti, a brilliant Italian mathematician had in fact introduced the exact same idea twelve years earlier in a paper published in an Italian insurance journal – see De Finetti, B. (1940). Il problema dei «pieni» (The problem of full risk insurance), *Giornale dell' Instituto Italiano degli Attuari*, *11 (1)*, 1–88.

9 See Chesterton, G. K. (1908). *Orthodoxy*. Toronto, Canada: John Lane Company.

## CHAPTER 11

1 *Hamlet*, Act 2, Scene 2.

2 Kahneman, D. and Tversky, A. (1979). Intuitive prediction: Biases and corrective procedures, *TIMS Studies in Management Science*, *12*, 313–327.

3 Gladwell, M. (2005). *Blink: The Power of Thinking without Thinking*. London, UK: Penguin Books. In fact, the report of a colloquium held in 1992 in Athens where nineteen experts expressed their opinions about the authenticity of the Kouros indicates considerable disagreement among these experts (see chapter 12 for additional discussion of blinking and the Getty Kouros).

4 Howe, M. J. A. et al. (1998). Innate talents: Reality or myth? *Behavioral and Brain Sciences*, *21*, 399–407.

5 Gigerenzer, G. et al. (1999). *Simple Heuristics that Make Us Smart*. New York, NY: Oxford University Press.

6 Shaw, G. B. (1950). *Man and Superman: A Comedy and a Philosophy*. Bel Air, CA: Amereon Limited.

7 Bacon, F. (1994). *Novum Organum: With Other Parts of the Great Instauration*. Chicago, IL: Open Court. (Original work published 1620.)

8 Ariely, D. (2008). *Predictably Irrational: The Hidden Factors that Shape Our Decisions*. New York, NY: HarperCollins.

9 Gigerenzer, G. (2002).*Calculated Risks: How to Know when Numbers Deceive You*. New York, NY: Simon & Schuster, p. 92.

10  Hogarth, R. M. (2006). Is confidence in decisions related to feedback? Evidence from random samples of real-world behavior. In K. Fiedler and P. Juslin (ed.), *Information Sampling and Adaptive Cognition*. Cambridge, UK: Cambridge University Press.

11  Ericsson, K. A. et al. (1993). The role of deliberate practice in the acquisition of expert performance, *Psychological Review, 100 (3)*, 363–406.

12  Colvin, G. What it takes to be great: Research now shows that the lack of natural talent is irrelevant to great success. The secret? Painful and demanding practice and hard work, *Fortune*, October 19, 2006. See also Colvin, G. (2008). *Talent is Overrated: What Really Separates World-Class Performers from Everybody Else*. New York, NY: Penguin Books.

13  Csikszentmihalyi, M. (1997). *Creativity: Flow and the Psychology of Discovery and Invention*. New York, NY: Harper Perennial.

14  Daniel Kahneman, cited in *Monitor on Psychology, 38 (9)*, October 2007, p. 13.

## CHAPTER 12

1  Howard, J. W. and Dawes, R. M. (1976). Linear prediction of marital happiness, *Personality and Social Psychology Bulletin, 2*, 478–480.

2  Dawes, R. M. and Corrigan, B. (1974). Linear models in decision making, *Psychological Bulletin, 81 (2)*, 95–106.

3  Showers, J. L. and Chakrin, L. M. (1981). Reducing uncollectible revenue from residential telephone customers, *Interfaces, 11 (6)*, 21–34. Unfortunately, the authors of this study don't reveal details of the formula they developed (e.g., they don't specify the variables).

4  Einhorn, H. J. (1986). Accepting error to make less error. *Journal of Personality Assessment, 50*, 387–395.

5  Grove, W. M. et al. (2000). Clinical versus mechanical prediction: A meta-analysis, *Psychological Assessment, 12 (1)*, 19–30.

6  Flyvbjerg, B. in association with Cowi (2004). *Procedures for Dealing with Optimism Planning Bias in Transport*. The British Department of Transport, UK.

7 McNeil, B. J. et al. (1982). On the elicitation of preference for alternative therapies, *New England Journal of Medicine, 306,* 1259–1262.

8 Blanchard, K. H. and Johnson, S., (2000). *The One Minute Manager.* New York, NY: Harper Collins Business; Hansen, M. V. and Allen, R. G. (2002). *The One Minute Millionaire: The Enlightened Way to Wealth.* New York, NY: Harmony Books; Johnson, S. and Candle Communications (1995). *The One Minute Father.* New York, NY: Collins; Johnson, S. and Candle Communications (1995). *The One Minute Mother.* New York, NY: Collins; Blanchard, K. H, Hudson, D., and Willis, E. (2008). *The One Minute Entrepreneur: The Secret to Creating and Sustaining a Successful Business.* New York, NY: Doubleday.

9 Ray, J. A. (2006). *The Science of Success: How to Attract Prosperity and Create Harmonic Wealth® Through Proven Principles.* Carlsbad, CA:. Sunark Press.

10 Ormerod, P. (2007). *Why Most Things Fail: Evolution, Extinction and Economics.* New York, NY:Wiley.

11 Herbold, R. J. (2007). *Seduced by Success: How the Best Companies Survive the 9 Traps of Winning.* New York, NY: McGraw-Hill.

12 Gladwell, M. (2005). *Blink: The Power of Thinking without Thinking.* London, UK: Penguin Books.

13 The Goulandris Foundation and the J. Paul Getty Museum (1993). *The Getty Kouros Colloquium: Athens, 25–27 May 1992.* Athens, Greece: Kapon Editions.

14 Tetlock, P. E. (2005). *Expert Political Judgment: How Good Is It? How Can We Know?* Princeton, NJ: Princeton University Press.

15 See, for example, Damasio, A. R. (1994). *Descartes' Error: Emotion, Reason, and the Human Brain.* New York, NY: Avon; Bechara, A. et al. (1997). Deciding advantageously before knowing the advantageous strategy, *Science, 275,* 1293–1295; and Slovic, P. et al. (2002). The affect heuristic, in T. Gilovich, D. Griffin, and D. Kahneman (ed.). *Intuitive Judgment: Heuristics and Biases.* New York, NY: Cambridge University Press.

16 See also Hogarth, R. M. (2001). *Educating Intuition.* Chicago, IL: The University of Chicago Press.

# CHAPTER 13

1 White, A., 2007, see www.le.ac.uk/pc/aw57/world/sample.html

2 Diener, E. and Seligman, M. (2004). Beyond money: Toward an economy of well-being, *Psychological Science in the Public Interest, 5 (1)*,1–31.

3 Kahneman, D. et al. (2006). Would you be happier if you were richer? A focusing illusion, *Science, 312 (5782)*, 1908–1910; Diener, E. (1984). Subjective well-being, *Psychological Bulletin, 95*, 542–575; Layard, R. (2005). *Happiness: Lessons from a New Science*. New York, NY: Penguin.

4 Layard, *Happiness: Lessons from a New Science*.

5 Seligman, M. E. P. (2002). *Authentic Happiness: Using the New Positive Psychology to Realize Your Potential for Lasting Fulfillment*. New York, NY: Free Press.

6 Easterlin, R. E. (1974). Does economic growth improve the human lot? Some empirical evidence. In P. A. David and M. W. Reder (ed.), *Nations and Households in Economic Growth: Essays in Honour of Moses Abramowitz*. New York, NY: Academic Press.

7 Layard, *Happiness: Lessons from a New Science*. For completeness, we add that some recent work has challenged conclusions such as these and, in particular, the implications depicted by our graph of life satisfaction versus per capita GDP. However, the statistical issues involved in interpreting this recent work are quite challenging and we believe it will take some time before the "correct" relation between happiness and income is understood. See B. Stevenson and J. Wolfers, *Economic Growth and Subjective Well-being: Reassessing the Easterlin Paradox*, Working Paper, University of Pennsylvania, May 2008.

8 Offer, A. (2006). *The Challenge of Affluence: Self-Control and Well-Being in the United States and Britain since 1950*. New York, NY: Oxford University Press.

9 Oswald, J. A. (1997). Happiness and economic performance, *Economic Journal, 107 (445)*, 1815–1831.

10 Kahneman, D. et al. (2004). A survey method for characterizing daily life experience: The day reconstruction method, *Science, 306 (5702)*, 1776–1780.

11 Kahneman, A survey method for characterizing daily life experience.

12 Kahneman, A survey method for characterizing daily life experience.

13 Seligman, *Authentic Happiness*, pp. 3–4.

14 Seligman, *Authentic Happiness*, p 10.

15 Steptoe, A. et al. (2005). Positive affect and health-related neuroendocrine, cardiovascular, and inflammatory processes, *Proceedings of the National Academy of Science of the United States*, 102 (18), 6508–6512.

16 Veenhoven, R. (ed.) (1989). *How Harmful Is Happiness? Consequences of Enjoying Life or Not*. Universitaire Pers Rotterdam, The Hague, Netherlands.

17 Rablen, M. D. and Oswald, A. J. (2007). *Mortality and immortality*. University of Warwick Discussion Paper No. 2560.

18 Redelmeier D. A. and Singh, S. M. (2001). Longevity of screenwriters who win an academy award: a longitudinal study, *British Medical Journal*, 323 (7327), 1491–1496.

19 Lyubomirsky, S. (2008). *The How of Happiness: A Scientific Approach to Getting the Life You Want*. New York, NY: The Penguin Press.

20 www.reflectivehappiness.com

21 Farahmand, B. at al. (2008). Golf: a game of life and death – reduced mortality in Swedish golf players, *Scandinavian Journal of Medical Science in Sports*, published online May 28, 2008.

22 Norem, J. K. (2002). *The Positive Power of Negative Thinking: Using Defensive Pessimism to Harness Anxiety and Perform at Your Peak*. New York, NY: Basic Books.

23 Csikszentmihalyi, M. (1997). *Creativity: Flow and the Psychology of Discovery and Invention*. New York, NY: Harper Perennial.

24 Csikszentmihalyi, M. (1990). *Flow: The Psychology of Optimal Experience*. New York, NY: Harper & Row.

25 Gilbert, D. (2006). *Stumbling on Happiness*. New York, NY: Vintage Books.

26 Ubel, P. et al. (2001). Do nonpatients underestimate the quality of life associated with chronic health conditions because of a focusing illusion? *Medical Decision Making*, 21, 190–199.

27 As reported by Pam Bellock, Looking for happiness? It may be very near; when the heart sings, part of the cortex gets busy, *The New York Times*, July 24, 1999.

28 Strack, F., Martin, L. L., and Schwarz, N. (1988). Priming and communication: Social determinants of information use in judgments of life satisfaction, *European Journal of Social Psychology, 18 (5)*, 429–442.

29 Juster, F. T. (1985). In F. Juster and F. Stafford (ed.), *Time, Goods, and Well-Being*. Ann Arbor, MI: Institute for Social Research, 397–414; Flood, L. (1997). *Household, Market, and Nonmarket Activities; Procedures and Codes for the 1993 Time-Use Survey, Vol. VI*. Uppsala Univ. Dept. Economics, Uppsala, Sweden.

30 Wallis, C., The new science of happiness, *Time*, January 9, 2005.

31 Powdthavee, N. (2008). Putting a price tag on friends, relatives, and neighbors: Using surveys of life satisfaction to value social relationships. *Journal of Socio-Economics, 37 (4)*, 1459–1480.

32 See Gardner, J. and Oswald, A. (2006). Do divorcing couples become happier by breaking up? *Journal of the Royal Statistical Society: Series A, 169(2)*, 319–336.

## POSTSCRIPT

1 This book was first published in April 2009. The postscript was added in March 2010.

2 On November 4, 1979 the CBS Program 60 Minutes aired a program about how 46 million Americans were vaccinated by being made to believe that a flu pandemic was imminent. The video of the 60 minutes can be seen in YouTube while a transcript of it can be found in the link: http://www.globalresearch.ca/index.php?context= va&aid=14433

3 *Daily Mail*, (2010). The doctor's receptionist paralysed by the swine flu jab, February 1, p. 29.

4 Brownlee, S. (2010). Cancer screening may do more harm then good, *NBC*, March 15. http://www.nbcwashington.com/news/health/ Cancer_screening__Doing_more_harm_than_good_.html

5 Gardner, A. (2009). Recent cancer screening changes leave many

confused: But experts say science is behind reasoning that testing less is OK. *US News and World Report*, November 24.

6 Begley, S. (2010). This won't hurt a bit: How we can save billions by cutting out unnecessary procedures that kill tens of thousands a year. *Newsweek*, March 15.

7 Browning, E. S. (2010,). Worries rebound on bull's birthday. *Wall Street Journal*, March 9.

8 Boyce, C. J., Brown, G. D. A., and Moore, S. C. (2010). Money and happiness: Rank of income, not income, affects life satisfaction. *Psychological Science, 21(4)* 471–475.

# INDEX

Note: Page numbers which refer to tables are shown in italics.

Schrodeus Fund
16.26 10/yr since inception
1993

www.dancewithchance.com
Birthday statistics